LEGENDARY LOCALS

OF

MARANA, ORO VALLEY, AND CATALINA

ARIZONA

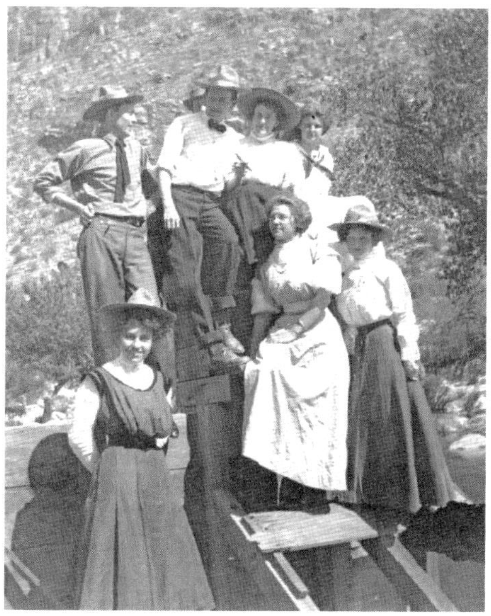

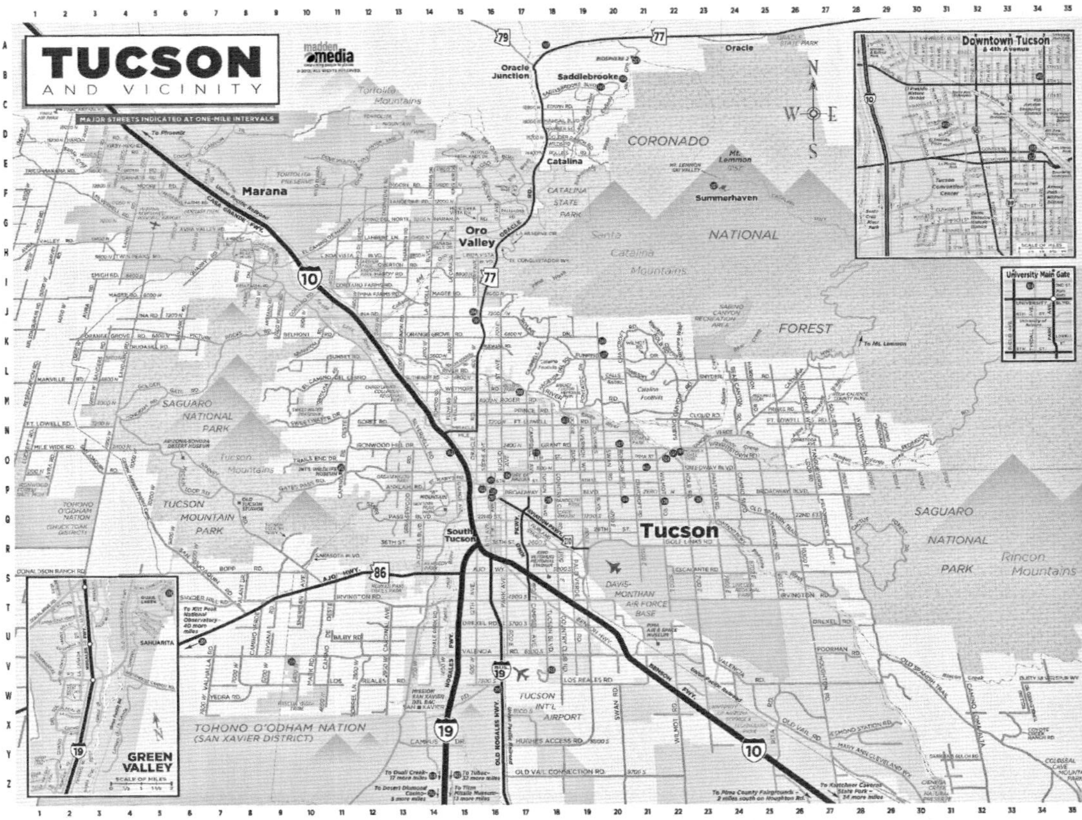

Page 1: Pusch Women
See page 45

Page 2: Marana, Oro Valley, and Catalina
This map shows the corridor of Legendary Locals: the towns and village of Marana, Oro Valley, and Catalina, located north of Tucson, Arizona. (Map reprinted with permission. Copyright Madden Media, Inc., 2012. All rights reserved.)

LEGENDARY LOCALS

OF

MARANA, ORO VALLEY, AND CATALINA

ARIZONA

BARBARA MARRIOTT

LEGENDARY LOCALS

ISBN 978-1-4671-0016-8

Published by Legendary Locals, an imprint of Arcadia Publishing
Charleston, South Carolina

Printed in the United States of America

Library of Congress Control Number: 2011944362

For all general information, please contact Arcadia Publishing:
Telephone 843-853-2070
Fax 843-853-0044
E-mail sales@arcadiapublishing.com
For customer service and orders:
Toll-Free 1-888-313-2665

Visit us on the Internet at www.arcadiapublishing.com

Dedication
To Mike Shook.

On the Cover: From left to right:
(TOP ROW) George Pusch, statesman and rancher (Courtesy of the Oro Valley Historical Society; see pages 42, 43), Catherine Reidy, 1930s businesswoman (Courtesy of the Reidy Family; see pages 54, 55), Buster Bailey, mountain man (Courtesy of the Oro Valley Historical Society; see page 47), Betty Proctor, society leader (Courtesy of the Arizona Historical Society #9682; see page 50), Hal Burns, designer of Lindbergh's Cacti plane (Courtesy of the Hal Burns Family; see pages 52, 53).
(MIDDLE ROW) Frank McDuff, founding member of Marana (Courtesy of the Town of Marana; see pages 20, 21), Higinio Aguirre, ranch owner (Courtesy of the Arizona Historical Society #6913; see page 16), Ora Mae Harn, community leader (Courtesy of the Town of Marana; see page 32), James and John Collins, pioneer family (Courtesy of the Town of Marana; see page 32), Jim Cloer, naturalist (Courtesy of Jim Cloer; see pages 110, 111).
(BOTTOM ROW) D.C. Warren, actor (Courtesy of the Town of Marana; see pages 26, 27), Carlos Rivera, cowboy (Courtesy of the Rivera Family; see pages 98, 99), Maren Seidler, Olympic athlete (Courtesy of Maren Seidler; see pages 112, 113), Chief Eskiminza, Apache leader (Courtesy of the Arizona Historical Society #30378; see pages 78, 79), Eulalie "Sister" Bourne, (Courtesy of Arizona Historical Society, see page 95).

CONTENTS

ACKNOWLEDGMENTS

This book is possible because of the efforts of many; most of their names can be found in the credit lines. There were three very special people—Dawn Doubek, Liz Rivera, and Lois Nagy—who patiently worked with me on obtaining pictures and information. My thanks to Mayor Hiremath and his Oro Valley staff, and Mayor Horna and his Marana staff, including Vicki Hathaway. Others who found and supplied pictures were Joyce Garcia, Kathy Stevens, and Clark Reddin from the Biosphere II. Josh Hungry and Mary Kay Stein, Miley Clark, Nancy Johannesmeyer, and Naomi L. Torres contributed to the Marana section. Thanks to the Oro Valley Historical Society, who can always be counted on. I am deeply appreciative of everyone who nominated a legend, and to those who gave me information. They all provided some wonderful history about some unique people. Thank you everyone.

INTRODUCTION

Just north of Tucson, Arizona, two towns and a village form a corridor running northeast to southwest. Despite their geographic proximity to Tucson, the lifestyle in these communities is quite different from the ways of the city. They are a microcosm of the West. While they share that trait, and some physical features, each is unique, with distinctive features not shared by the other two towns. These distinctions drew certain types of pioneers who helped define their communities, kept defining them, laying the groundwork for the Legendary Locals, those who left an imprint because they did more, or did something special.

The land mostly determines its own destiny. Its contours, climate, and natural resources are what entice people, and there are few places that offered more of a challenge than the Arizona desert. The land also defines the character of its settlers, welcoming those who can live and thrive on it, rejecting those who cannot compromise. Only a special kind will remain; those who can turn the land to their advantage with their minds and bodies. It is the melding of the land's demands with those who can answer them that builds a society, and it is the Legendary Locals who turned the land into communities. But, first of all, the land must offer something to the potential settler. In the desert, it is water that is the most precious commodity and lure.

In southeast Arizona, the Santa Cruz and San Pedro Rivers bracketed southern Arizona and ran north and south. The Santa Cruz was a generously flowing river that kept the plains around Marana lush. Smaller streams in the area flowed with robust energy, especially during the monsoon season. When an earthquake struck in 1887, the Santa Cruz went underground. But by that time, it had made its mark on the people who would work and dwell on its banks.

The first evidence of sustained life in these areas came between AD 900 and AD 1400, when the ancient people, the Hohokam, occupied the vicinity. Water drew them here, along with the fertile plains that helped them produce a plentiful supply of corn, squash, and beans. Their disappearance from the area, the abandonment of their sites, is a mystery.

Although the early people left the land, its waters and fertile plains remained, beckoning those who loved the land and knew how to work it. The ancient crops disappeared and were replaced by cotton, which brought the original migrant workers. Black slaves and their descendants came west to pick. When machinery replaced the pickers, some stayed, finding other jobs, settling around the valley. When new crops were introduced, farmhands arrived to do the work. Some of them also put down roots and raised families.

The rivers, streams, and plains that are now part of Marana offered more than fertile farming land. These waterways also offered easy to follow routes through mountainous land, and the early Spanish conquistadors and explorers followed their path through the desert, heading west to conquer and settle the lands of California. It was this route that was pioneered by Juan Bautista de Anza, and followed by the Butterfield Stage, and the Mormon Battalion. It is the route that was trekked by hordes of gold seekers as they headed west. Some arrived in the lush Santa Cruz valley and decided to stay.

When they came west, the trains also followed this historic route. The tracks were built in the flat lands between the mountains, and the railroad established bases near much needed water supplies. With the trains came the train employees and their families.

Mountains were also a lure. The many ranges, small and big, sent waters gushing down to the valleys to keep the flowing rivers full. Wild game roamed the peaks and ridges, and in torrid summers, these elevations offered relief to many. For the prospectors, these mountains meant the possibility of riches. Around the Santa Cruz plains, the mountains offered up rich ores of silver and copper. Another group followed, the men and women who supplied needed services to the farmers, train families, and miners. For if there are settlements there are needs, and if there are needs there is money to be made filling those needs.

With the lure of mountains, plains, and the Santa Cruz, the town of Marana slowly grew from ancient villages, to mining and railroad camps, to farming settlements, then into a town: a town that retains its roots in copper and cotton as an important part of its economic base. The Legendary Locals here are people who came for the treasures of the land, and by working with the land made a town. The history of Marana is rooted in the land, as are its people.

Marana has the largest land area of our three communities with 126 square miles. Its topography, which contains an abundance of large flat land, and its position in southern Arizona between the city of Tucson and the route to California, brought it to the attention of explorers, railroad magnates, and settlers.

The communities to the east of Marana did not have the luxury of a river. Their water was the Canada del Oro Wash, a contrary and unpredictable source that depended on the rains and snow run-offs. In Oro Valley, it was not the fertile plains that attracted the early settlers and fortune hunters, it was the Canada del Oro, the mountain ranges towering over them, and nature's small pockets of land filled with cacti, small streams, and borders of grassland. Between the Tortolita and the Santa Catalina Mountains, there isn't much room to farm. However, there is plenty of room for cattle.

Not too many frontier types came to Oro Valley. Most who did came from towns and cities. At first, they came to make their fortune and future in cattle; later it was the promise of a piece of land for themselves and their children. And always, although they were in the wild, there was the near-enough town of Tucson, which offered them their necessities. These people were less the rugged frontiersmen than their San Pedro Valley neighbors, but they were determined to improve their lives.

Slowly, the Canada del Oro shriveled until it became a dry wash that ran occasionally. Most of the ranchers were driven away by lack of abundant water. The settlers stayed. Undeterred, they sank wells and continued on with their lives and improving their rancheros. The land was still there, with its vistas, and its underground water. With the Homestead Act, the abandoned cattle ranches were soon populated by another breed, the settler looking for a piece of land—not to work it, but to live on it and create a quality lifestyle for his family.

After the Homestead Act, there was even less land for cattle, and later when the developers arrived small communities covered the open spaces. Country clubs, golf courses, art societies, and schools sprung up, and along with them the type of people who value these things. Here in the lands of Oro Valley, the Legendary Locals met the challenges to provide for their families while striving to maintain the beauty and peacefulness of the hills and mountains that had lured them. Merchants and industry moved into the area to provide an economic base that did not interfere with the beauty of the land. Today, Oro Valley is surrounded by some of the best nature has to offer: mountains, the Coronado National Forest, the Honey Bee Canyon archaeological site, the mighty Saguaro, and an abundance of state and federal parks.

To add to nature's bountiful cornucopia, the residents of Oro Valley have enhanced their town with public art, thus creating one of the prettiest small towns in America. It was the love of the finer things in life, and the desire and determination to capture these things, that made legends in Oro Valley.

The Santa Catalina Mountains march in a line from south to northwest. They are rugged and dominating, reaching a peak of over 9,000 feet. They face the smaller Tortolita and Galiuro Mountains, which in comparison look more like large rocky hills. There is water here for those who want to look for it and work for it. It arrives with running creeks and a flowing Canada del Oro during monsoon season. But, mostly you have to dig for it, and pamper your supply.

The beauty of the mountains and the wild land called the original settlers. They found it ideal for raising cattle. The mountain slopes offered an almost unlimited supply of grazing land. Cattle didn't care if they had to climb to find the sweet grass. But when the droughts hit and the grasses dried up along with the water, most of the big ranchers gave up their land. Ranching is not an easy life; it knows no set hours and is all-consuming, offering a life of little else but ranch work. But for men and women who enjoy the challenges offered by nature, and raising cattle, there is no other life. Determined and tenacious, ranchers respect nature and deal with what she gives them. They understand the delicate balance of their lives and how they are at the whim of weather and the land. They also appreciate the magnificent beauty nature offers up for free.

Catalina, the smallest of our communities, lacks the fertile soil and abundant minerals of Marana, and it does not have the close proximity to a city and all that it offers that Oro Valley enjoys. What it has is the determination of the individual to make it on his or her own, and because of its isolation, a sense of neighborly responsibility.

When the ranches disappeared, the land was taken over by communities of people who appreciated the beauty of the land snuggled at the base of mountain ranges. At first, the new settlers wanted only the independence this solitary spot offered them. But the climate and the land soon enticed those who were able to retire from their working life and relax. Communities sprung up that captured the beauty of the land. While the use of the land changed mostly from work to play, the spirit of caring neighbors did not. Catalina offered its heart to help their village and neighbors.

Some say there is no history, only biographies. They may be right. The history of wars is compiled through the reported actions of the warriors. The history of cultures is about the collective and individual behaviors of their people. All these people were ordinary until their stories were told; then they became a part of history. What they did, how they did it, and in some cases the reasons behind their actions tell stories not only of individuals, but also of communities and their values.

Legends are made not only by actions, but by the perception of the community. All the Legendary Locals in this book have been nominated by their communities, family members, or acquaintances.

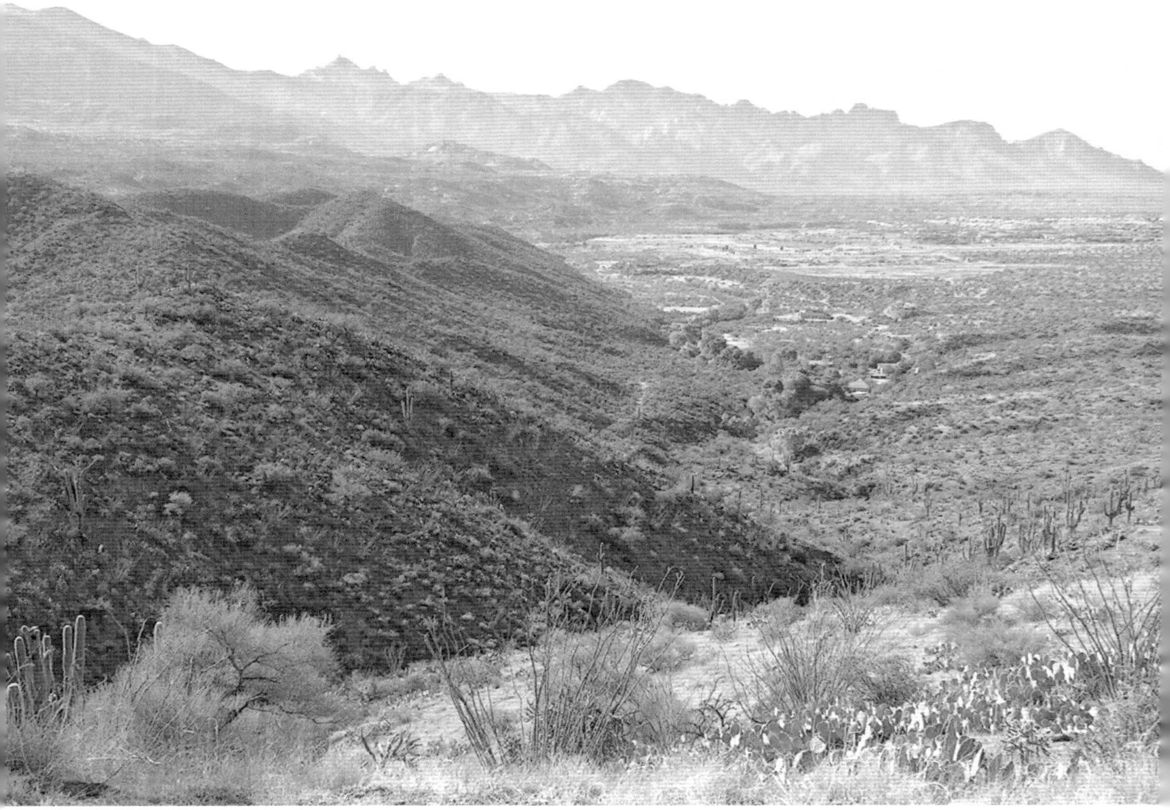

The Land

The lands of Marana, Oro Valley, and Catalina echo with history from the Santa Catalina Mountains to the cotton fields and around the roving cattle. It is a land that made the special people who are legendary locals. (Author's collection.)

CHAPTER ONE

Marana: Blending Cultures with the Land

Marana sprawls over 126 square miles and is the largest of the three places featured in this book. Located at the western end of the Marana–Oro Valley–Catalina corridor, the town, incorporated in 1977, gets its name from a Mexican word that means dense brush, which is what the railroad workers found when they came to build the train tracks that brought the first train to southwest Arizona Territory in 1880.

The town has been considered a prime spot for settlements since early times because of its location near the waters of the Santa Cruz River, where three tributaries, the Rillito River, Canada del Oro Wash, and the Altar-Brawley Wash, join. Because of its proximity to water, this floodplain can trace human settlements back to the Clovis culture about 11,000 BC.

For Juan Bautista de Anza, captain of the Spanish Tubac Presidio, the countryside of Marana was a roadway that led to claiming the lands of California. His expedition of 200 colonists and an additional 100 soldiers, priests, and various experts passed through Marana. This small army of pioneers and explorers camped near Pointer Mountain. Historical records show they also made camp at the old Indian village of Oit Par, which is near the current Pinal Air Park, and in the native village once situated at Picacho Peak.

Marana's geography, especially its proximity to water, is what has drawn such a diversification of people and industry to this spot. It has always been a welcoming place for people of all cultures.

The footprints of western history are etched across the dirt of Marana. It was host to ancient Indian cultures, and evidence of the Hohokam people, who go back to about AD 1000, can still be found by archaeologists in the remains of ancient villages, petroglyphs, and artifacts. It has been a path to the fulfillment of dreams for many including Father Kino, who arrived here in 1694 to explore the land for Spain and to bring Christianity to the indigenous people.

Picacho Peak has the distinction of being the site of the most western Civil War battle. In May 1862, Confederate troops occupied Tucson, and Union troops planted the American flag high at Picacho Peak to stake their claim in the area. The challenge to the Confederate soldiers could not be ignored. The ensuing battle lasted an hour and a half. Three Union soldiers were killed, but at the end of the day the Yankees prevailed and reclaimed the land. In 1846, another military group came through Marana. The Mormon Battalion marched through on its way to San Diego.

John W. Butterfield also took advantage of the roadway to California created by de Anza. The Butterfield Stage used the route to deliver mail and passengers between St. Louis and San Francisco. The trip took 25 days.

Marana has always provided a chance for people from many cultures to realize their ambitions. The Chinese came to work the railroads and stayed to enrich the economy and culture of these desert lands. Many years later, Buck Sam Chu also found Marana to his liking, especially the cotton industry. Black American migrant workers brought their knowledge of cotton crops from the East Coast and turned it into one of the town's major economic factors. They settled in an area called Rillito. Actor D.C. Warren, who appeared in the Clint Eastwood film, *The Outlaw Josey Wales*, grew up there. When machinery replaced the pickers, farmhands arrived to work the crops.

For much of its history, Marana was sparsely populated, but today it is a busy modern town of 35,000 citizens. Its major economic contributors are agriculture, copper mining, and cement products. The Cal Portland cement plant facility produces one half of the cement products in Arizona and the Silver Bell Mine is a major producer of high-grade copper.

Historically Marana is noted for the state of Arizona's 3 Cs . . . Copper, Cotton, and Cattle. There isn't much ranching done in Marana today, but the White Stallion Ranch, a dude and semi-working ranch founded by the True family, is an entertaining reminder of the town's historic ranching past. Further reminders of its ranching heritage are found in the Marana auction stockyards and the many competitive rodeo events conducted throughout the year. In fact, one of its citizens, Sherry Corvi, is a barrel-racing champion holding several national titles.

Ora Mae Harn saw to it that Marana did more than accept other cultures. She worked to develop a community spirit. Aware of the plight of some of the improvised farm and mine workers, she put her efforts into expanding and improving the health clinic, and setting up a food bank. Leading by example, she invited families to her home to enjoy a sit-down dinner during holidays.

Frank McDuff arrived in 1937 and built the first cotton gin. Pat Garrett came to town and worked to guarantee water for the town's crops for future generations. The community-minded Honea family arrived five generations ago to farm, and one of their descendants has served for over 20 years on the town council. Sarah Gorby became internationally famous for her rehabilitation of wildlife, and Red Skelton entertained the soldiers at Marana's Army Air Training Base during the Second World War. A modern addition to the town's economic and cultural base is the Ritz Carlton Resort at Dove Mountain, where professional golf's Accenture Match Play Championship takes place.

In Marana, Yaqui Indians, the descendants of the ancient Hohokam, walk among the sons and daughters of old western prospectors, railroad men, ranchers, and miners. Marana is a place where individual cultural differences are celebrated. However, each culture is only a facet of the whole . . . a town that prides itself on what it was, is, and will be. Most importantly, it takes pride in its people. Marana is still a gracious host to all cultures, ways of life, and talents, and it has produced a plethora of Legendary Locals.

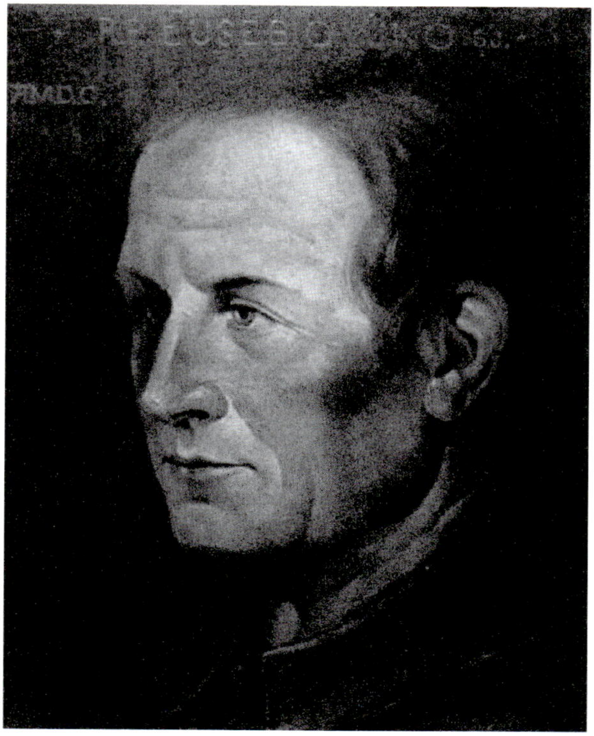

Eusebio Kino and the Yaquis

In 1691, Father Eusebio Kino followed the Santa Cruz River and arrived in what would later become the town of Marana. There he met with the Yaquis, who had repelled the conquest of the Toltecs, Aztecs, and earlier Spanish units. But their curiosity was great and they welcomed Father Kino. Educated in the sciences and adept at learning languages, he brought them more than Christianity. He worked with the Yaquis, encouraging them to group into communities for protection from the marauding Apaches. Father Kino taught the Yaquis agriculture practices that included irrigation techniques and gave them seed for winter crops. Father Kino died in 1711, but the Yaquis are still a part of Marana. Today 39 families live on a sub-reservation in the town. The Yaqui photograph is in the public domain. (Courtesy of the National Archives.)

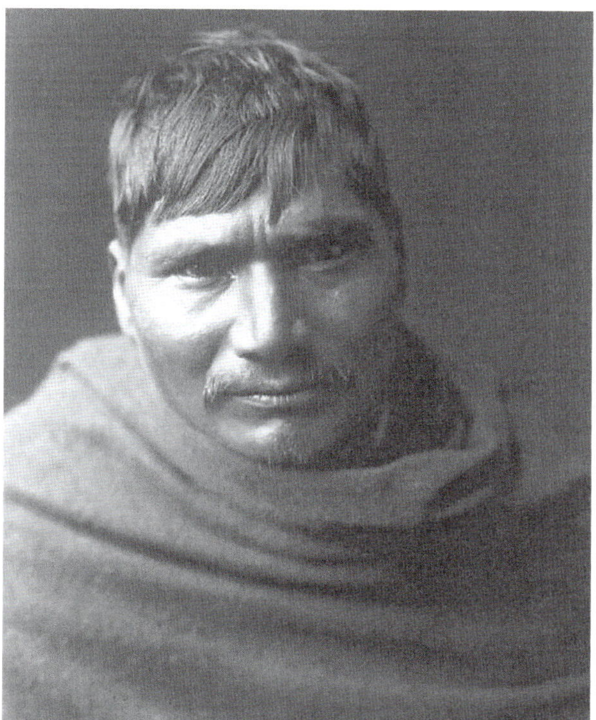

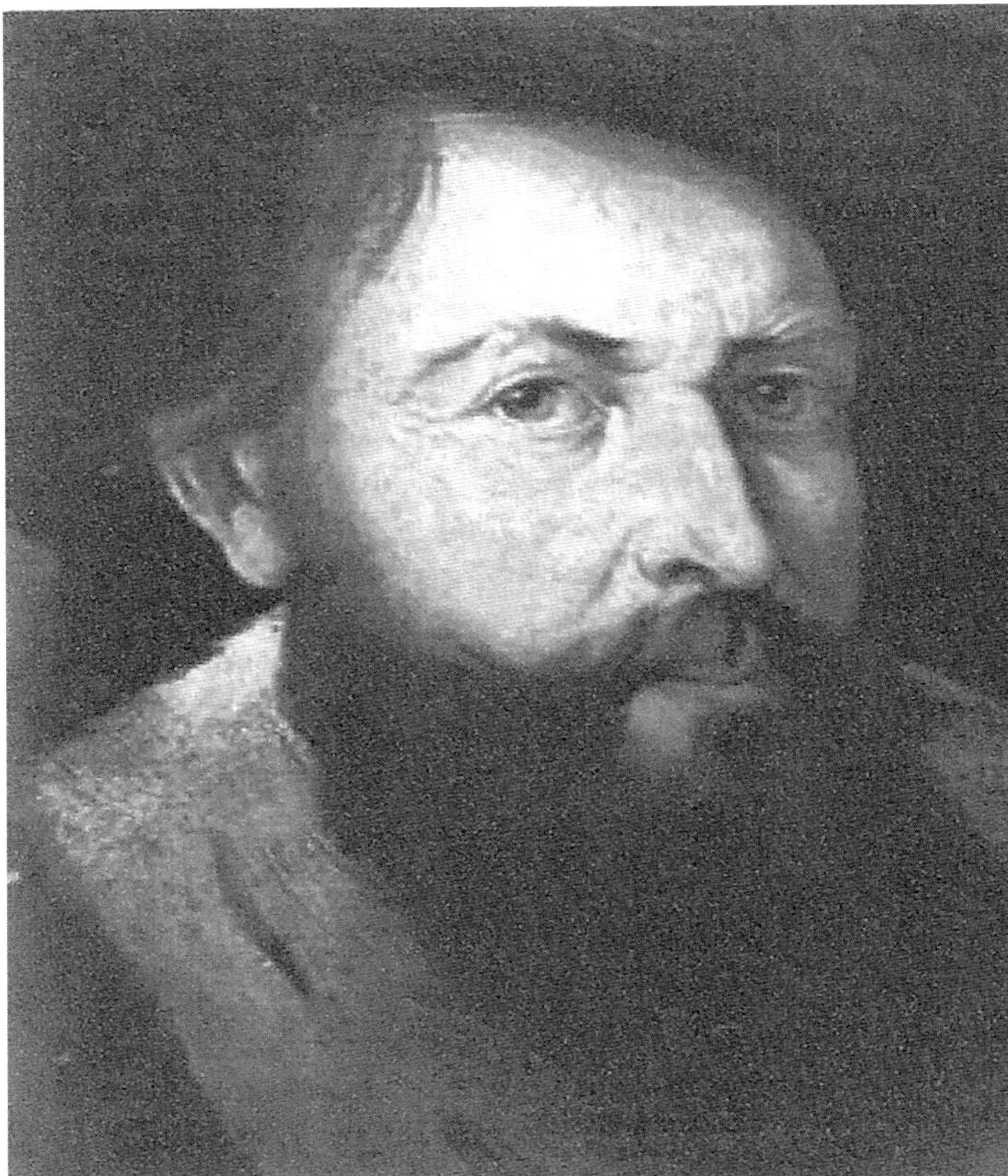

Juan Bautista de Anza
In 1775, de Anza was given orders by Spain to colonize the San Francisco Bay area. He started out from the Presidio in Tubac, Arizona, with the colonizers. The expedition included 30 soldiers and their families, cowboys, muleteers, guides, burros, and 1,000 head of cattle. These 300 people made camp in southern Marana near Pointer Mountain. There two mule handlers tried to desert the expedition and were punished, which earned this place the name Llano del Azotado (flat of the criminal publicly whipped). Near what is now Pinal Air Park, the expedition set up their second Marana campsite. Their third stop was at the native village at Picacho Peak. De Anza's route earned Marana the distinction of being part of the Juan Bautista de Anza National Historic Trail. (Author's collection.)

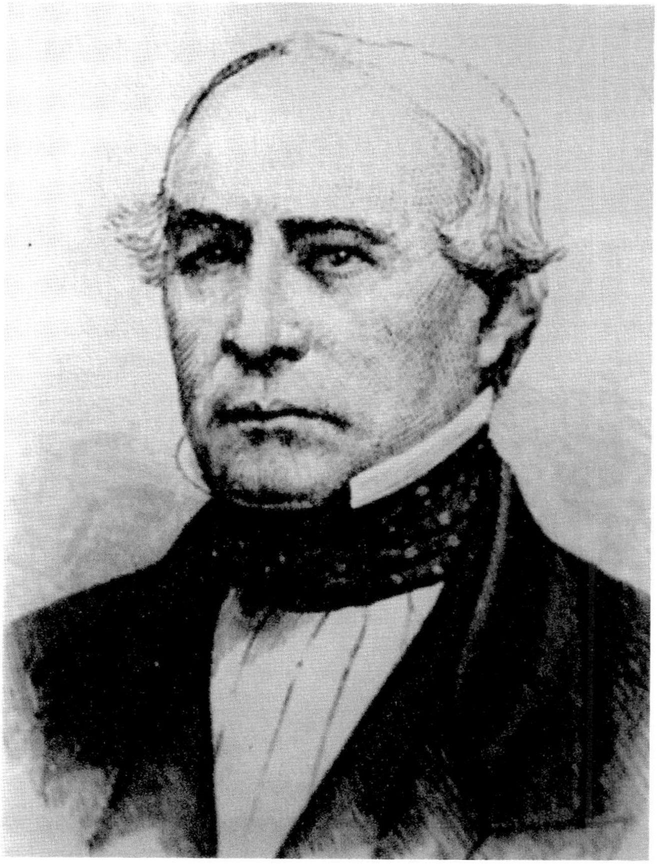

Highway to the West
From 1859 to 1861, John W. Butterfield's overland stage operated a southern route between St. Louis and San Francisco. The first Butterfield Concord coaches simultaneously departed both cities on September 15, 1859, and arrived at their destinations within 25 days. The route included remount stations at Pointer Mountain, Nelson's Desert Ranch, and Picacho Pass. There were no overnight stops; the stage traveled 24 hours a day, halting to change horses. Although it was a mail route, there were passengers. Fare for the entire trip was $250. Passengers were allowed 25 pounds of luggage, two blankets and a canteen. At the relay stops, passengers ate dried meat, bread, and coffee. The relay station is gone, but Butterfield helped Marana make its mark in transportation history. (Butterfield, author's collection; Station, courtesy Arizona Historical Society #51108.)

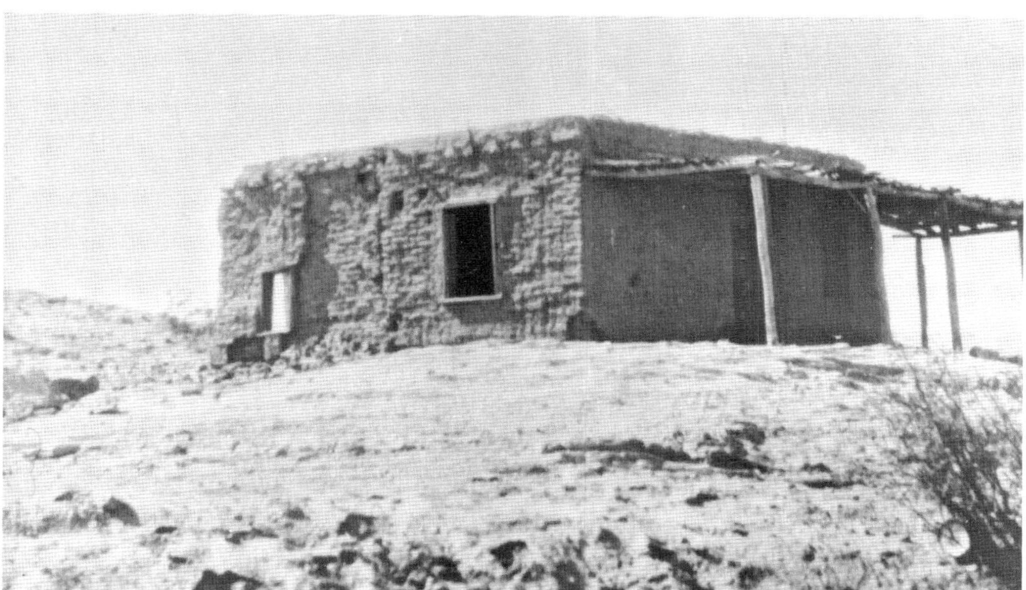

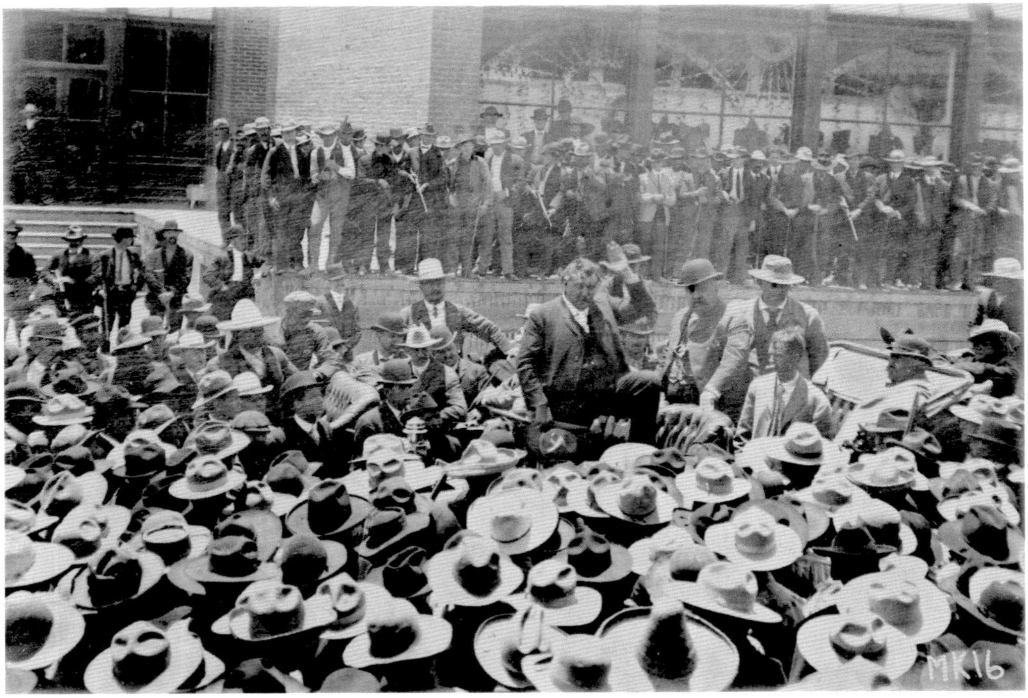

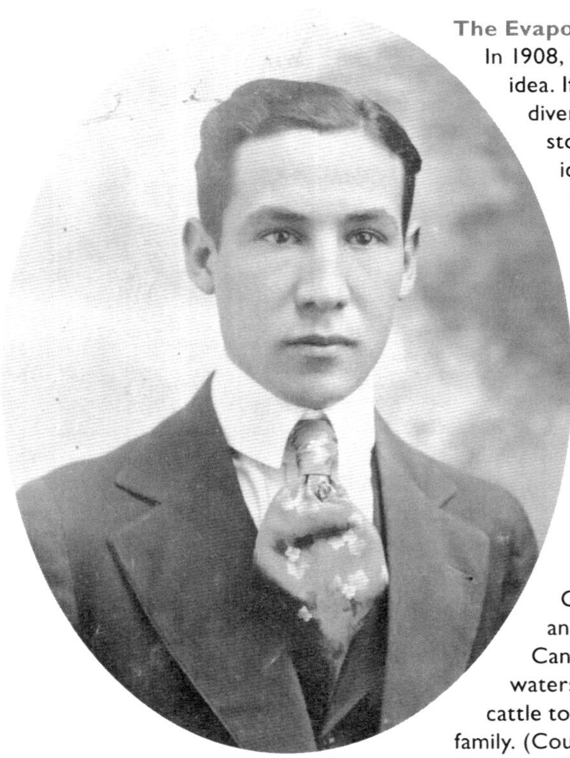

The Evaporated Water Project

In 1908, "Colonel" William C. Greene had a brilliant idea. If the Santa Cruz Reservoir Company diverted floodwaters from the river, it could be stored, then distributed to farmland. This great idea failed when the floodwaters destroyed the Marana dam. The colonel, standing in the center, is shown addressing striking miners in 1906 just across the Arizona border. (Courtesy Southern Methodist University, Central Libraries, DeGolyer Library.)

The Cattle Dons

In 1907, the Aguirres ranched in the Red Rock and Catalina areas. When the Canada del Oro dried up, the family moved their Catalina cattle to Red Rock until the waters and grasses returned. Unfortunately, the Canada del Oro grasses died off and the robust waters never did come back. Marana owes its cattle town reputation to Higinio and the Aguirre family. (Courtesy Arizona Historical Society #6913.)

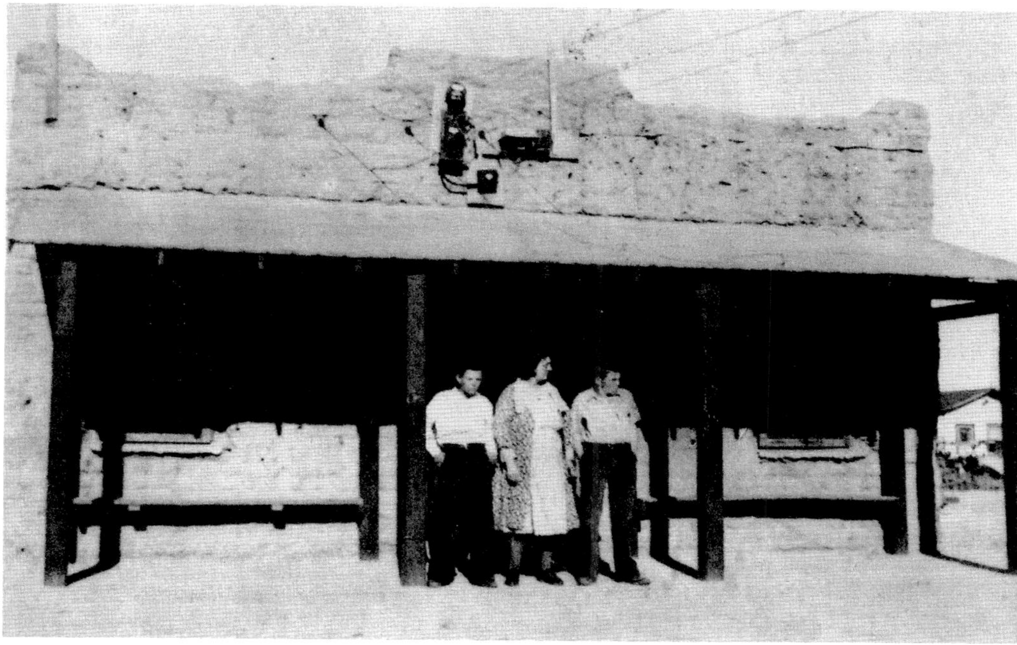

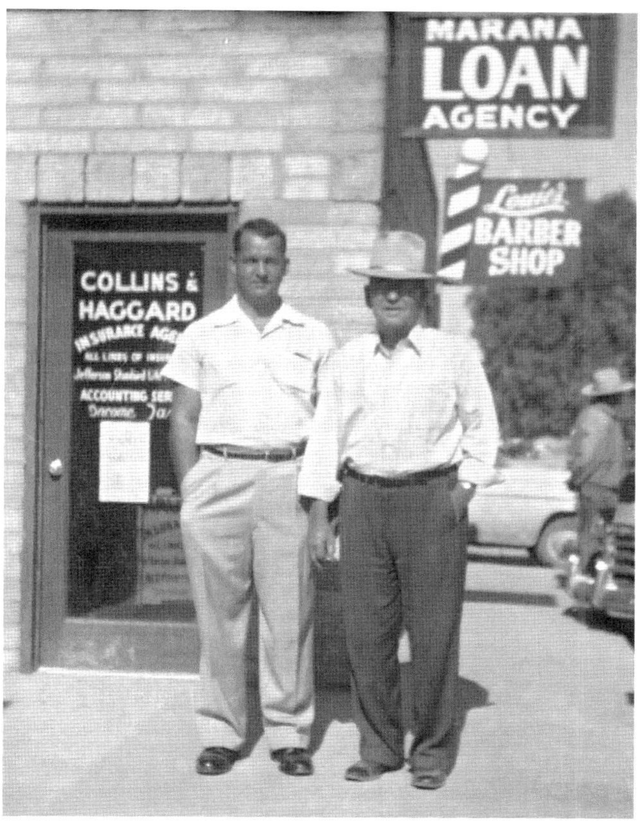

Mistress of the Post
Although Marana had a post office in 1887, it wasn't until the 1930s that they had their first postmistress. This post office was located in an adobe hut on what is now I-10, but was once the town center. Here, she is pictured in front of the original post office between two unidentified men. (Courtesy of the Town of Marana.)

The Mail Man
In the 1940s, James Collins became Marana's postmaster. Postmaster Collins served in that position for over 10 years. He and his brother John were members of one of the pioneering families of the town. Among other things, his brother John drove the school bus. The Collins brothers are shown outside their family insurance business. (Courtesy of the Collins family.)

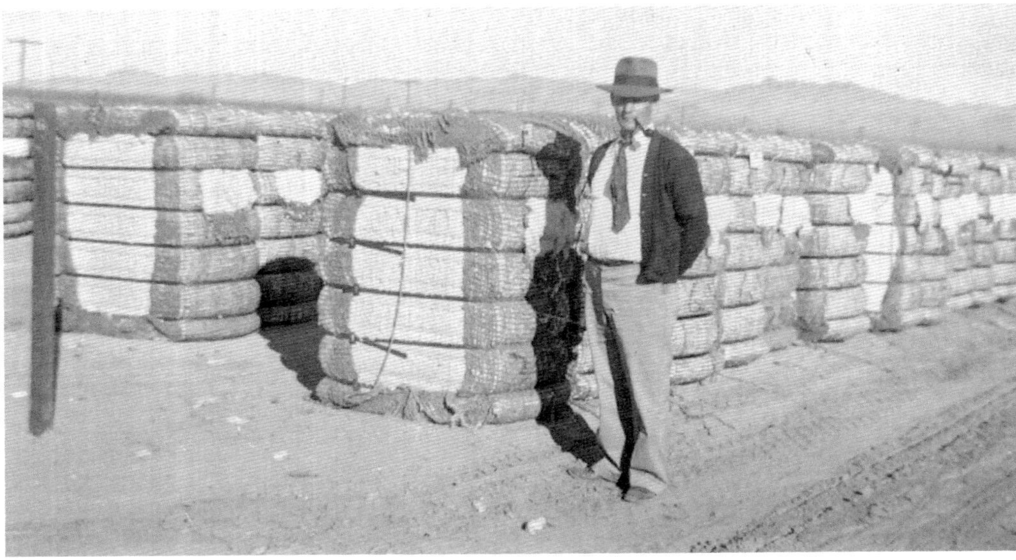

The Insect Man

The important job of "Contrary Bill" from the Arizona Bureau of Entomology was to be sure that the Marana cotton was not infected with insects and to ensure the quality of the crop. This representative was an exacting man, earning him the nickname of "Contrary Bill." He is shown here in the 1950s inspecting a cotton crop in the Marana gin yard. (Courtesy Town of Marana.)

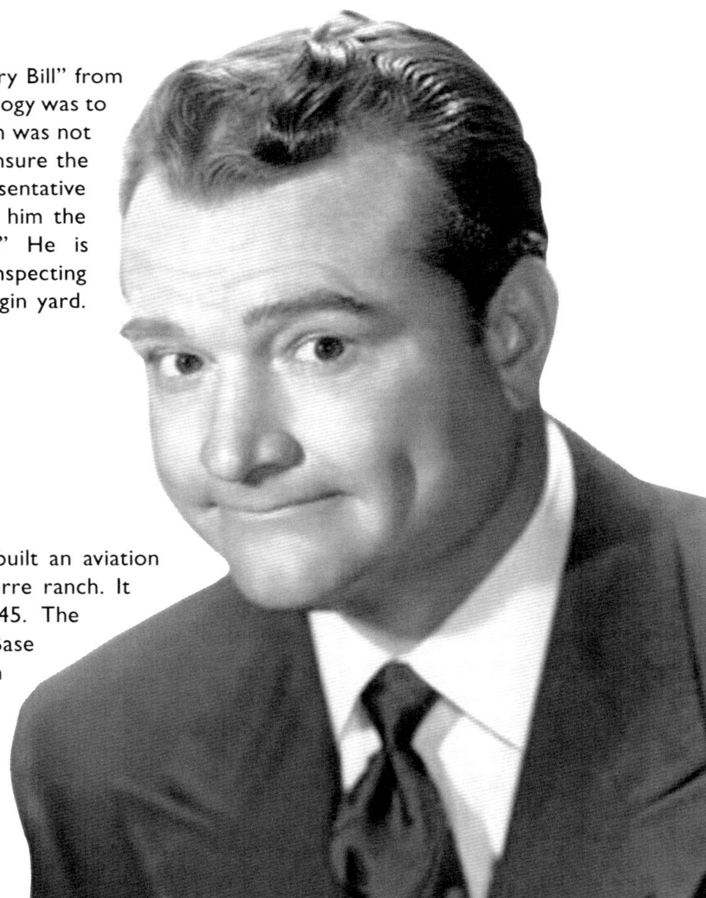

A Comic and a Soldier

In World War II, the Army built an aviation training base on the old Aguirre ranch. It was active from 1942 to 1945. The Marana Army Air Training Base was one of the largest in the country, training over 10,000 aviation personnel. Red Skelton entertained his Army buddies here, then went on after the war to become a celebrated radio, TV, and movie star. (Author's collection.)

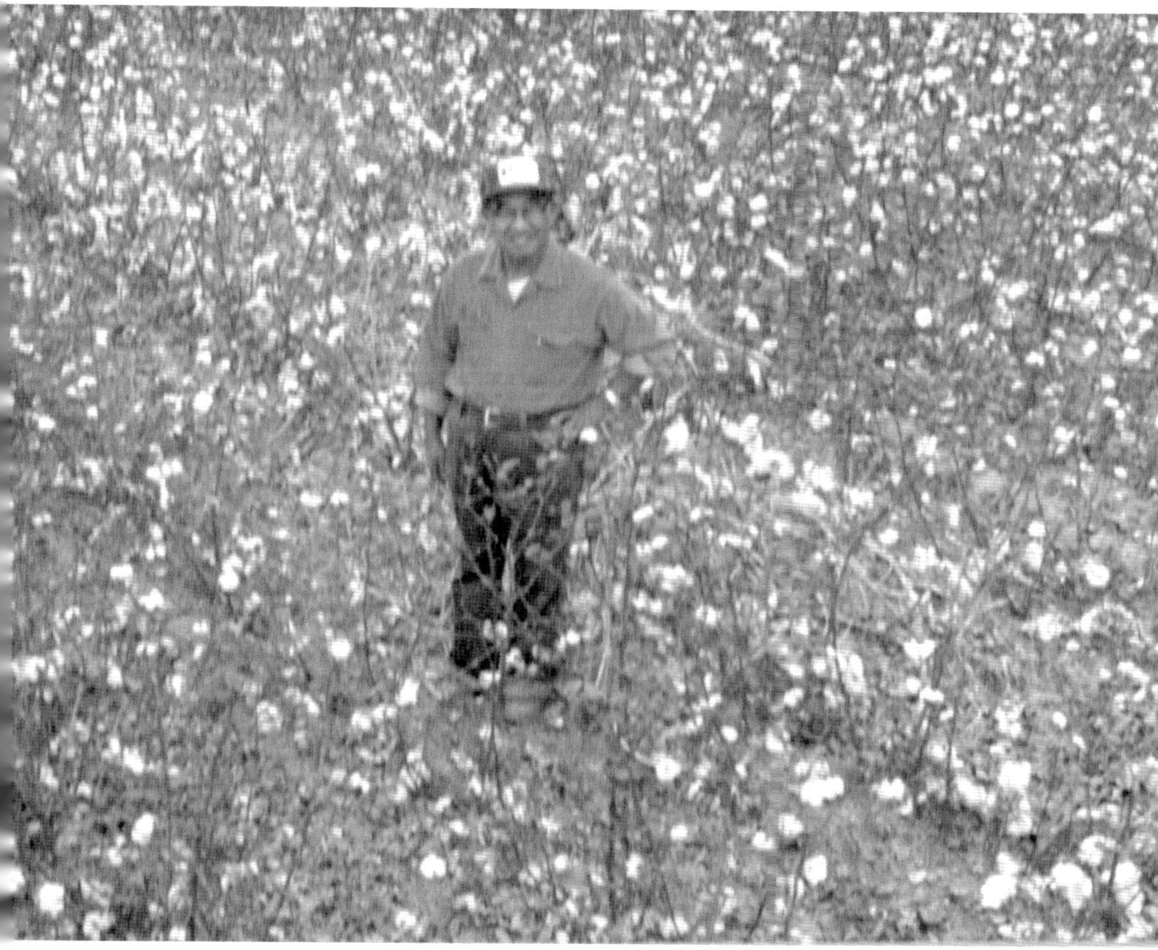

The King of Cotton

Marana was most fortunate when Buck Sam Chu decided to call it home. This extraordinary man came to the United States from China in 1939 to attend the California Institute of Technology. His studies at the university earned him a master of science degree with a double major in mechanical engineering and aeronautical engineering. During World War II, Chu was employed by Hughes Aircraft designing wing-mounted engines for Douglas Aircraft and the Hercules. The Hercules was Howard Hughes's personal favorite and was nicknamed "The Spruce Goose." Unfortunately, it was never put into production and only lived in fable. When "May" Tae-Shar, Chu's wife, arrived from China after the war, the family settled in Tucson. In 1952, the Chu family moved to Marana and purchased the grocery store located on what is now the frontage road. They operated the Village Market in what was then the small village of Marana. When construction was started on I-10, the store was moved to West Trico-Marana Road where the market operated until 1971. Sam Chu became interested in Marana farming in 1959. He was to remain active in agriculture until his retirement in 1984. Immensely successful in growing long-staple cotton (Pima cotton), Chu took great delight in his fields. His pleasure is evident in this picture from around 1970 of Chu standing in the middle of what looks like a snowstorm but is in reality one of his fields ready for harvesting. Today, the cotton grown in Marana has a worldwide market and is considered some of the finest in the country. As Marana grew, it became evident that incorporation was necessary. Sam Chu, a visionary, worked as one of the original incorporators. (Courtesy Chu Ong family.)

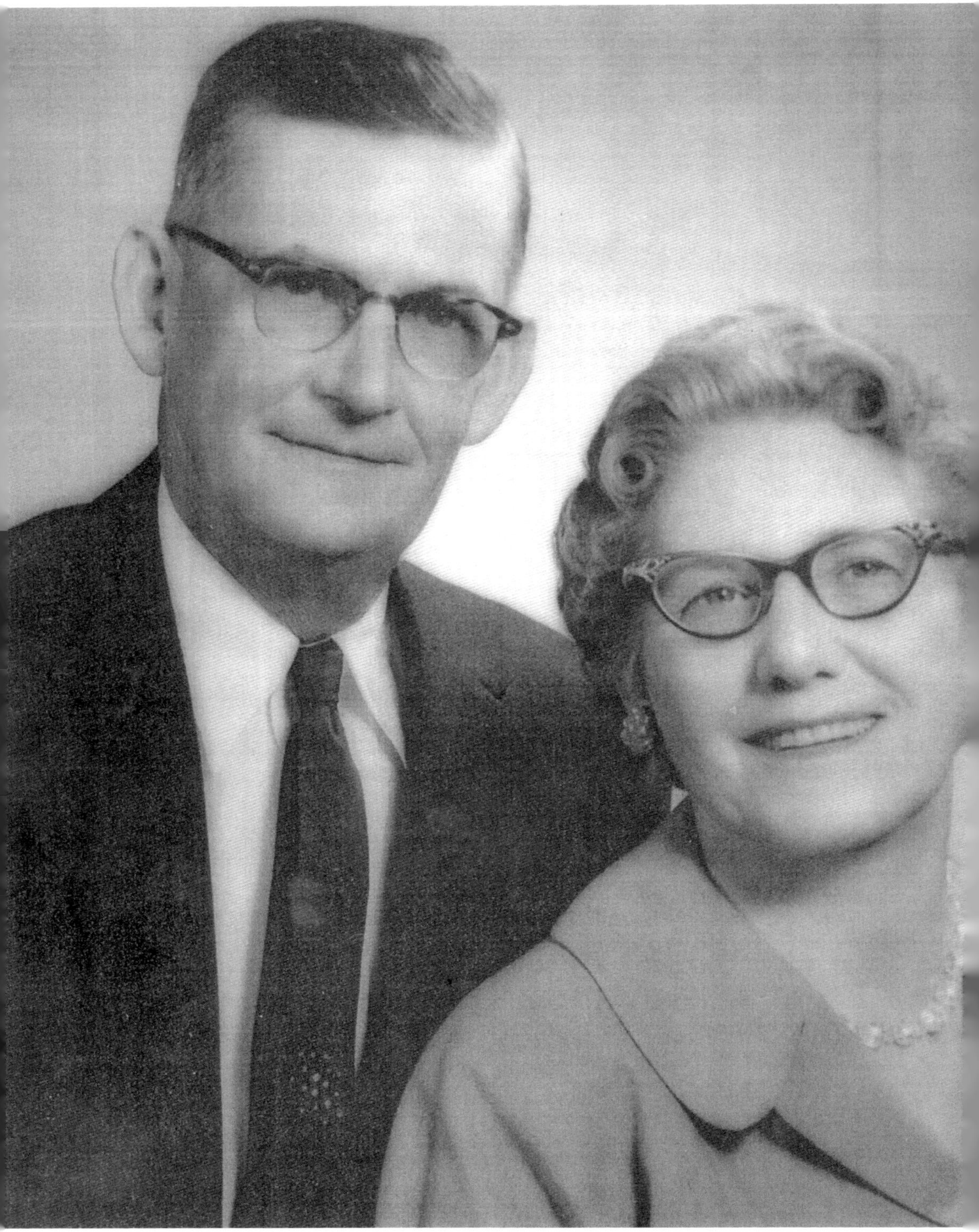

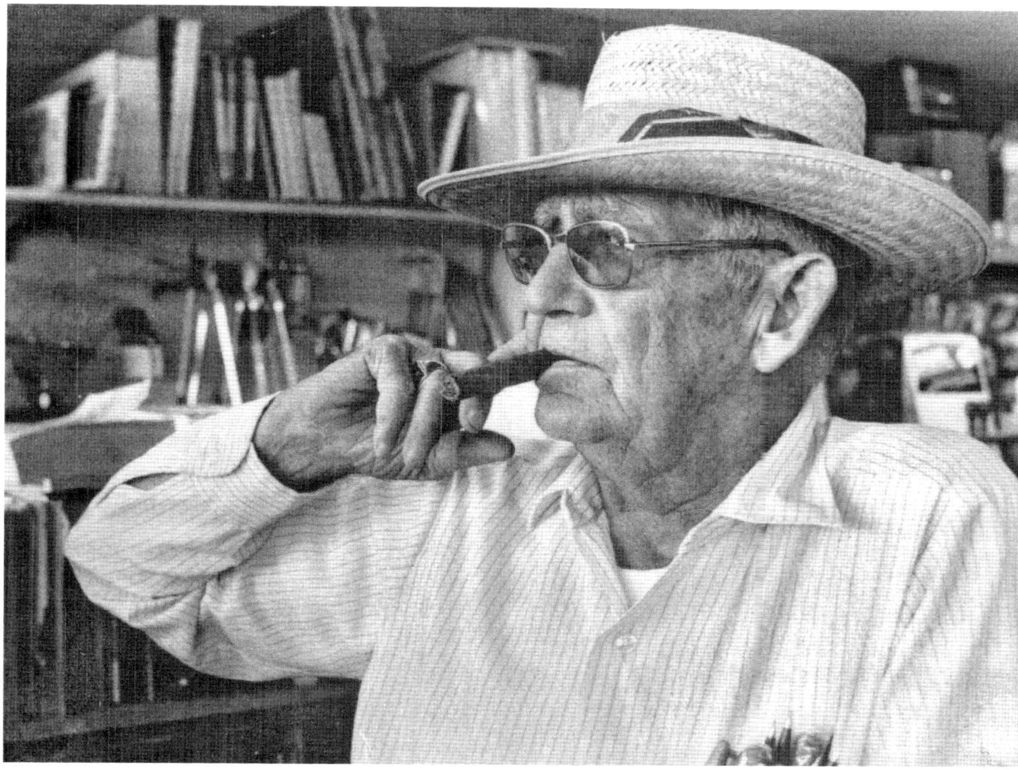

The Town's Foundation

There are few places in Marana that have not experienced the work and concern of the McDuff family. When cotton came to Marana, Frank McDuff built the first cotton gin. The Producer Cotton Gin was constructed in 1938 out of adobe bricks. It was gin, office, and warehouse. Nannie McDuff, the family matriarch and Frank's wife, became part of Marana in 1937. For 28 years, she ran the school cafeteria, taking special food courses to ensure the schoolchildren received nutritious food and that the operation ran efficiently and smoothly. She was an active supporter of the 4H and was made an honorary member of the Future Farmers of America for her support of the organization. Nannie McDuff also was largely responsible for the building of the Church of Christ in Marana. (Courtesy Town of Marana.)

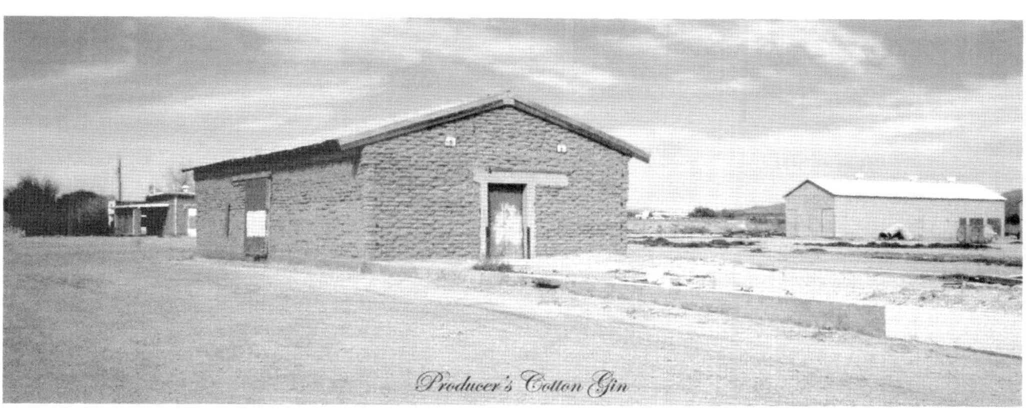

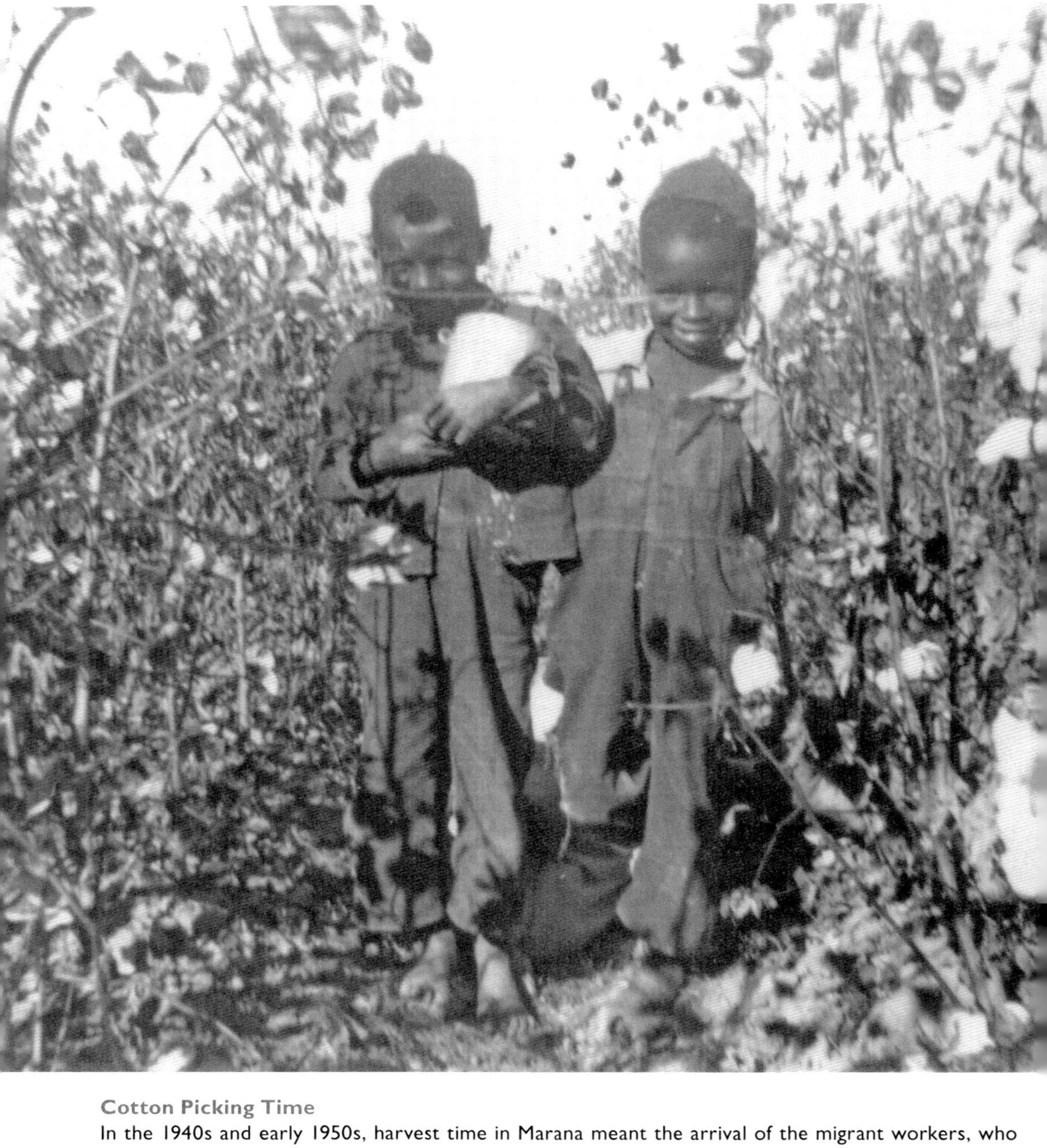

Cotton Picking Time

In the 1940s and early 1950s, harvest time in Marana meant the arrival of the migrant workers, who arrived in buses, cars, and trucks. Whole families would work in the fields. The adults would pick and weigh; children would be given jobs such as carrying water to the workers. A good worker could pick 150 to 200 pounds of cotton a day. Pulling the cotton balls off the stems and stuffing them into sacks, worn around their shoulders, the workers would walk the rows. Bent over their work, they could hardly be seen in the fields. The migrant workers were given housing and little else and moved on after the fields were picked. In the late 50s, the mechanical picking machine put the migrant workers out of business. (Courtesy Town of Marana.)

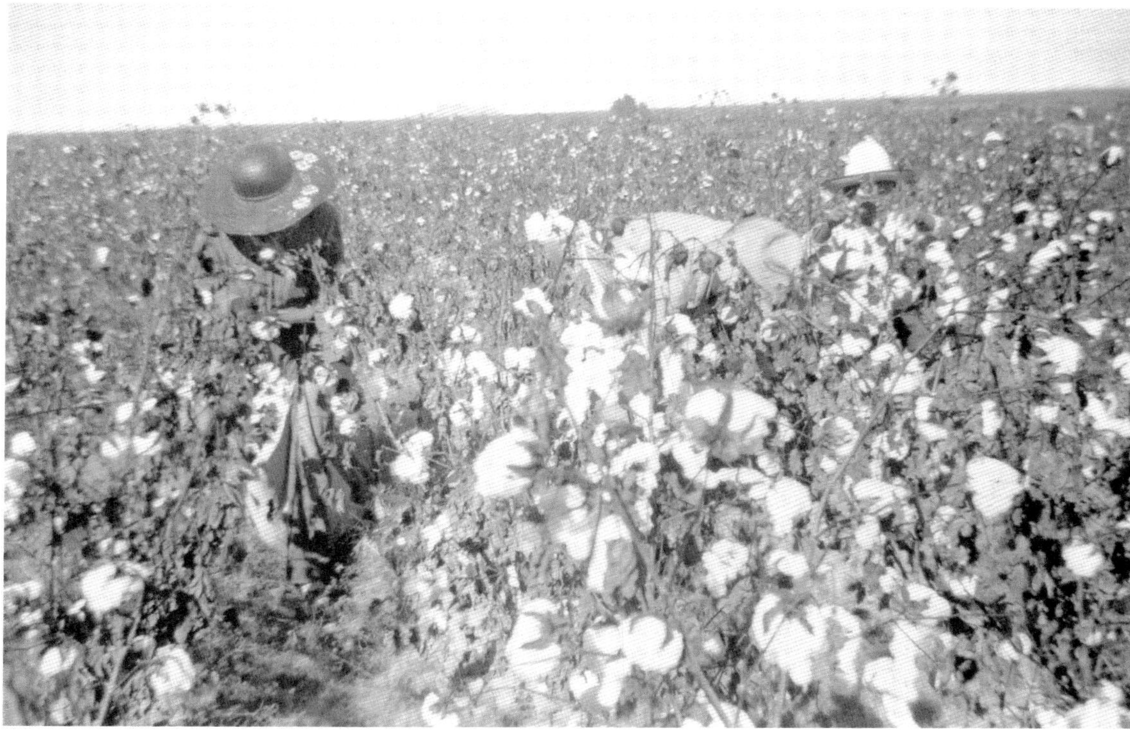

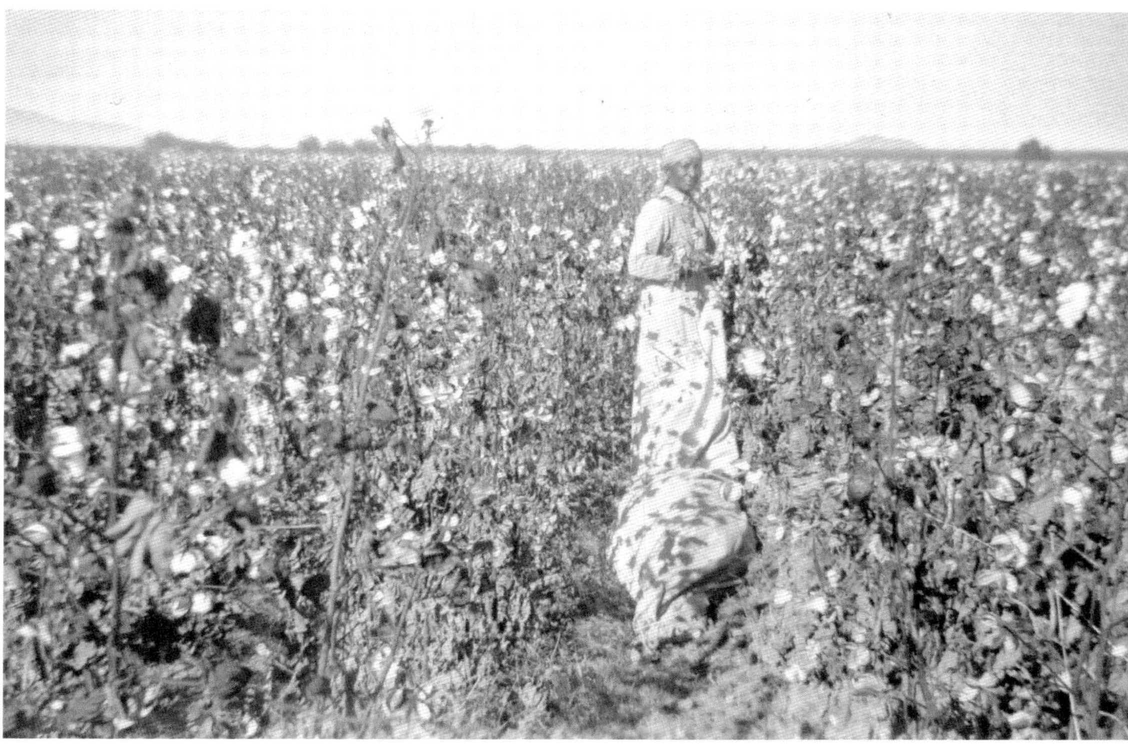

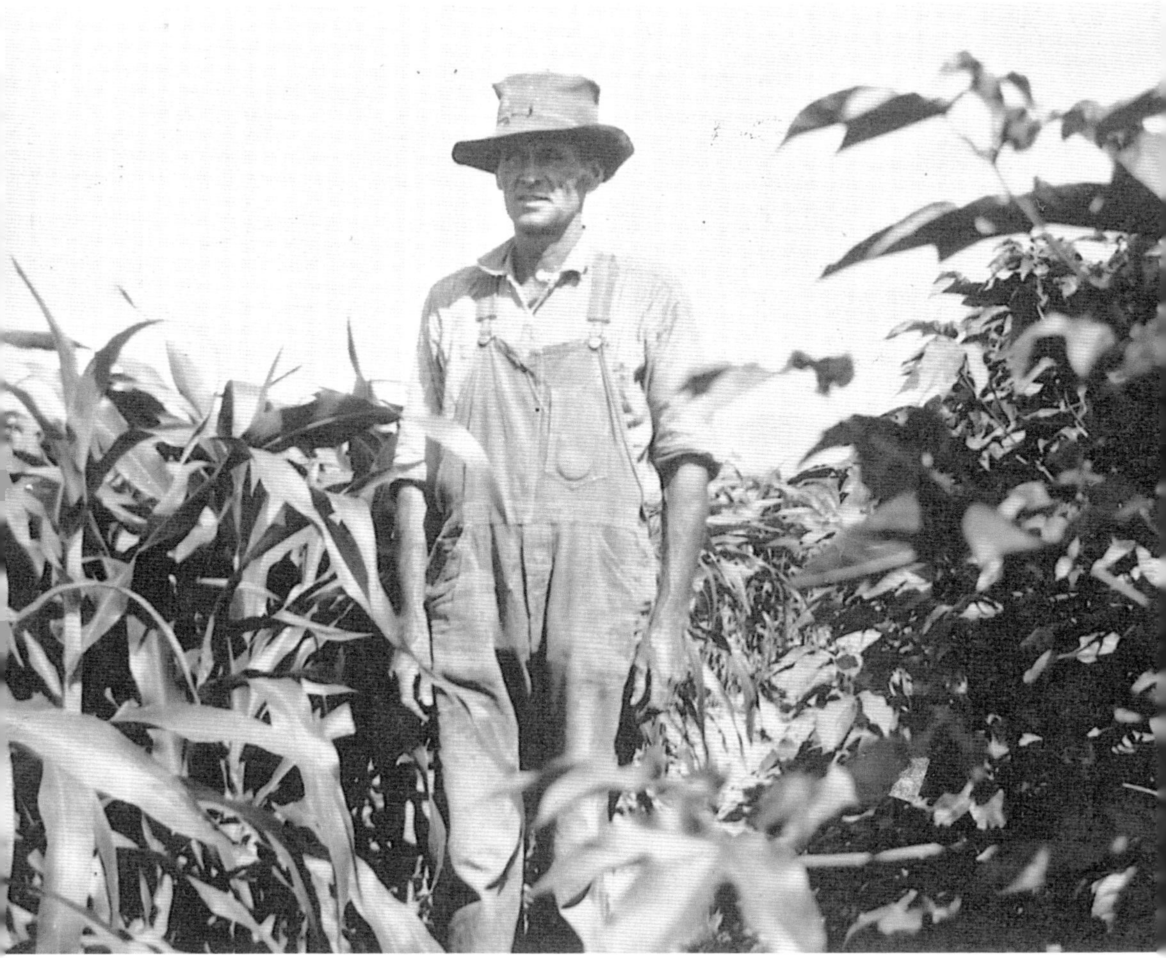

Working the Fields
Around 1955, machines replaced the cotton workers and migrant field hands disappeared. The migrant workers were replaced by farmworkers, who came to Marana and stayed year-round, raising their families here. Although these nameless farmhands had better living conditions than the previous migrant workers, they only got paid when there was work. Today, however, workers are provided with housing, utilities, and a year-round income. The early farmworkers were a part of Marana's history and kept it from becoming another western ghost town. Marana is still an agriculture town and its farmers are an important part of the town's economic base. Central Arizona Project (CAP) waters from the Colorado River keep the town's fields green with crops and white with cotton. The image below depicts the process of weighing the cotton. (Courtesy of the Town of Marana.)

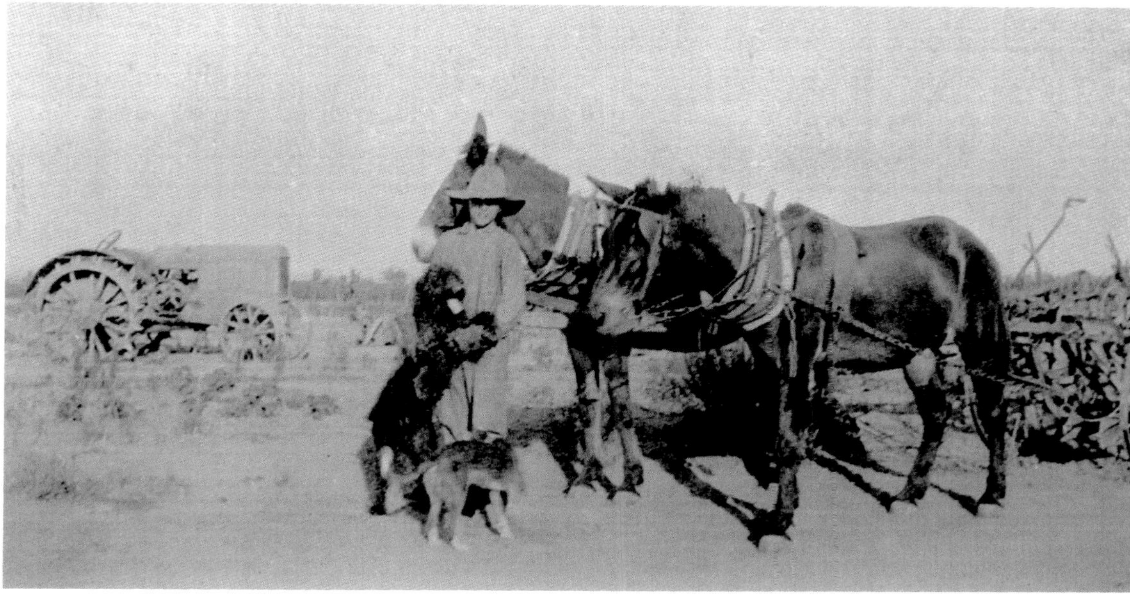

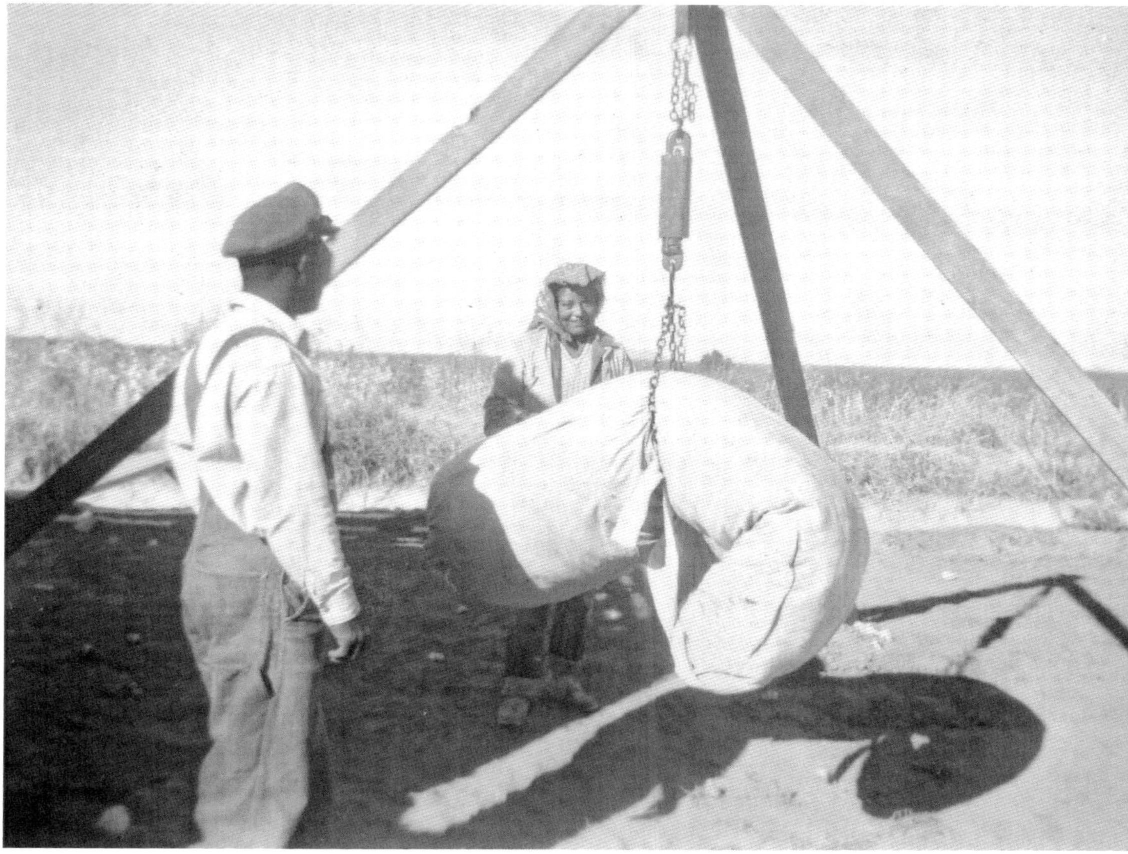

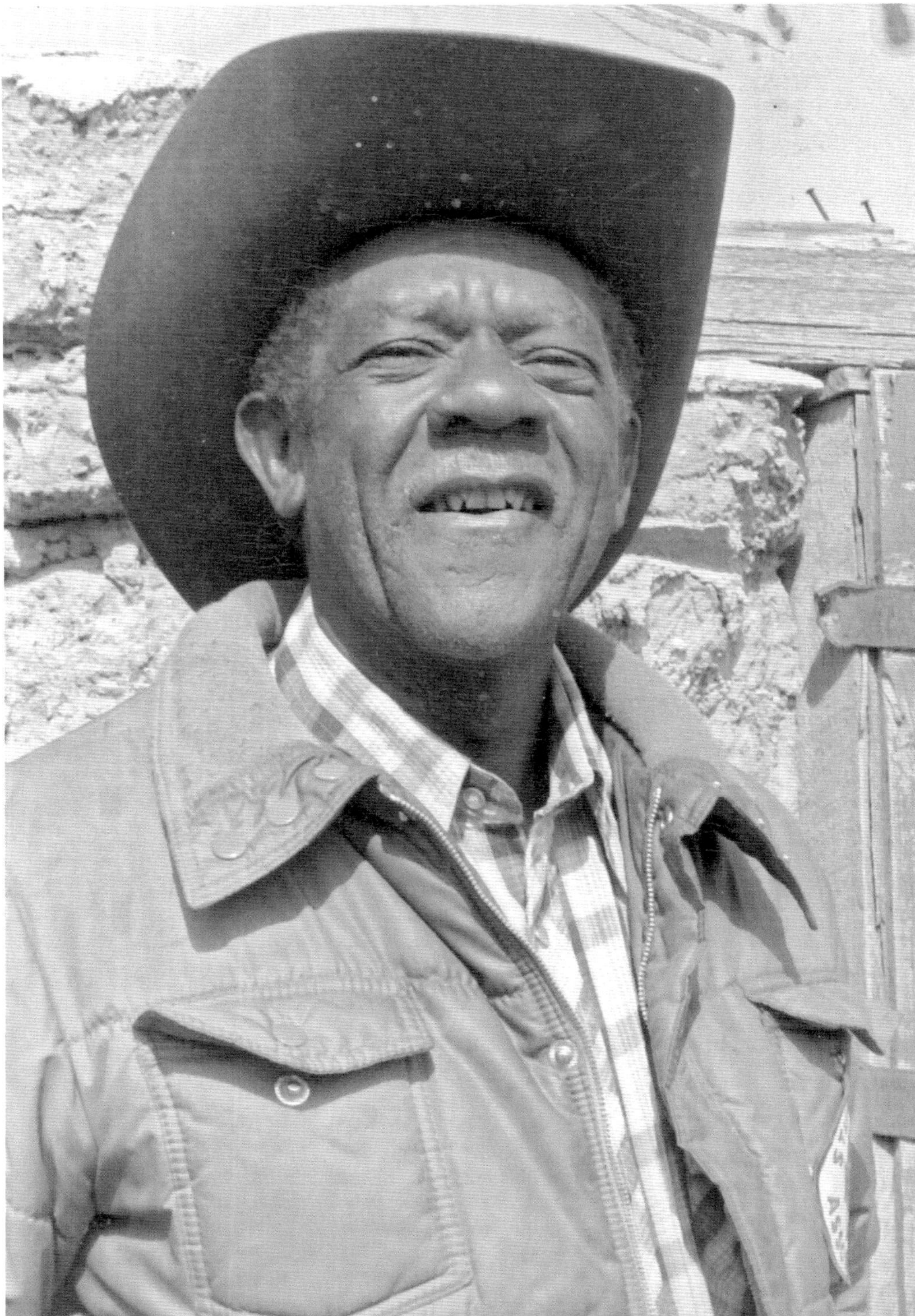

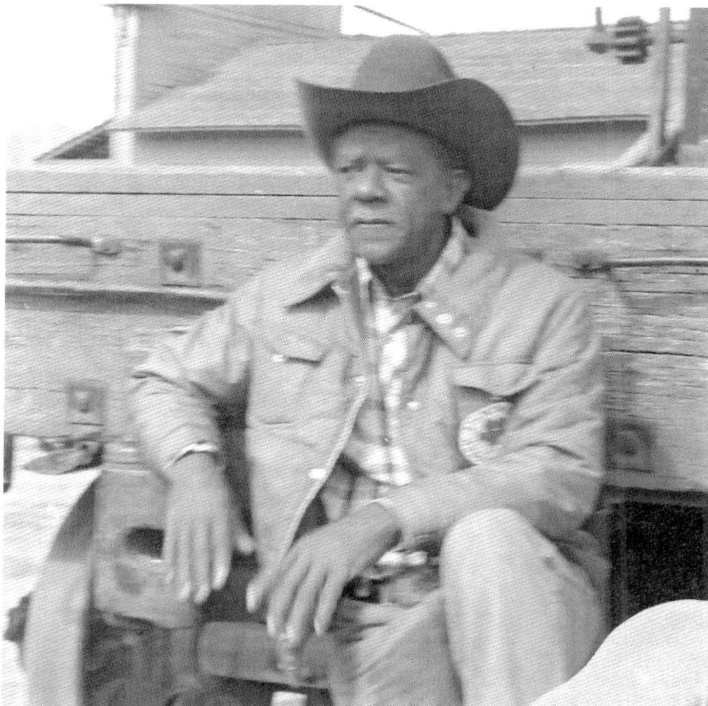

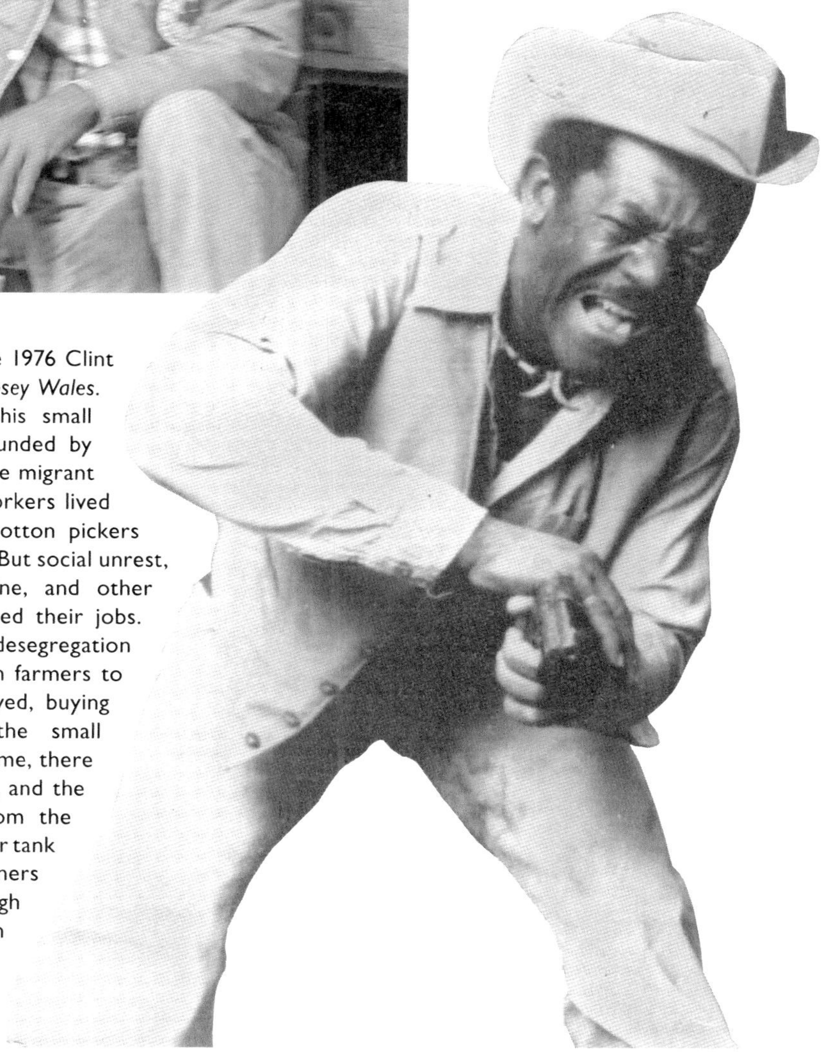

The Outlaw Josey Wales
D.C. Warren had a part in the 1976 Clint Eastwood classic *The Outlaw Josey Wales*. Warren hails from Rillito. This small community, completely surrounded by Marana, got its start during the migrant worker days of the 1940s. Workers lived in housing supplied for the cotton pickers and later for the farmworkers. But social unrest, the cotton harvesting machine, and other technological changes eliminated their jobs. The raging dispute over school desegregation caused many African American farmers to leave the area. But some stayed, buying property and establishing the small community of Rillito. At that time, there was no water supply in Rillito, and the residents got their water from the Southern Pacific Railroad's water tank by filling up their own containers and transporting them. Although Warren had only a small part in *Josey Wales*, he is remembered locally as the Hollywood actor from Rillito. (Courtesy Town of Marana.)

The First Elected Mayor

In 1950, Don Frew's job with El Paso Natural Gas brought him to the Marana area. Making the community his own, he worked to help Marana in its early years. From 1961 to 1964, he served on the Marana School Board. He was the bus director and purchasing director for the school district. After incorporation, he served as its first elected mayor. (Courtesy Frew family.)

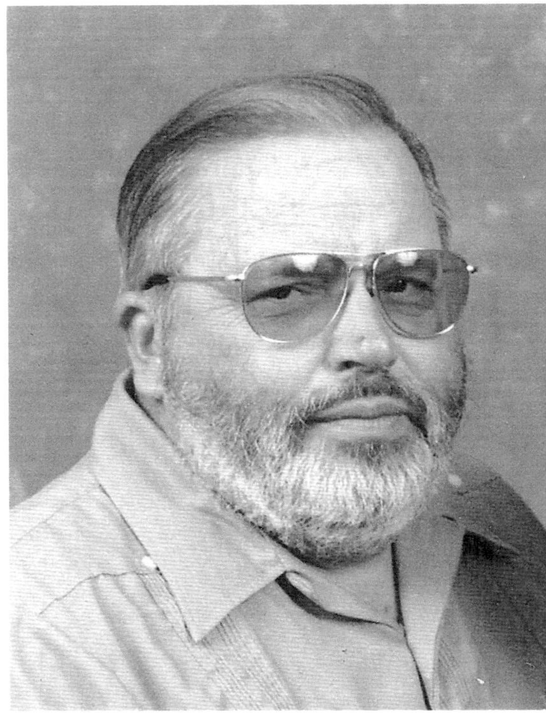

The Post Office Fans

The dedication of the Marana Post Office in 1976 provided an occasion for some Arizona basketball fans to meet. The fans include (from left) Bob Honea, postmaster, the DC postal representative, and US congressman Mo Udall. Honea's family came to Marana to farm and raise horses and is still there serving the community. (Courtesy Town of Marana.)

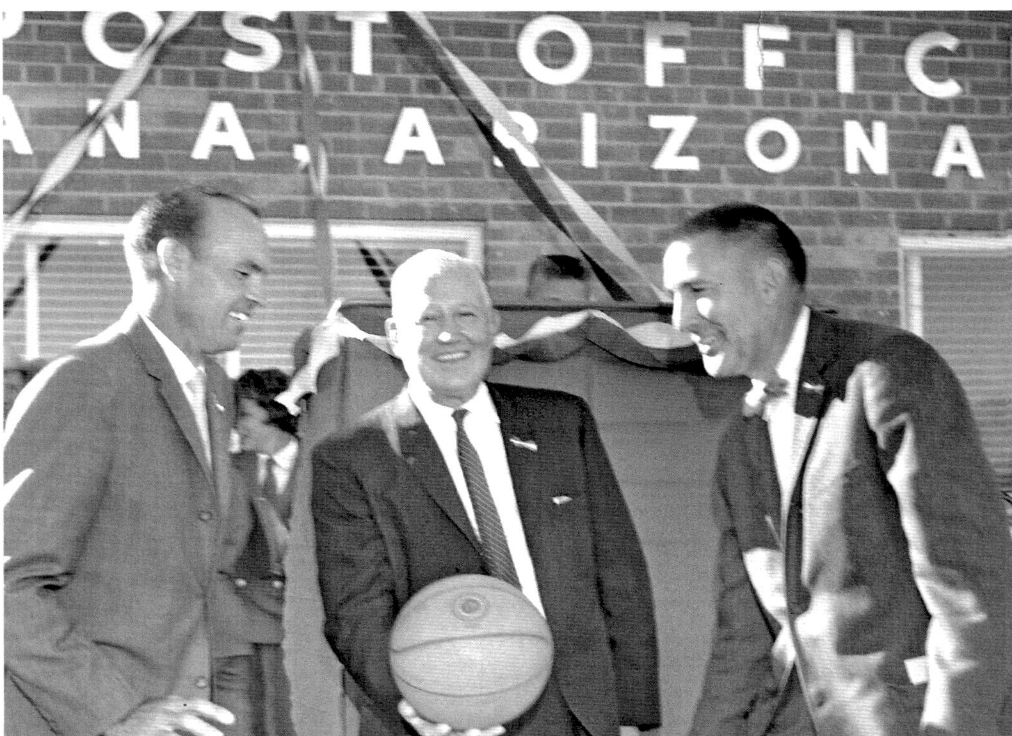

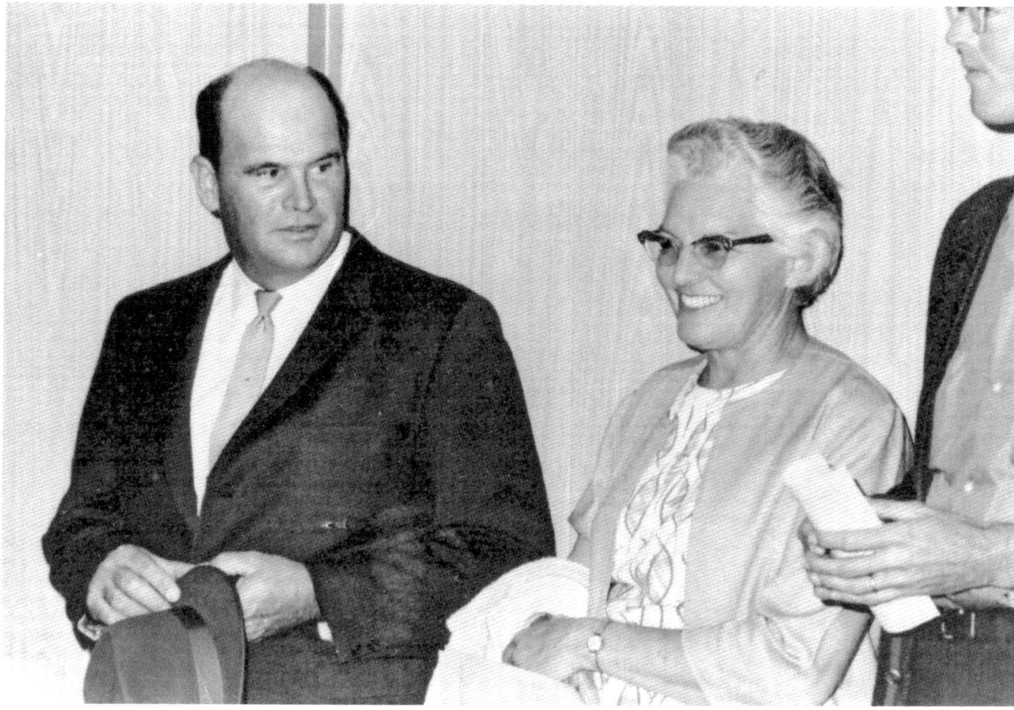

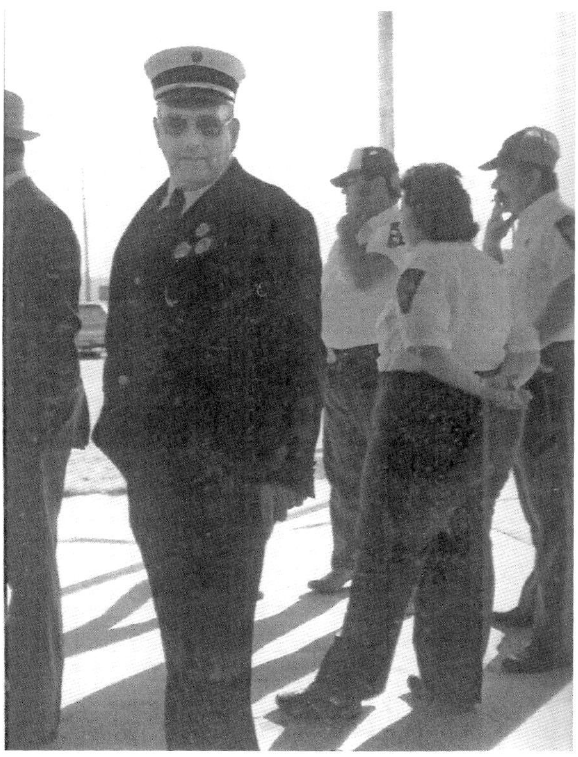

The Water Man

W.H. Pat Garrett brought water to Marana in 1956. With drought conditions threatening the agriculture industry, Garrett brought CAP water to the town. He was president of the Arizona Municipal Water User Association and two times president of the Marana School Board. Garrett helped create the Marana Health Clinic, and was one of the incorporators of the town. (Courtesy Garrett family.)

The Fire Man

As Marana grew, the need to protect its ever increasing population and industries also grew. In 1980, the fledging town of Marana responded and established an official volunteer fire department, complete with a vintage 1957 fire truck. Its first leader was Chief Bill Gaudette. Gaudette established the original policies and protocol that make Marana's current modern fire department so efficient. (Courtesy Town of Marana.)

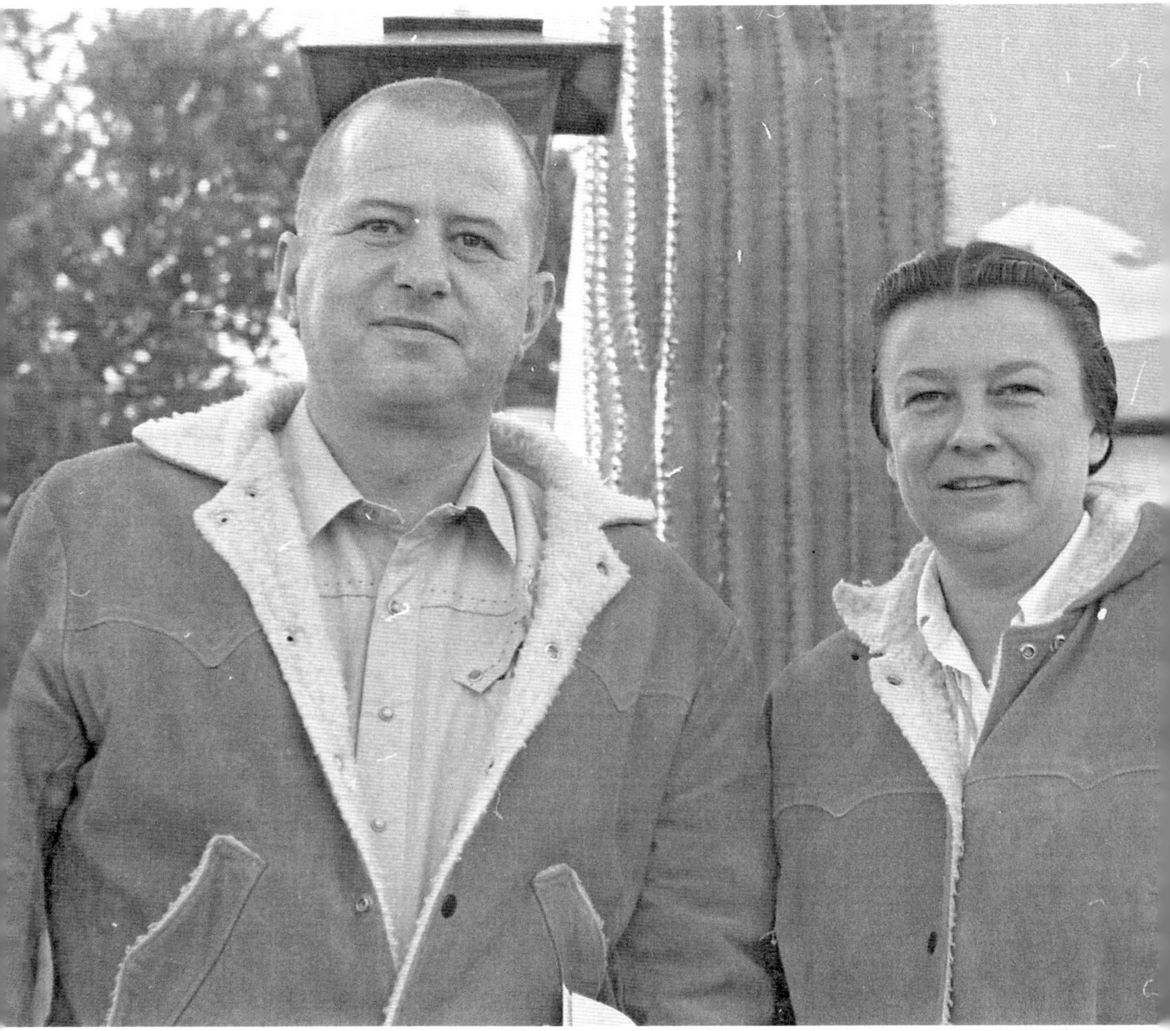

The True Way

The White Stallion Ranch started out as a cattle ranch. Around 1930, chickens and turkeys were added, and at one time there were pens for 30,000 birds. In 1940, Max Zimmerman, a Chicago liquor store owner, bought the ranch and turned it into a guest ranch. By 1948, Mrs. Zimmerman had had enough of the annual trip from Chicago to Marana and the Zimmermans decided to sell. In the ensuing years, it changed hands several times. In 1958, the Townes bought the ranch and it again became a guest ranch. In 1965, after a visit to the White Stallion Ranch, Allen True decided to buy the property. His wife Cynthia said no, but his persistence wore her down and finally she relented, saying, "OK. If I can look at the mountains every morning go ahead, throw our lives away." True purchased the property, put in floor to ceiling windows for mountain views, and worked to upgrade the ranch. The ranch now has 3,000 acres. Their sons, Russell and Michael, took over ranch operations, pouring youthful energy into expanding and renovating. Today, the White Stallion Ranch is known worldwide. It offers some of the best barbecue found in the West and all of it is served under a brilliant Arizona sky. It has been the site of TV movies, commercials, and a *Sports Illustrated* swimsuit shoot. The Trues have brought international recognition to Marana with their famous dude ranch. (Courtesy of the White Stallion Ranch.)

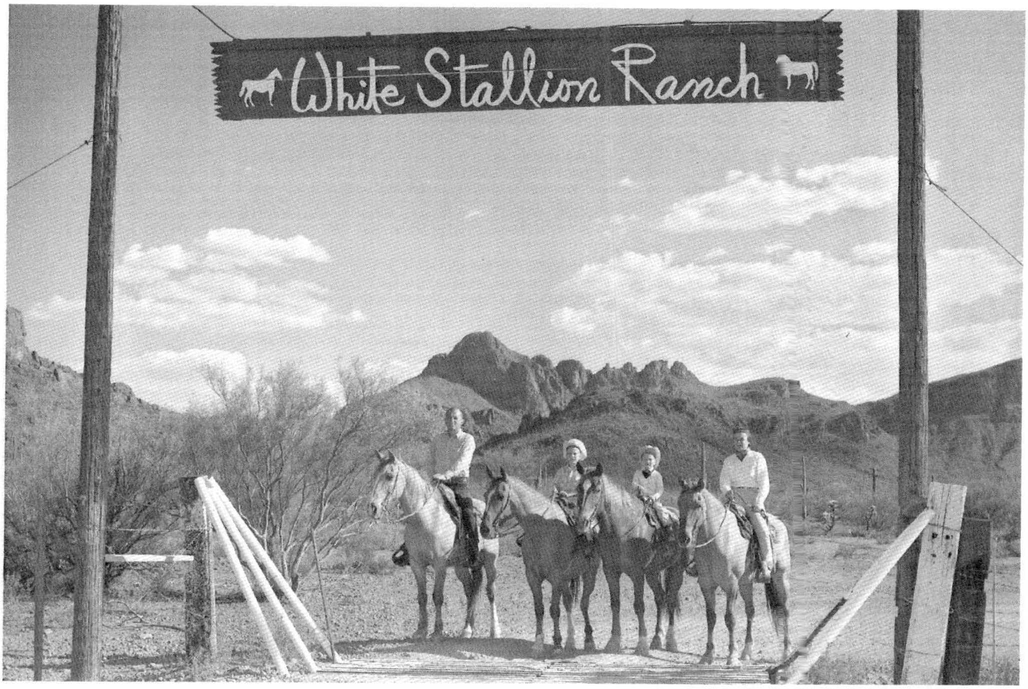
White Stallion Ranch

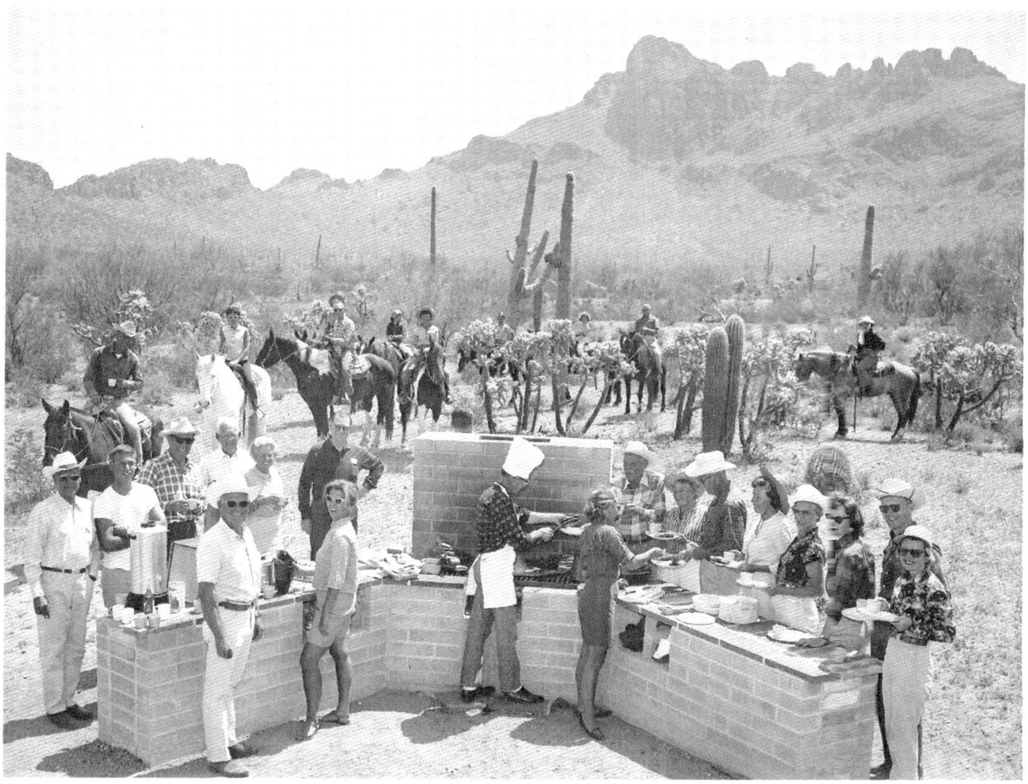

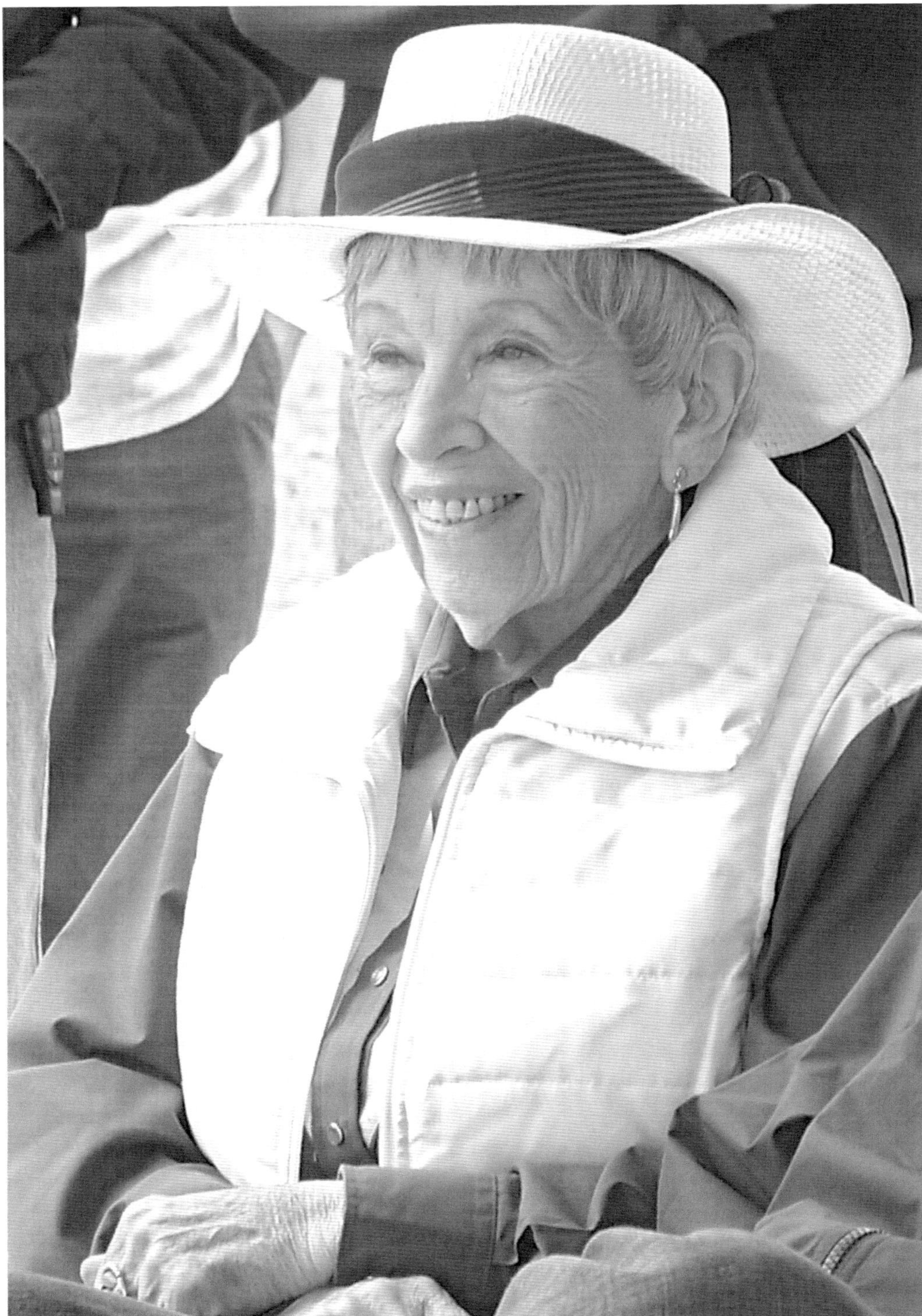

The Heart of Marana (LEFT)

It was not unusual for the 70-year-old Ora Mae Harn to zip off to South Africa to deliver money for AIDS orphans. Her heart was huge, and so was her energy. In her lifetime, she was assistant director of the Marana Community Food Bank, and served on the board of directors for the Marana Arts Council, the Marana Rotary, and the Marana Foundation for Educational Excellence. She helped expand the Marana Health Center to include food and clothing, energy assistance, aid to the elderly and disabled, and school-based clinics. She was a member of the town council for 13 years and fought to provide protection against the flooding Santa Cruz River. Her motivation was simple: just do what needs to be done. Her home, like her heart, was always open. At Christmas, she would invite families who would not otherwise be able to have a holiday meal to her home for a sit-down dinner. Harn, her husband Jerry, and three children moved to Arizona when a doctor suggested it would help her daughter's asthma. They first lived in Silver Bell, but in 1973 moved to Marana. Harn got a job as a cafeteria worker and school bus driver. She started volunteering at the Marana Health Center, which was then a small wooden building that served indigents and farmworkers. Seeing the need for a bigger facility, she worked hard for the expansion. In 1979, she was hired as the center's director of community services. In 1983, the Santa Cruz flooded. Three people died in the flood. Harn, her daughter, son-in-law, and grandson linked arms and forged their way through cold waist-deep water to higher ground. That experience, plus hearing the stories of people who suffered in the flood, motivated her to work for flood protection. Ora Mae Harn, a petite woman, had a giant presence in Marana. (Courtesy Town of Marana.)

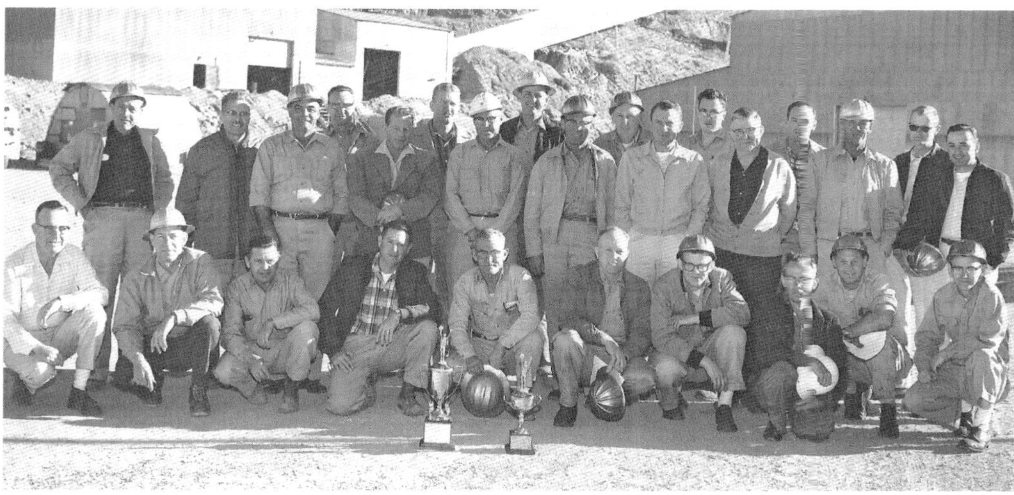

The Hell Hole of Arizona

In 1908, the *Tucson Citizen* headline read "Moral Wave Sweeping over Silver Bell Camp." This mining camp was accused of being the toughest town in Pima County. Many considered it to be tougher than Tombstone, Arizona. It was a town where "hell breaks loose every pay day." The law moved in to clean up the town by arresting three women who ran houses of ill repute. The area was owned by many mining claimants, including Tucson businessmen Zeckendof and Steinfeld. By the end of the 1800s, these two men had acquired a large number of claims. Around 1919, the Imperial Copper Company established a "town" called Silver Bell built on the remains of the rowdy mining encampment of the 1880s. Over the years, there have been many mine owners in the district with varying success. Silver Bell today is a far cry from the wild days. It is now winning awards as an example of an iconic operation. Fifty-three years after the scandalous headline, the State Mine Inspectors recognized American Smelting and Refining Company (ASARCO), now the owners, for having the Best Open Pit Safety Record of all Arizona mines. Receiving the award was a group of engineers and the driving force behind the award, the general supervisor D.R. Jameson (top row, second from left). (Courtesy of ASARCO.)

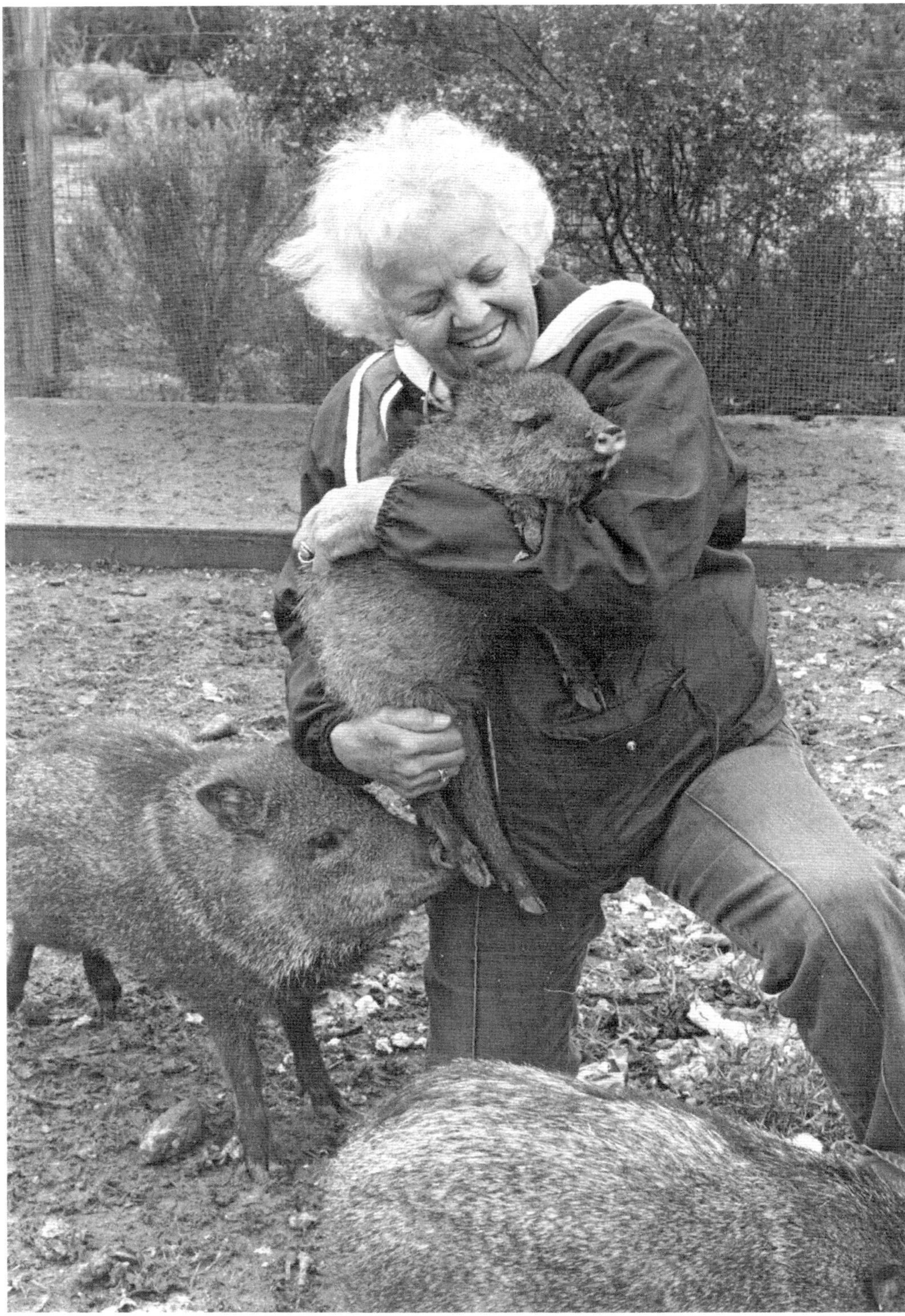

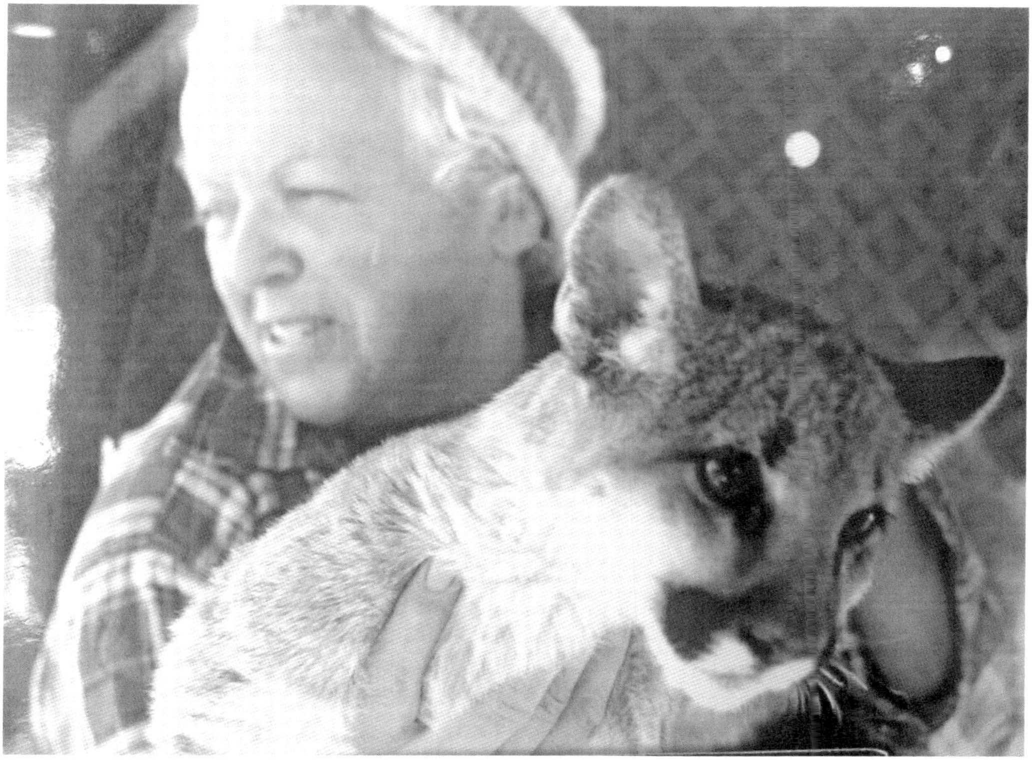

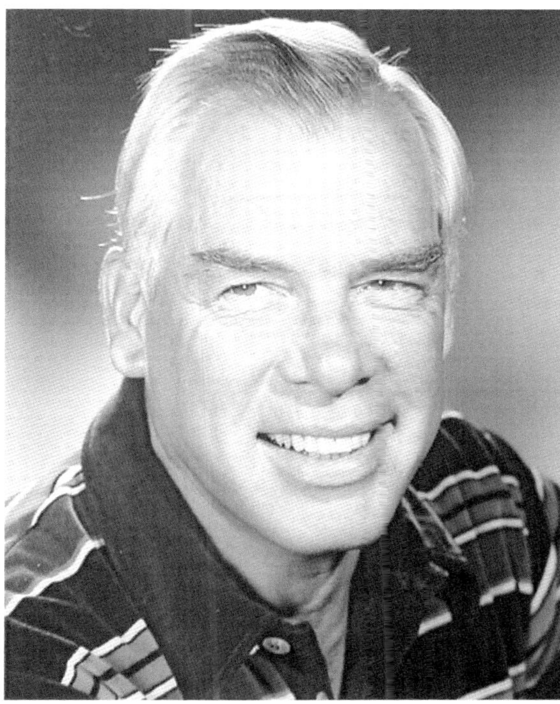

The Caregiver

Sarah Gorby loved animals. When Game and Fish authorities found out she was caring for injured wildlife in her home, they paid her a visit. The game warden was so impressed he recommended the state license Gorby. She was the first licensed Arizona wildlife caregiver. One day while walking out of a supermarket with baby javelinas at her heels, a man approached her inquiring about her "pets." She told him they were Mongolian Goosehounds. He soon discovered the true breed of the "pets." From then on, actor Lee Marvin was a supporter and a frequent visitor to her house, once remarking, "It is the only house where you have to wipe your feet after you leave." Her life was not easy. She grew up poor and married a man who was blind. Ultimately, she received international attention and praise for her work. (Gorby, Courtesy Lorna Kraemer; Marvin, author's collection.)

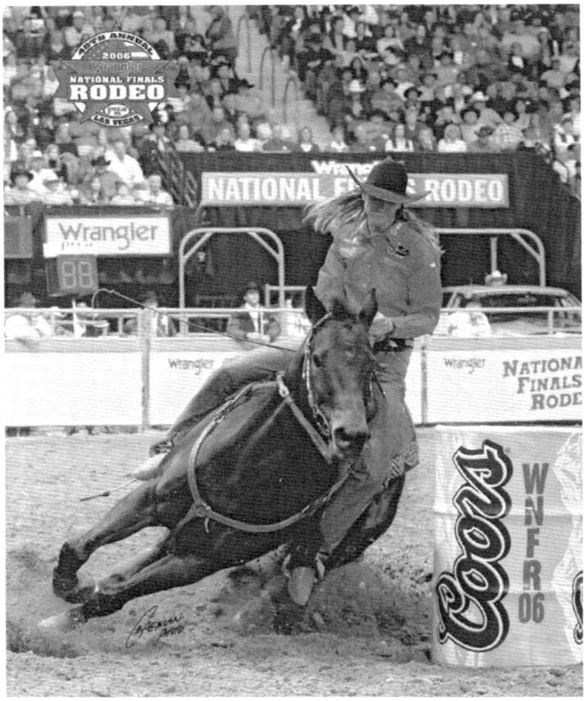

The Racing Champion

In a land where the cowboy is king, Sherry Cervi is the queen. Born and raised in Marana, Cervi started winning barrel races in the 5 to 18 classes. By the time she was 18, she had to her credit multiple Arizona Junior Rodeo Association championships. She is a multiple Arizona High School Rodeo Association champion and a three-time Women's Professional Rodeo Association (WPRA) world champion barrel racer. Barrel racing is the only professional rodeo event for women. She was selected to represent the United States in the 2002 Winter Olympics, counts over 11 major rodeo wins in her career, and was the first competitive woman barrel racer to earn over a million dollars. However, it hasn't always been just barrel racing for her. When at Marana High School, she played varsity basketball. (Courtesy race to the finish, Dan Hubbell Photography; at the barrel, Mike Coperman.)

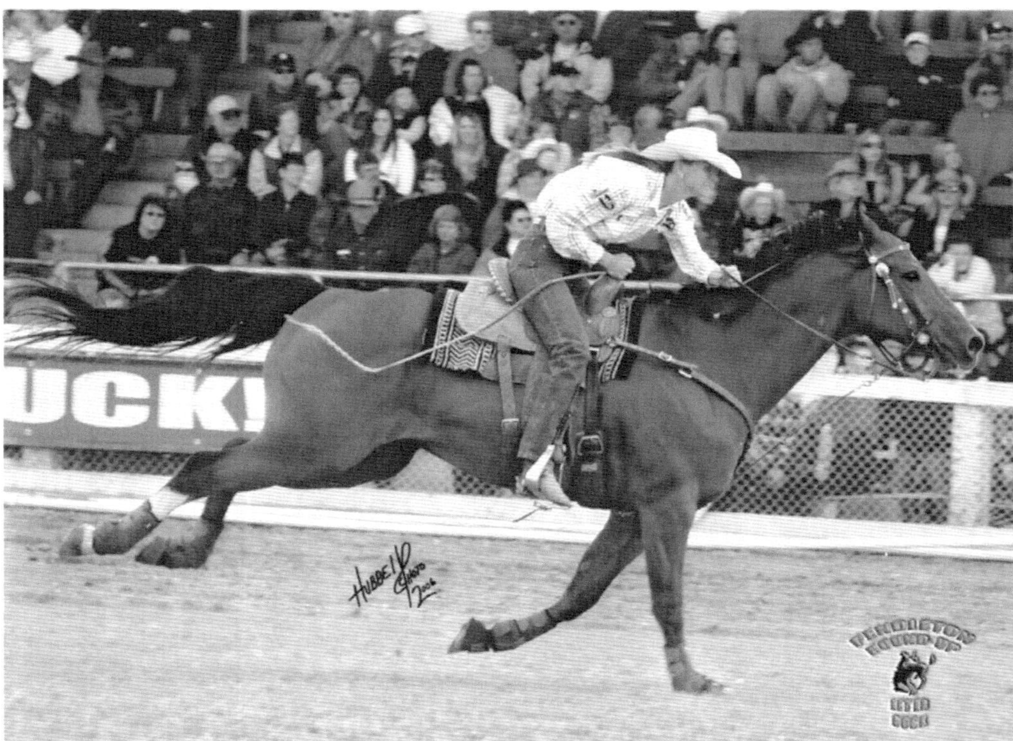

CHAPTER TWO

Oro Valley: Creating a Quality of Life

Originally an area of ranches and homesteads, Oro Valley has the largest population of the three communities in this book. On the east, it is snuggled against the western slopes of the Santa Catalina Mountains. On its northern side is the Tortolita Mountains, not as high as the Santa Catalinas, but still beckoning to the hiker and the naturalist. It is bisected by the Canada del Oro, which at one time ran all year. Today the "river" is a dry wash for most of the year.

Oro Valley counts among her ancestral population George Pusch and Francisco Romero, who were considered the first settlers in the remote desert area above Tucson. Romero and his wife established a ranch in the mid 1800s at the base of the Santa Catalina Mountains in what is now Catalina State Park.

Pusch arrived in 1874 and, along with his partner John Zellweger, started the Steam Pump Ranch. Both were successful Tucson businessmen, and Pusch served as a representative in the legislature that prepared Arizona for statehood. Zellweger sold out his interest to Pusch, and the Pusch family kept the Steam Pump until they were forced to sell after George's death.

The settlers had to be determined and independent to brave the rocky lands at the base of the Santa Catalina Mountains and breed their cattle on hilly, cacti-laden land. Yet when the early ranchers came to Oro Valley to make their fortune, they also brought with them an appreciation for the finer things in life and some of the niceties they had left behind.

It was the robust Canada del Oro that attracted these men, that and the availability of plenty of land. Although the land, for the most part, was rough mountainous terrain, most of it unsuitable for cultivation, its lush grasses were a delight for cattle who didn't mind the climb, or eating on a slant. The early arrivals saw in the running river a promise of wealth as ranchers and homesteaders.

After Pusch died, the family left the area and the Steam Pump Ranch was purchased by Jack Proctor. Proctor used the ranch as guest quarters. His daughter Betty Proctor later married retired professional baseball player Hank Leiber, and they moved into the Steam Pump, introducing high society to the area.

As the Canada del Oro dried up, the new arrivals became more interested in land. The Homestead Act of 1862 made land available to settlers, who arrived first to establish a home for their families and then stayed to create a community.

Homesteader Catherine Reidy helped her family through the Depression by capturing rattlesnakes and making jewelry and clothes from their skins and bones. The town was home to Bee Dee Daniels who, along with Doctor William Lackner, made his mark hunting mountain lions with his dog Copper. Copper was the inspiration for the movie *The Fox and the Hound.*

The character of Oro Valley was also shaped in the early 1900s by another type of pioneer, the mountain man. Buster Bailey named a mountain and located a spring, which helped him make the best home brew in the area. The beauty of the land attracted others, such as Doctor Frank Russell, who established an exclusive school for boys in its low-lying hills, and the Countess of Suffolk, who was as elusive as her name was haughty.

The beauty of the land drew many people to Oro Valley. It was this beauty and the favorable climate that Louis Landon believed would attract sportsmen to his golf community, and that attracted Ester and Lloyd Golder Sr. when they purchased local ranches. It was this beauty that lured hundreds of residents, in later years, to the retirement resorts built on the former Golder land.

When faced with the threat of being swallowed up by the city of Tucson, the settlers turned their attention to creating a town: not a citified town, but one where people could enjoy what nature offers, a town that would give their families a particular quality of life. They put their efforts into enhancing the community and its lifestyle. In the end, they created a town built upon what nature provided, enhancing the community and its residents' lifestyle.

The Oro Valley residents have seen to it that what nature surrounded them with is not lost. Teddy Roosevelt's efforts to establish a national park system are appreciated and enjoyed daily by those in Oro Valley as they view the Coronado National Forest vistas around them. Through their own efforts, they also established state and local parks. Oro Valley is surrounded by some of the best that nature has to offer: mountains, the Coronado National Forest, the Honey Bee Canyon archaeological site, the mighty Saguaro, and town and state parks. Although the land no longer abounds with ranches, Oro Valley has not neglected its economic base. It has welcomed several clean air industries, in particular the biotech industry.

Oro Valley has always valued the finer aspects of life, and today the town is home to writers, musicians, and artists. The town's public art program features multiple pieces by Matt Moutafis and other artists. A walk around town is like a visit to an art gallery, a gallery that shows its art along with nature's finest works . . . and it all started with Jim Kriegh, the father of Oro Valley. Today's residents owe their quality of life to the Legendary Locals who helped build the town.

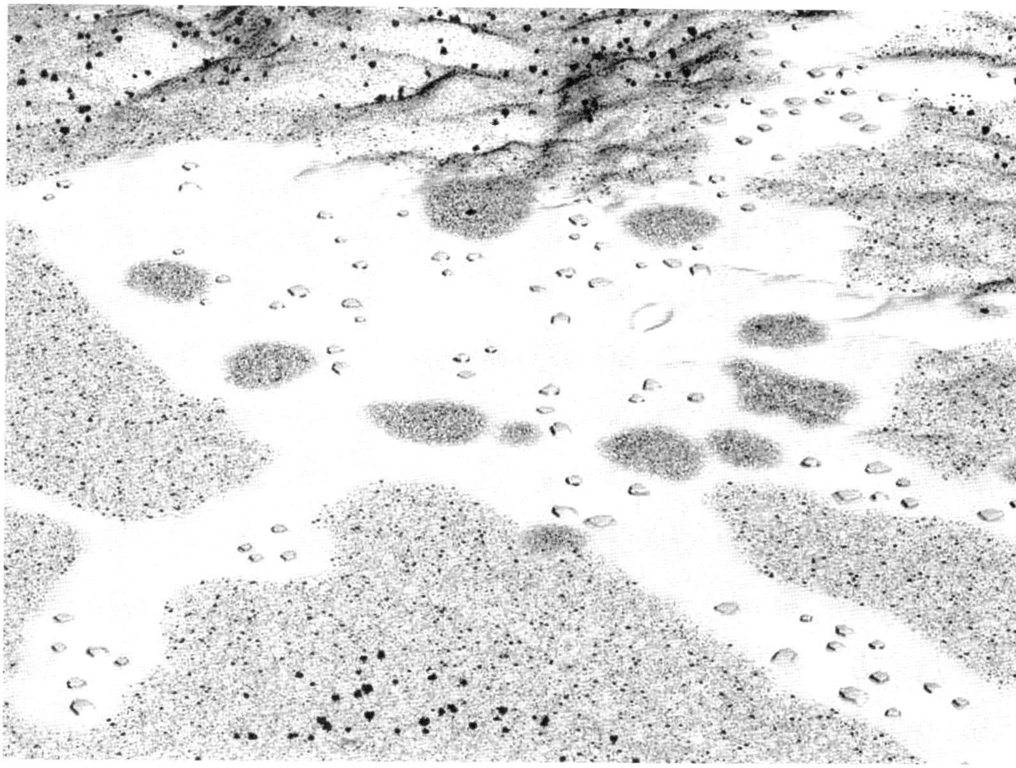

The First People

The first recorded people in the Oro Valley area were the Hohokam, who lived here between AD 450 and AD 1100. Why they left the area and where they went is a mystery. There is no evidence to show when they departed. Honey Bee Canyon is one of the largest sites, and over 500 pit houses have been excavated and analyzed there by archaeologists. The site includes a ball court, its exact use unknown. Were ball courts for religious ceremonies, entertainment, or political use—or perhaps something unsuspected? The Hohokam's petroglyphs abound in the area, showing animals, symbols, and people. It is obvious that the rock carvings etched into the Catalina Mountains are carefully done, not just graffiti of an ancient tribe. Researchers can only speculate on the meaning of the marks, but one message is loud and clear—the Hohokam were here. (Petroglyph courtesy Pat Spoerl, site courtesy Douglas W. Gunn, Desert Archeology.)

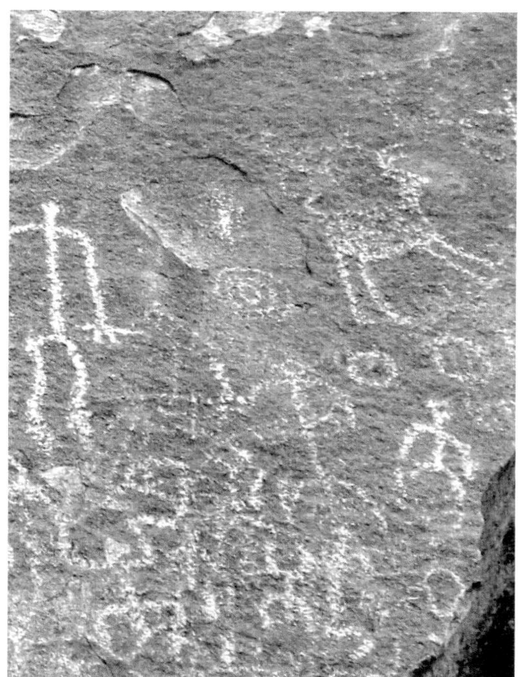

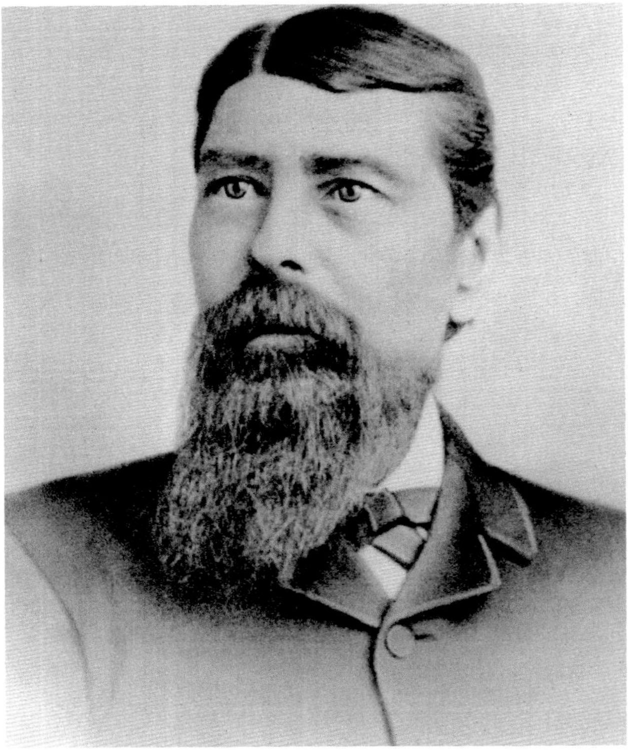

The Tough Pioneers

Around 1850, Francisco Romero and his wife Victoriano Ocoboa started their small ranch in the wilderness above Tucson. They built a one-room adobe house on the site of an ancient Hohokam village. But Romero's supply of cattle was constantly depleted by Apache raids. Dauntless, both Romero and Ocoboa fought off the raids, but it was a losing battle. As Francisco's arrow wounds mounted, and their cattle diminished, Victoriano insisted they move back to Tucson. The Romeros held on to the land and years later their son, Francisco, acquired more land, and successfully ran the Romero ranch. The ranch is now part of the Catalina State Park. Visitors can view the foundation ruins of the ranch house and spot some interesting pieces of Hohokam pottery. (Courtesy of the Arizona Historical Society, Francisco #27340, Victoriano #27339.)

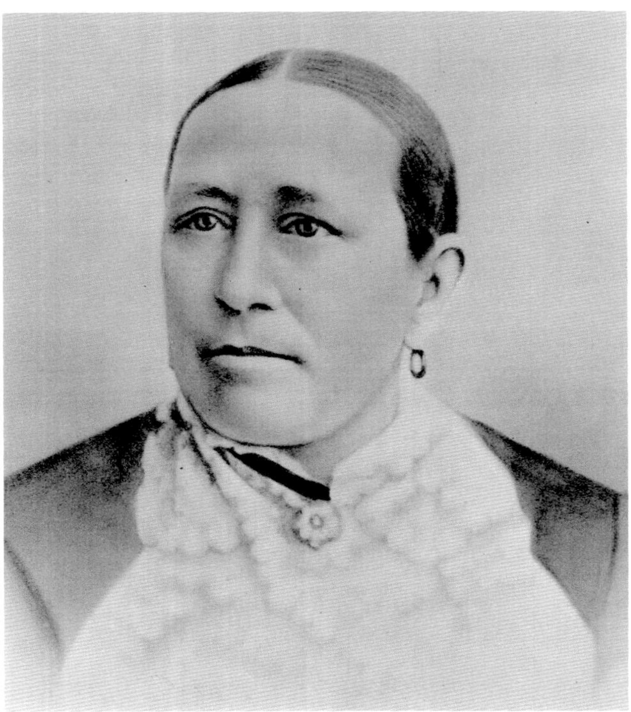

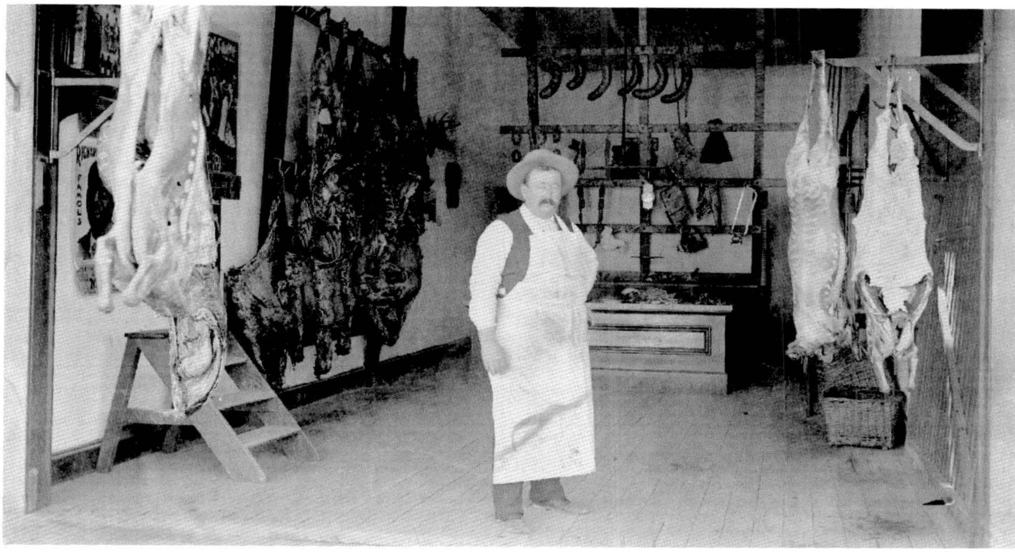

Businessman and Rancher
In 1874, John Zellweger arrived from San Francisco to join George Pusch in several business ventures, including a butcher shop. Together they also established a ranch, the Canada del Oro Ranch, which was situated next to the wash by the same name, and later became known as the Steam Pump Ranch. Eventually, Zellweger sold his interest in the ranch to Pusch. (Courtesy of the Arizona Historical Society #44173.)

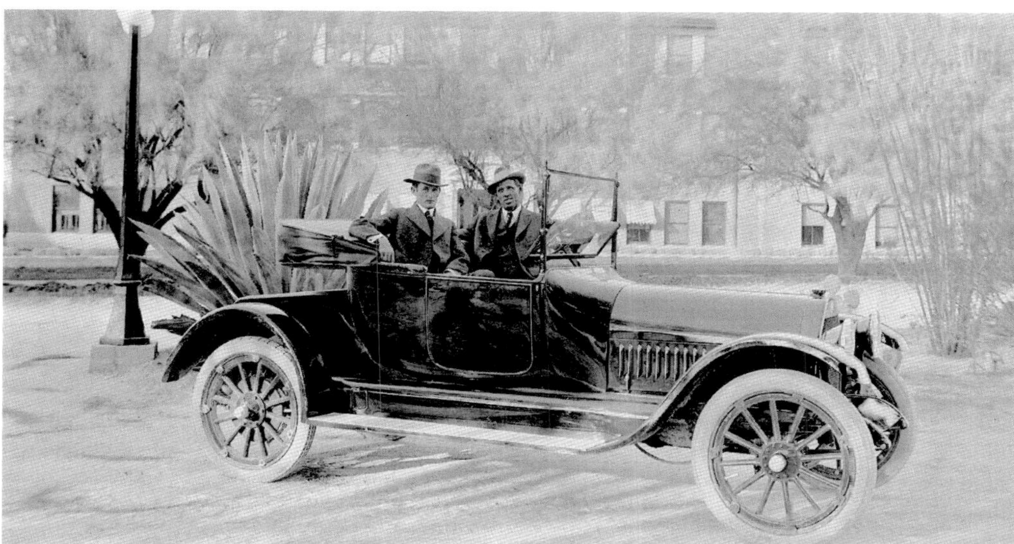

Man About Town
In the early 1930s, John Zellweger's son Frank (in the driver's seat) could be seen zipping around in one of the town's few sporty cars. The Zellweger and Pusch families also established the PZ Ranch near Aravaipa. Frank Zellweger was part of the Steam Pump social scene, which was very prominent in the Oro Valley area. (Courtesy Town of Oro Valley.)

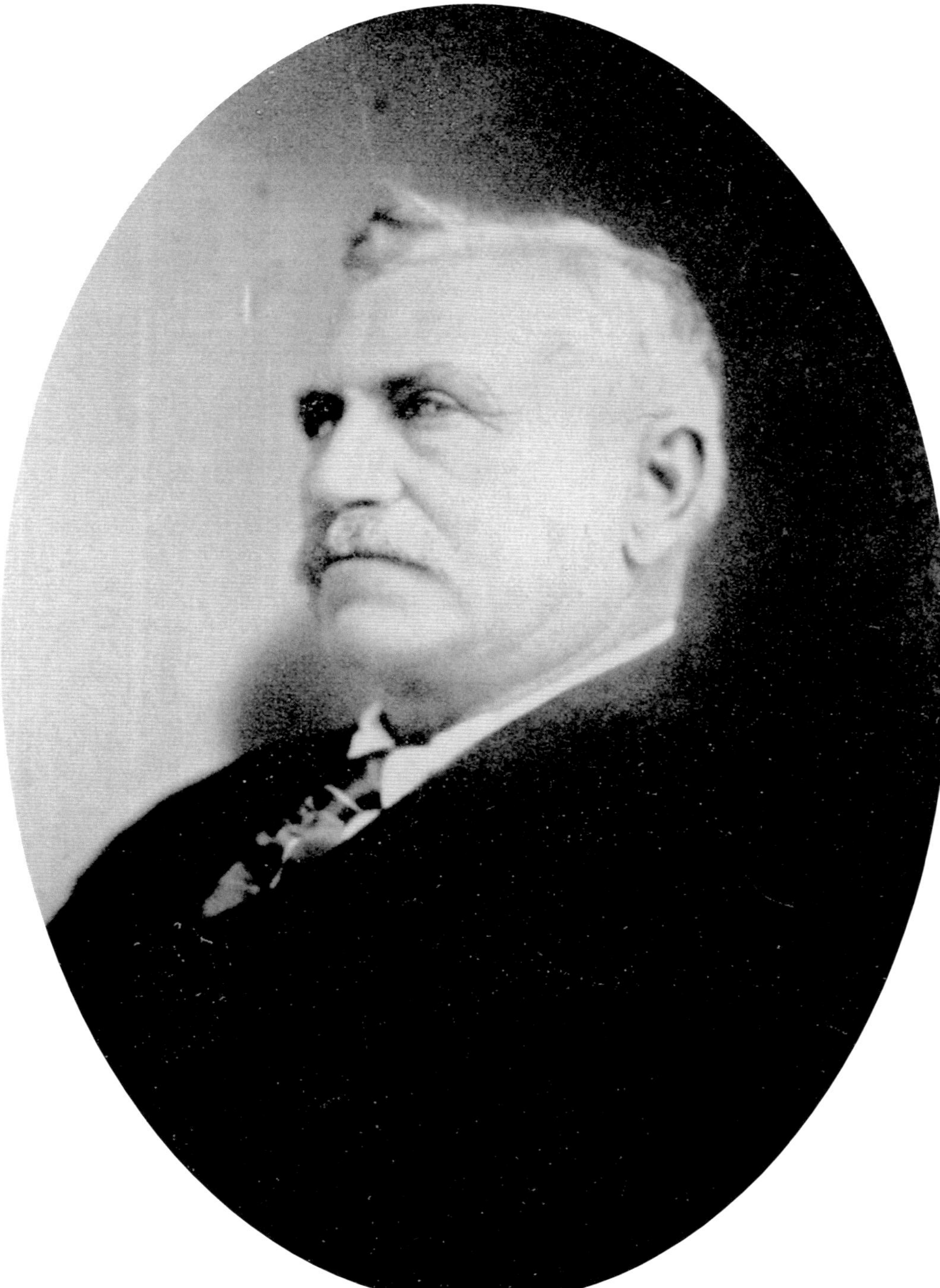

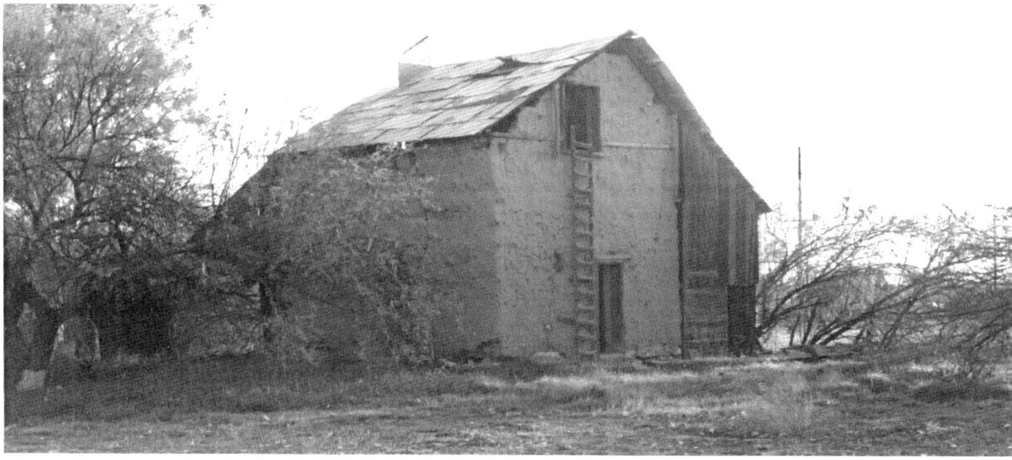

The Territorial Statesman

In the late 1800s, George Pusch was part owner of the Canada del Oro Ranch. He became a successful rancher and bought a steam pump for pumping water for the cattle. The property came to be known as the Steam Pump Ranch. The housing for the pump was made from adobe brick. Part of the pump house still stands, as does the main house of the ranch. Located on the main route between Tucson and Florence, travelers, Army troops, and cattle drives stopped at the ranch for water. It soon became apparent to Pusch that he could make more money selling water than selling cattle. Pusch was a member of the 1910 Constitutional Convention, shown here gathered for an official photograph. In total disagreement with the results of the convention, the Tucson delegation refused to sign the final document. However, in 1912 Arizona still managed to become a state. (Courtesy Oro Valley Historical Society.)

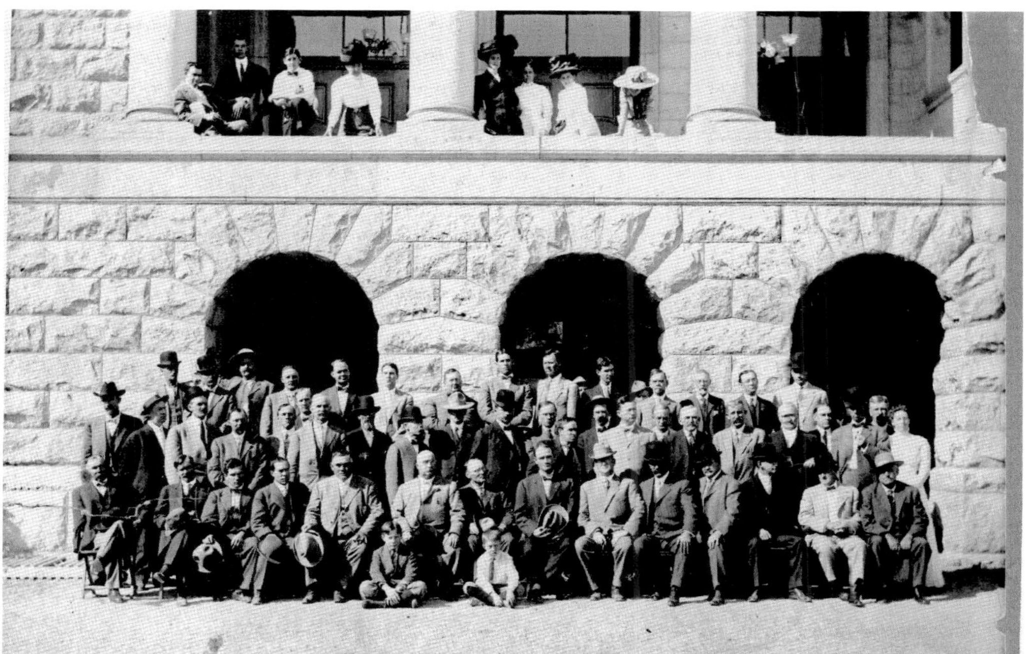

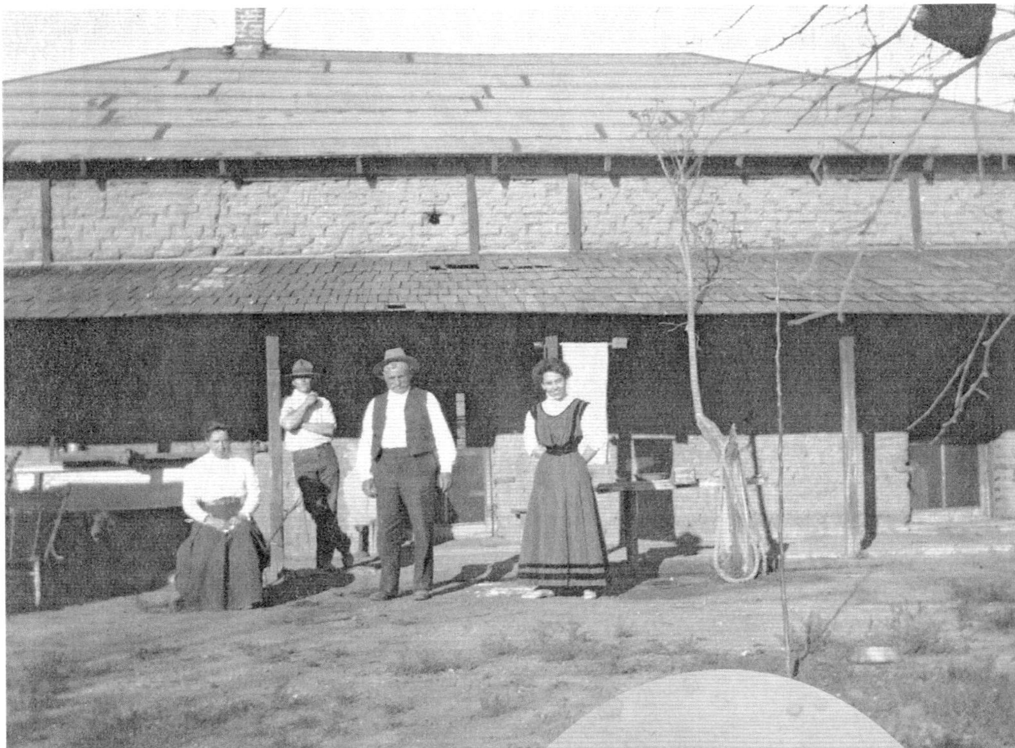

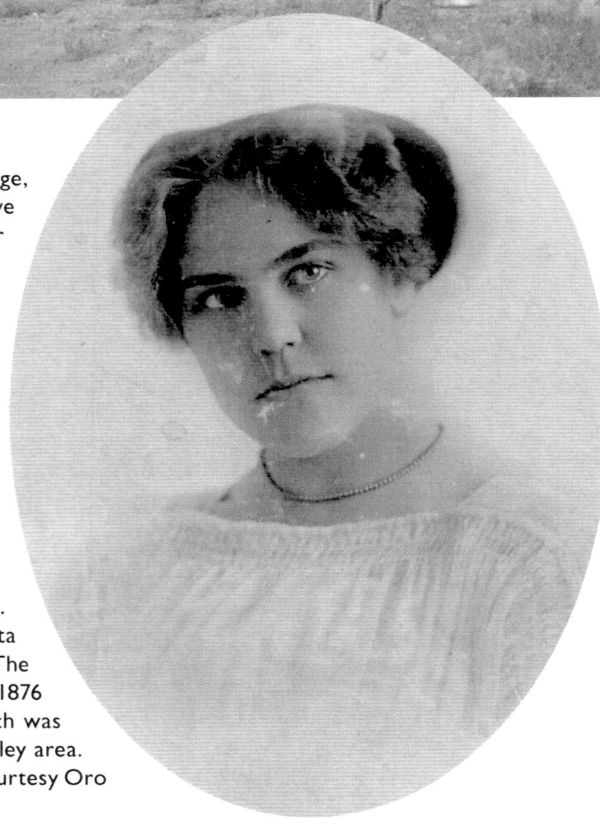

The Pusch Women

Mathilda Pusch (seated), wife of George, was noted for her kindness to Native Americans. She fed all who came to her door and allowed them to camp on the ranch. Gertrude Pusch Zipf was the oldest of the six Pusch children. She continued the legacy of family hospitality when at the Steam Pump. Her brother George is seen leaning on the post. The family owned a house in Tucson, and the PZ ranch in Aravaipa , but Gertrude favored the Steam Pump and spent much time as possible there. While at the University of Arizona, she invited her friends to join her at the ranch (right). Gertrude is standing bottom left. One of her joys was to ride in the Santa Catalina Mountains over Pusch Ridge. The Pusch family owned the ranch from 1876 until about 1933. The Steam Pump Ranch was the first successful ranch in the Oro Valley area. Today the site is owned by the town. (Courtesy Oro Valley Historical Society.)

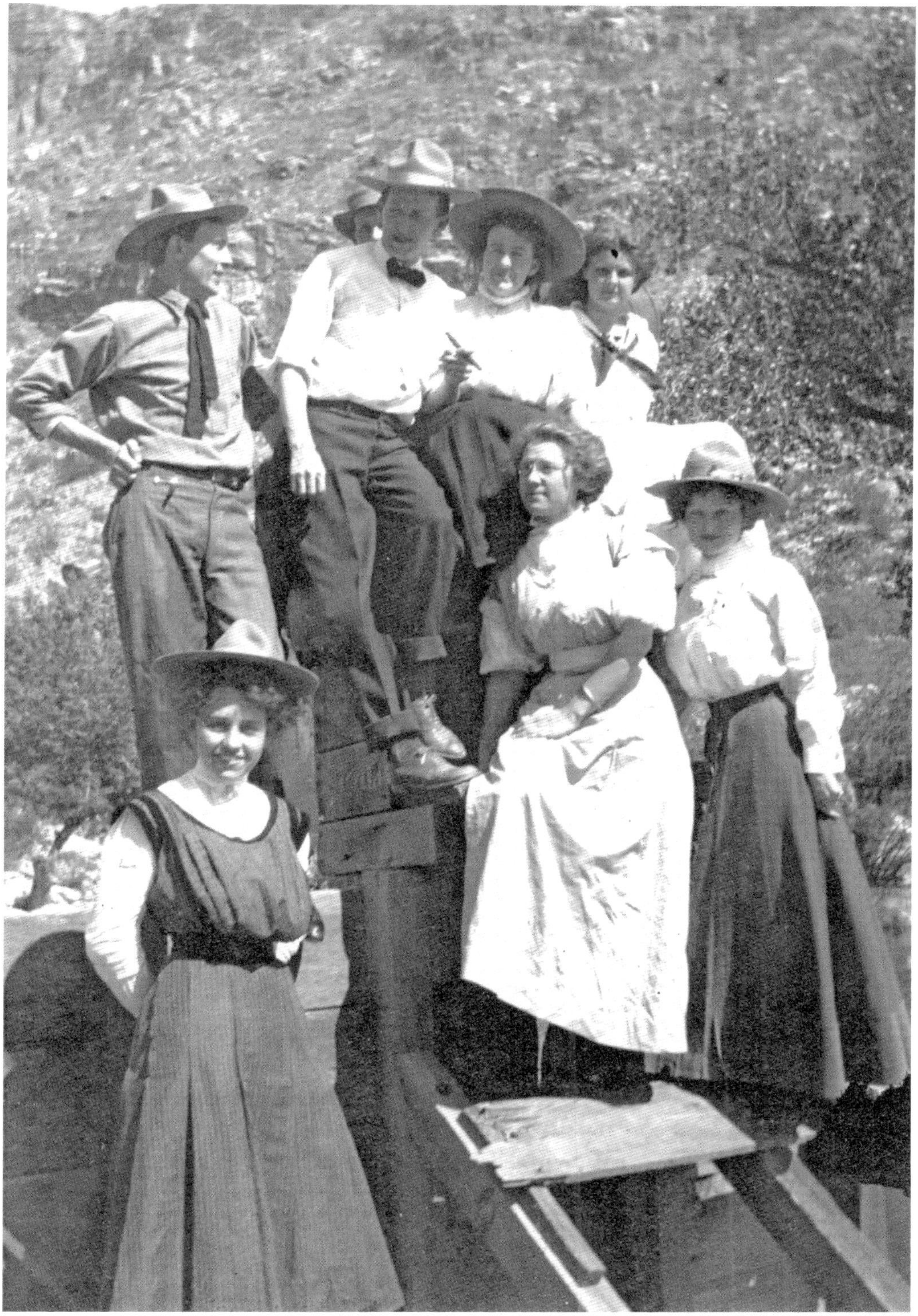

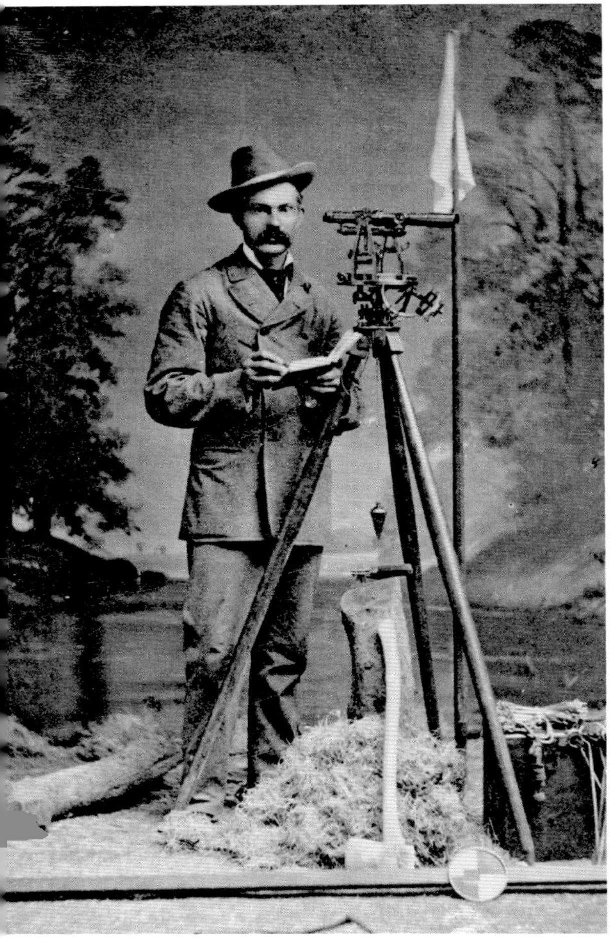

The Western Surveyor

George Roskruge was born in England and came to America in 1870. He served as the surveyor general for the Arizona Territory. His official map of Pima County, which was authorized by the board of supervisors, was drawn in 1893 and updated in 1899. He gave the county definition, an invaluable asset to the settlers. (Courtesy Arizona Historical Society #B93849.)

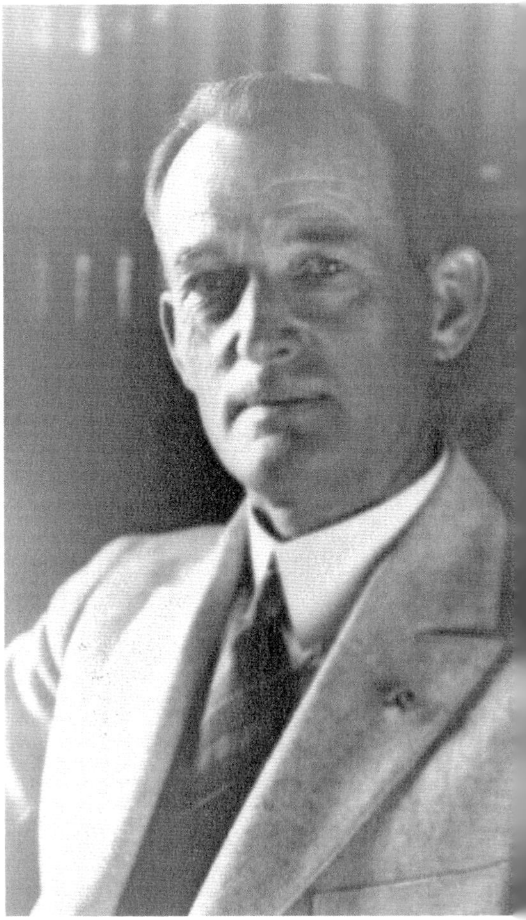

The Storyteller

Harold Bell Wright suffered from tuberculosis and frequently came to Arizona to escape the dampness of California. He was the first American author to sell over a million books. After visiting Gertrude Pusch at the Steam Pump, he took her story of two old prospectors and wrote *The Mine with the Iron Door* in 1923, which was made into a movie filmed locally. (Courtesy Arizona Historical Society #24957.)

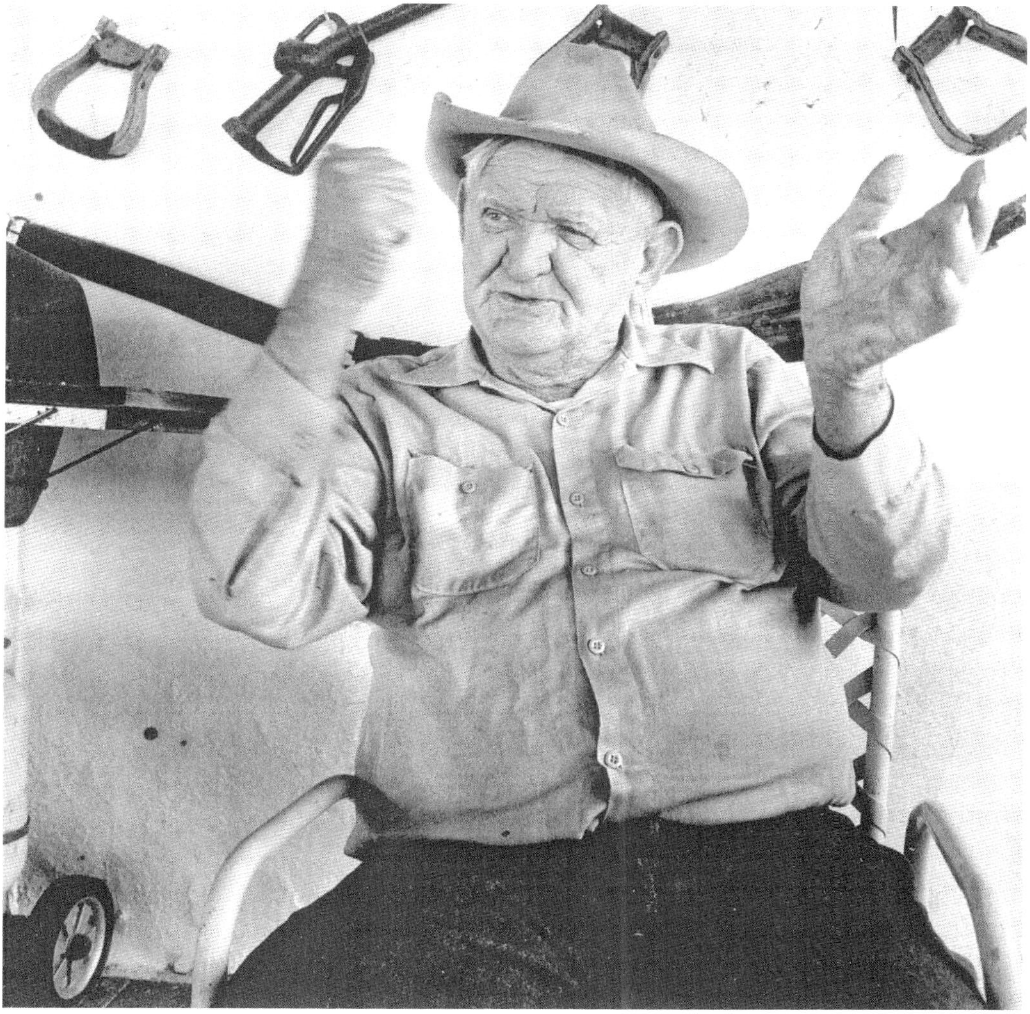

The Mountain Man

Buster Bailey carved out a piece of the Santa Catalina Mountains for his own haven. The Bailey family came to the mountains in June 1927. Buster was a big strapping kid of 16. When his family went back to Texas in the 1930s, Buster stayed. He worked the land and has a mountain named after him. He also dug a well on his property, on a site still called Buster Springs, which was known to have the sweetest water in the area. He did some ranching, and worked at any job he could find, from breaking broncos to mending fences to bailing hay. He worked at the Mount Lemmon Inn as a handyman for the owner Tony Zimmerman. He helped repair the fences at the Steam Pump Ranch, most of which are still standing. One of his most acclaimed talents was making moonshine. He was so good at it that during World War II, when he was stationed in the South Pacific, his commanding officer set him up with a still. The troops were making their own liquor from dangerous ingredients. Afraid for their lives, the officer ordered Bailey into the booze business. Buster loved the land and left copious notes on its history. Bailey fancied himself a poet, and although his poems never won any prizes, they show his wry sense of humor. Buster is gone, but Buster Mountain and Buster Springs remind locals of the importance of the land and the man who treasured the Santa Catalina Mountains. (Courtesy Arizona Historical Society #90746.)

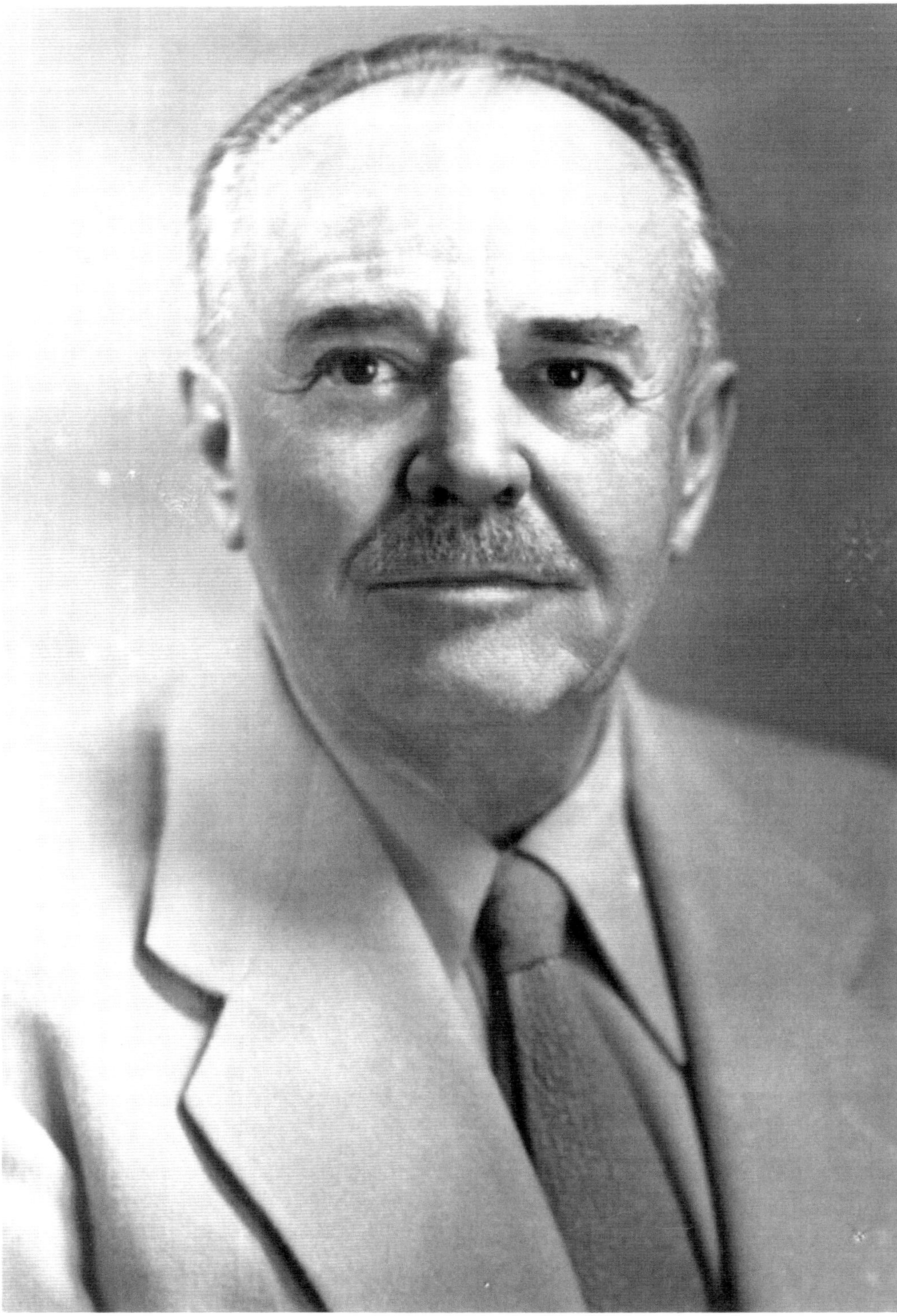

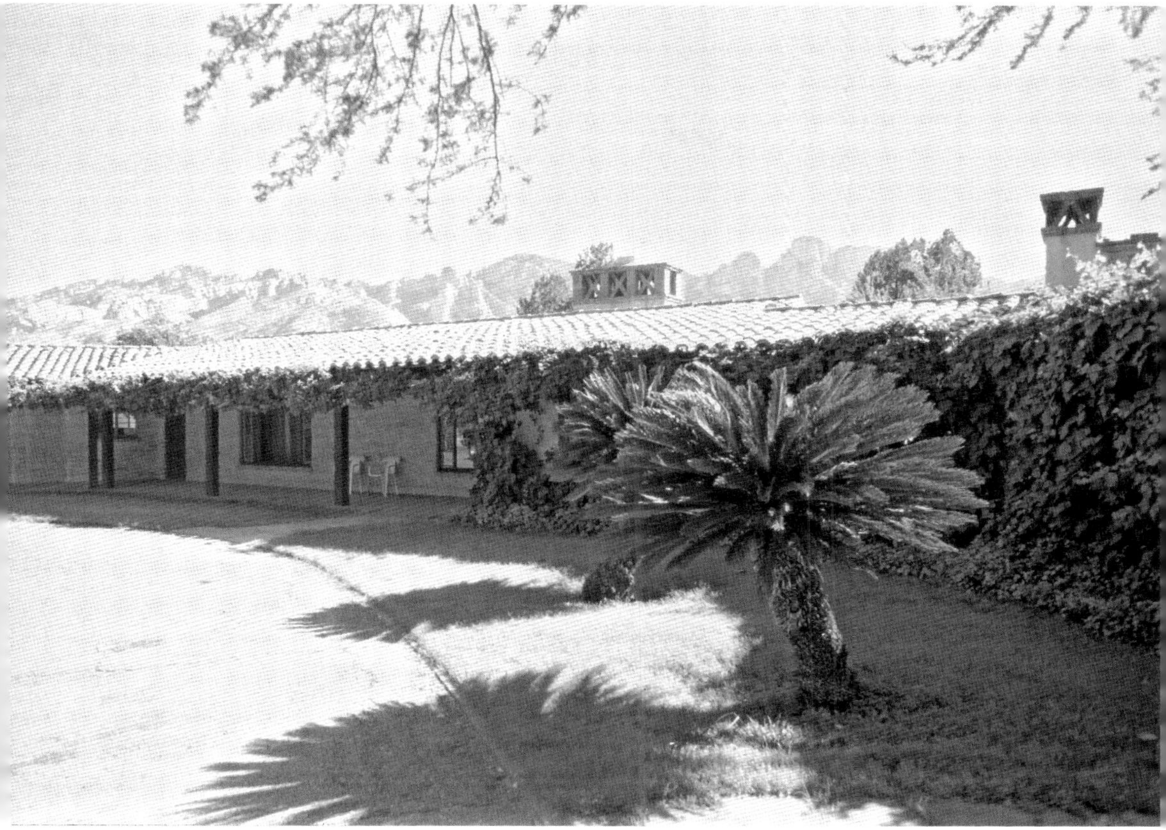

The Imaginative Architect

Josias Joesler had a huge impact on the look of the new West in the first half of the 20th century. He blended the best of traditional southwestern crafts with open spacious designs. His buildings flowed horizontally. He started designing his architectural masterpieces locally in 1927 and was hired by Mr. and Mrs. McAdams in the mid 1940s to design and build a house at the base of the mountains. The home is a low-slung flow of wood and adobe that blends into the terrain without offending the view. The home enhances the mountains rather than distracts from them. Arizona lost a creative genius when he died February 12, 1956. (Joesler Courtesy Arizona Historical Society # 65851, house Arizona Architectural Archives, College of Architecture and Landscape Architecture, University of Arizona.)

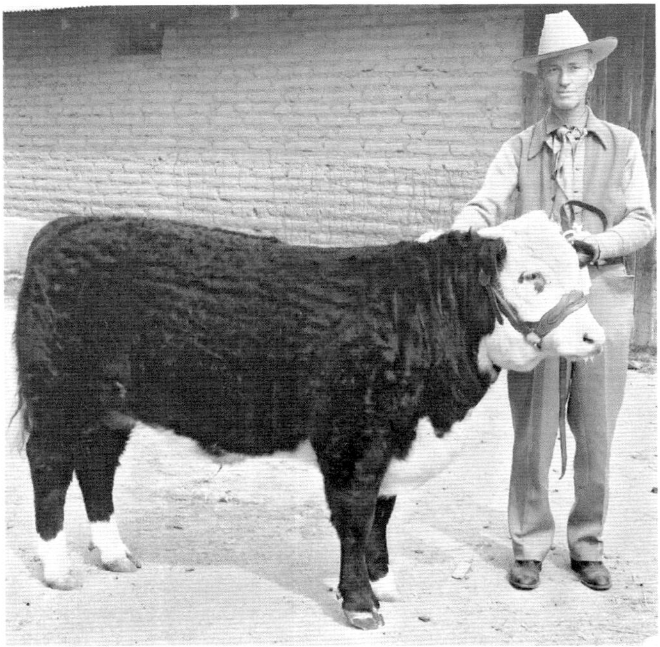

The Hotel Rancher

Jack M. Proctor acquired 2,000 acres of the Steam Pump Ranch in 1933 from the Pusch estate for $10,000. He raised cattle, pigs, and chickens. He used the animals and the vegetables he grew to feed the guests at the Pioneer Hotel in Tucson, which he managed for Lee Orndoroff. As a part-time rancher, his main interest was raising prize bulls. (Courtesy Oro Valley Historical Society.)

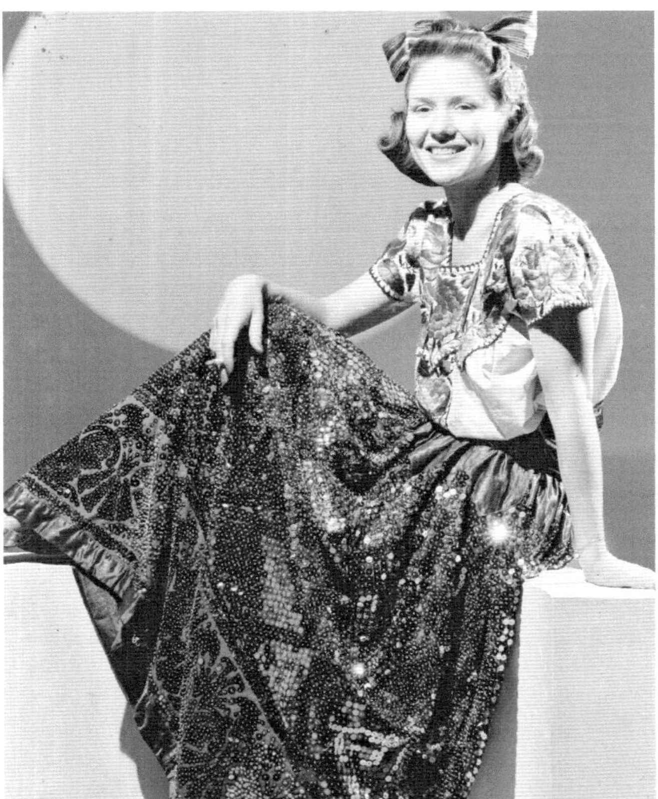

A Model Western Beauty

Jack Proctor's daughter, Betty, was a University of Arizona student and a favorite model of a prestigious fashion shop. At the university, she met the new assistant baseball coach, Hank Leiber. Leiber had recently retired from professional baseball. In 1940, Hank and Betty married, and they lived at the Steam Pump Ranch. (Courtesy Arizona Historical Society #9682.)

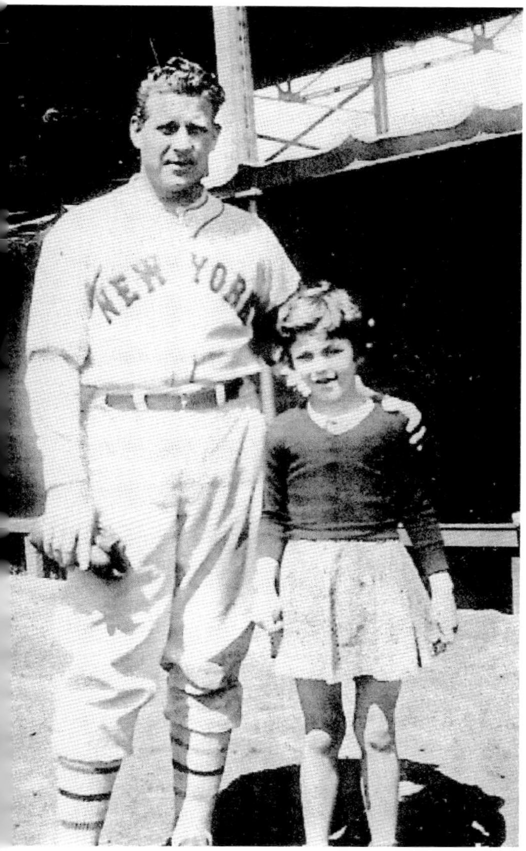

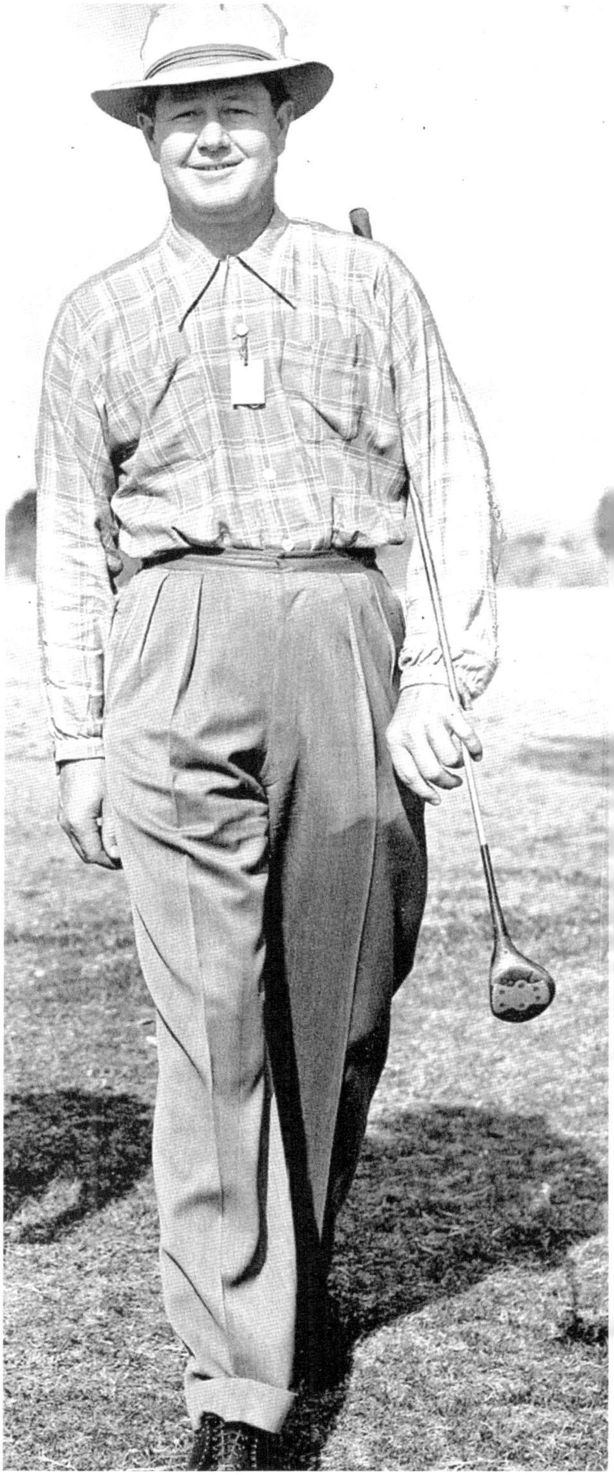

The Baseball Star

Hank Leiber lettered in football, basketball, and baseball at the University of Arizona. He decided to make baseball his professional career. In 1933, he began his career with the New York Giants, then was traded to the Chicago Cubs in 1938. He was a three-time All-Star. Leiber was beaned twice, once by Bob Feller, and the combined effects of the beanings and a calf injury forced him to give up baseball. (Courtesy Oro Valley Historical Society.)

A Drive for the War Effort

In 1942, Byron Nelson, the golf champion, came to town for a match. He teamed up with hometown baseball star Hank Leiber. Together Nelson and Leiber put on an exhibition golf match as a fundraising event for the Red Cross's World War II efforts. (Author's collection.)

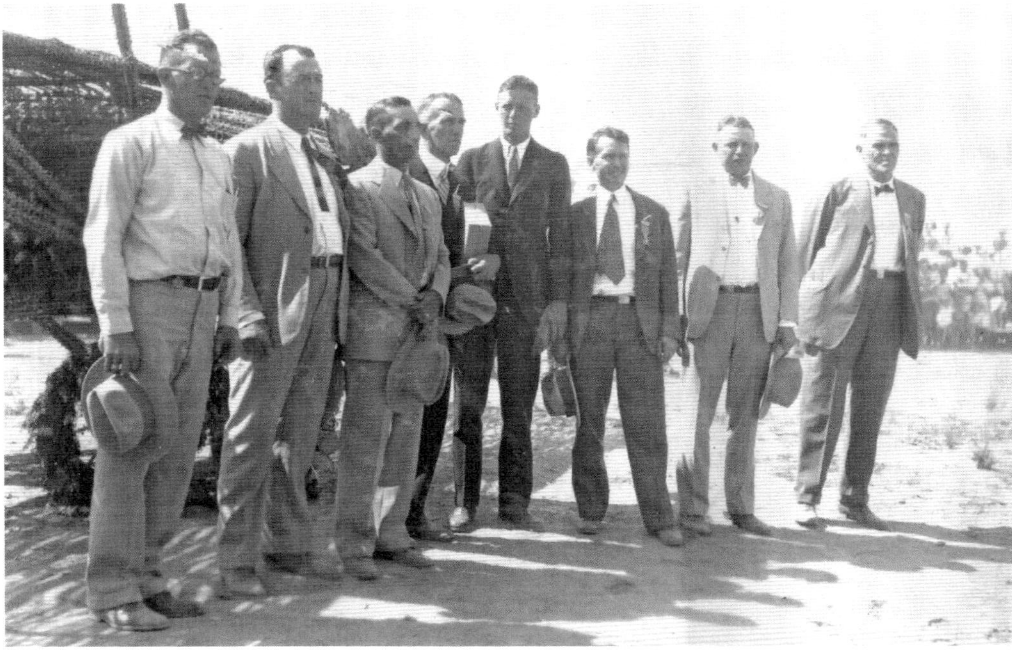

A Prickly Plane

Francis Hallett (Hal) Burns, a victim of mustard gas in World War I, came to Arizona for his health. He was a popular local florist and active in the community. He invited schoolchildren to his cacti farm and educated the children on the local flora. Burns was commissioned to produce a piece to honor the visit of Charles Lindbergh and the *Spirit of St. Louis*. He designed and made a replica of the famous aircraft, to scale, entirely of cacti. The cacti came from Burns's homestead in Oro Valley. On September 27, 1927, Lindbergh and his famous plane landed in Tucson and Lindy was greeted by the town's dignitaries, including Burns in shirtsleeves. The legendary pilot's comment on the cacti plane: "Surely you don't want me to get in that." (Courtesy Hal Burns Sr. family.)

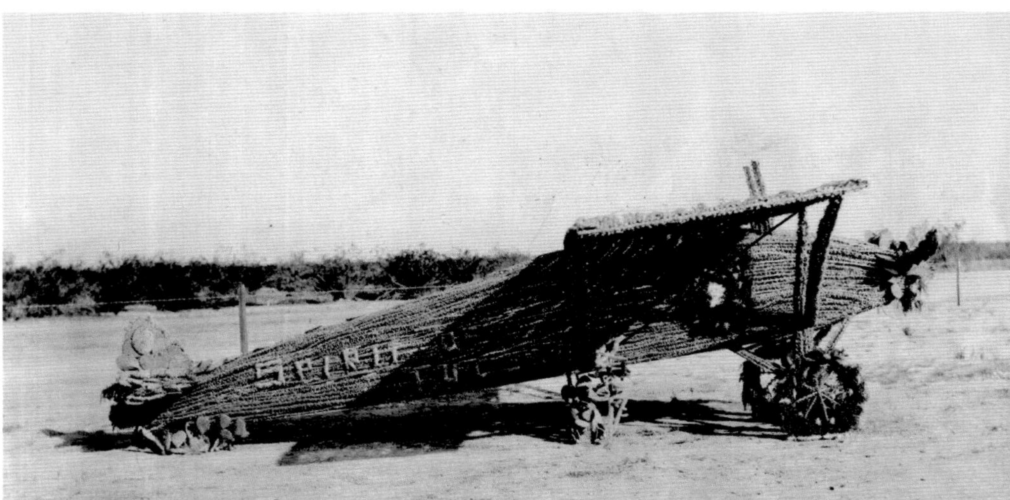

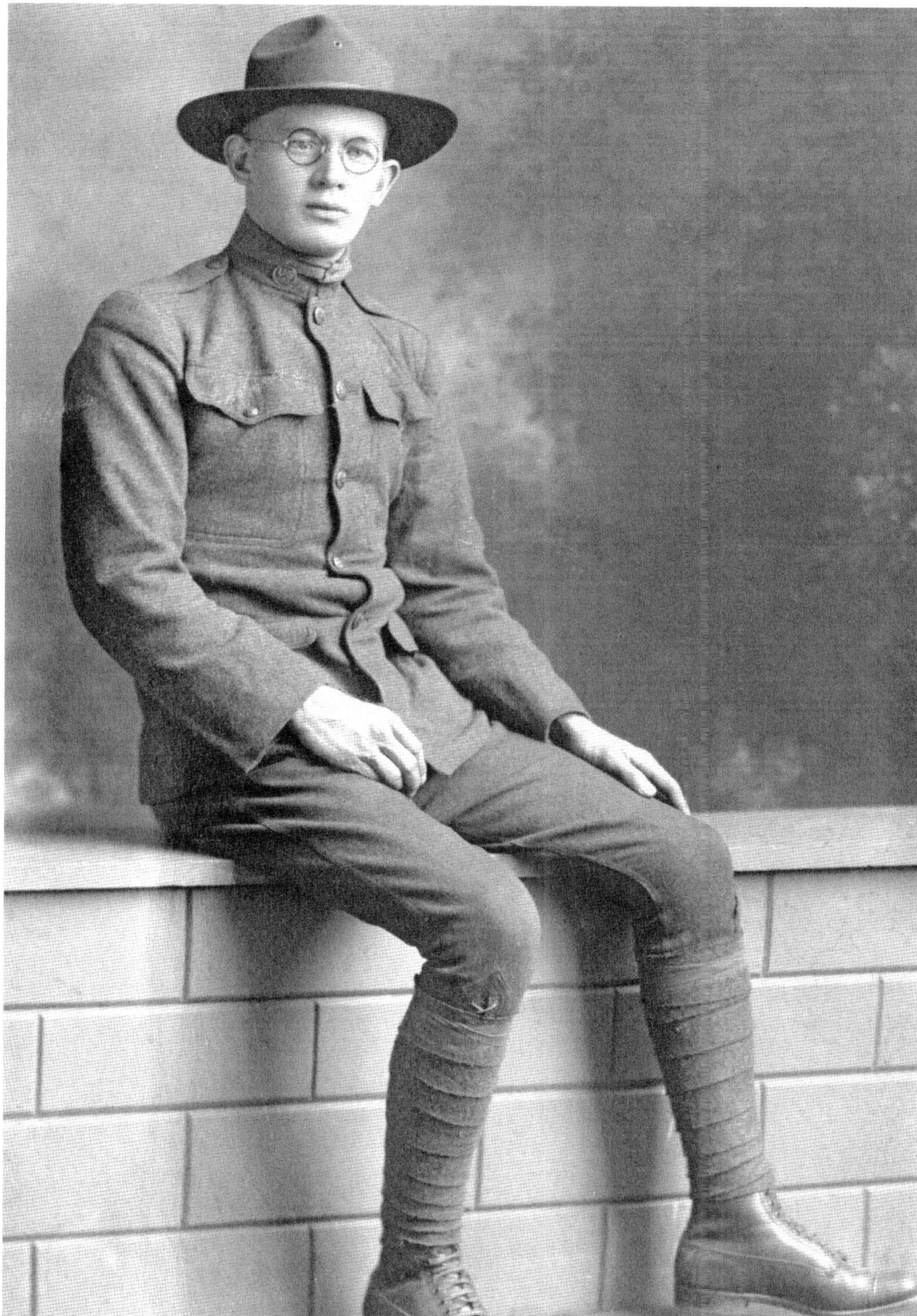

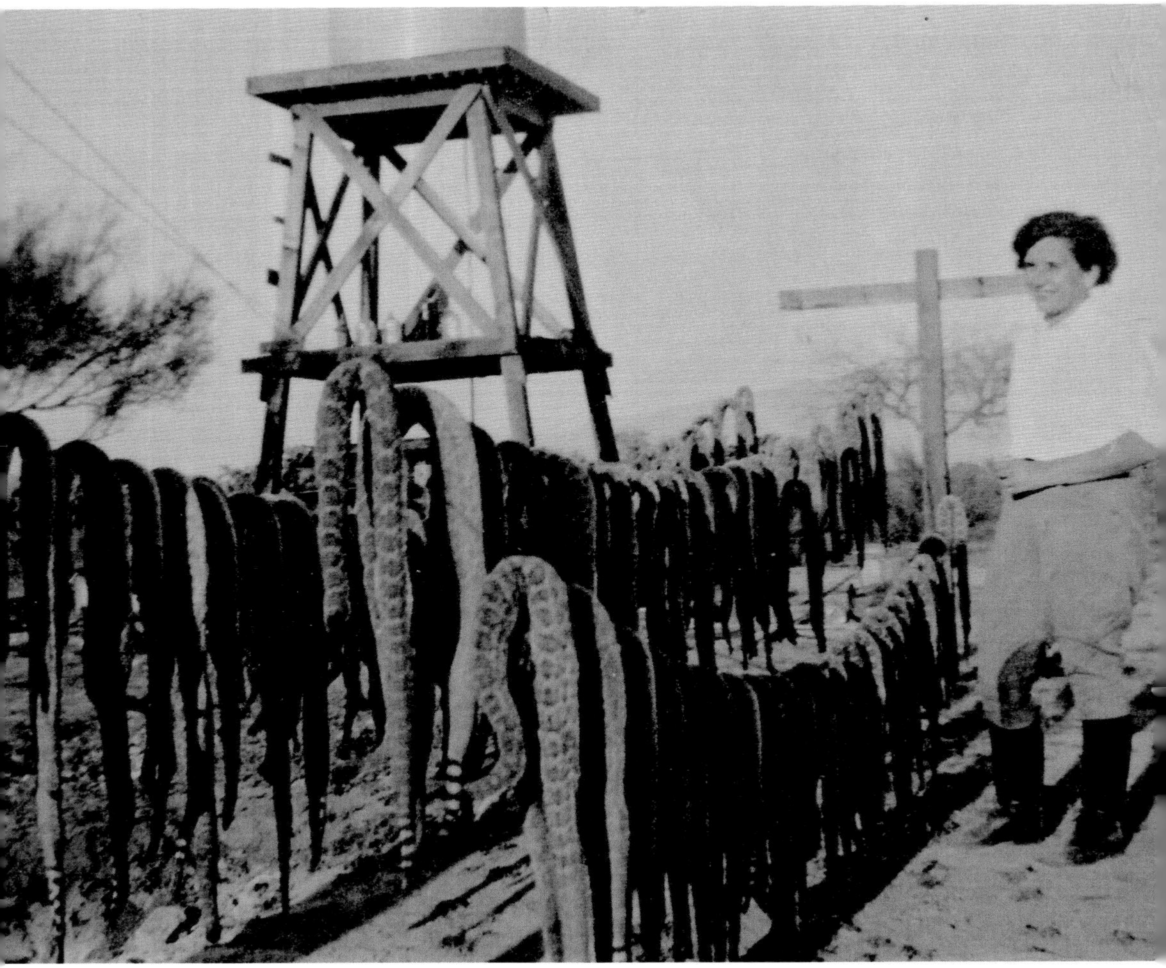

A Snaky Business

In the 1930s, Catherine Reidy found an innovative way to help her family during the Depression. She used a plentiful desert resource . . . rattlesnakes. Reidy made clothing and jewelry from the snakeskins that were sold in local shops. Her most popular items were the jewelry made from the snakes' backbones. Not all the snakes were skinned. Some of Reidy's snakes were milked by a University of Arizona professor for their venom, and a few were sold to zoos. Reidy and her husband Jim collected the snakes around their desert property. Other rattlers were brought in by the truckload by two brothers living in Oracle, Arizona, about 30 miles north of the Reidy homestead. Rattlesnakes were plentiful in the desert, and homesteaders were glad to get rid of a few. (Courtesy Jim and Catherine Reidy family.)

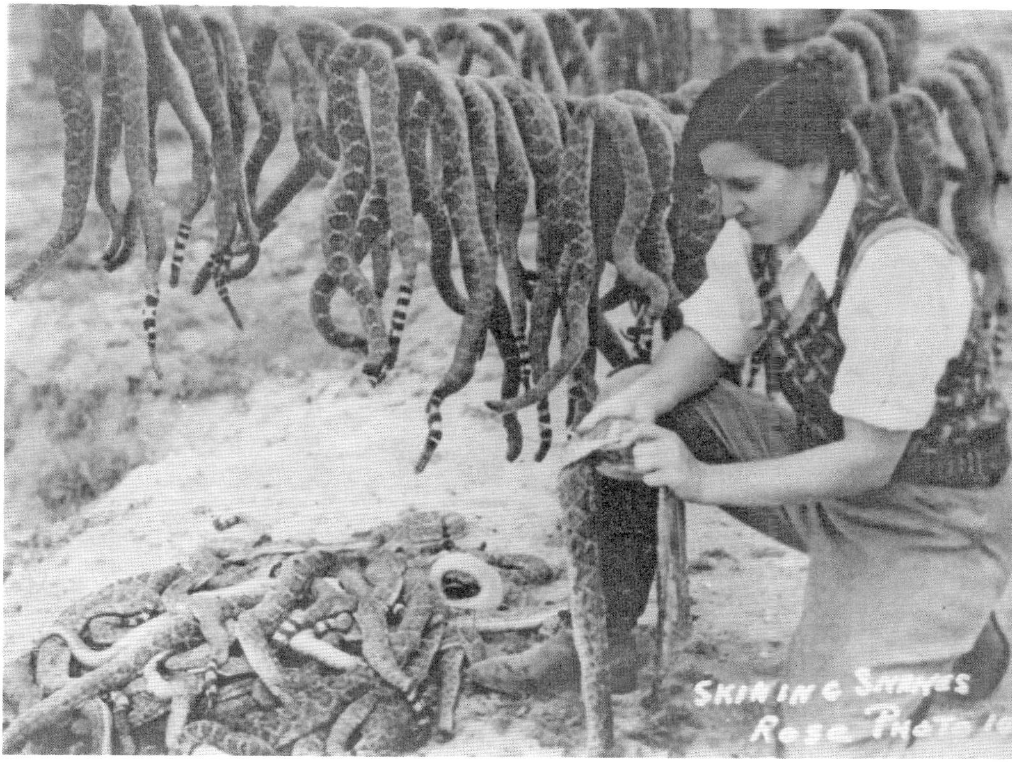
SKINING
Rose

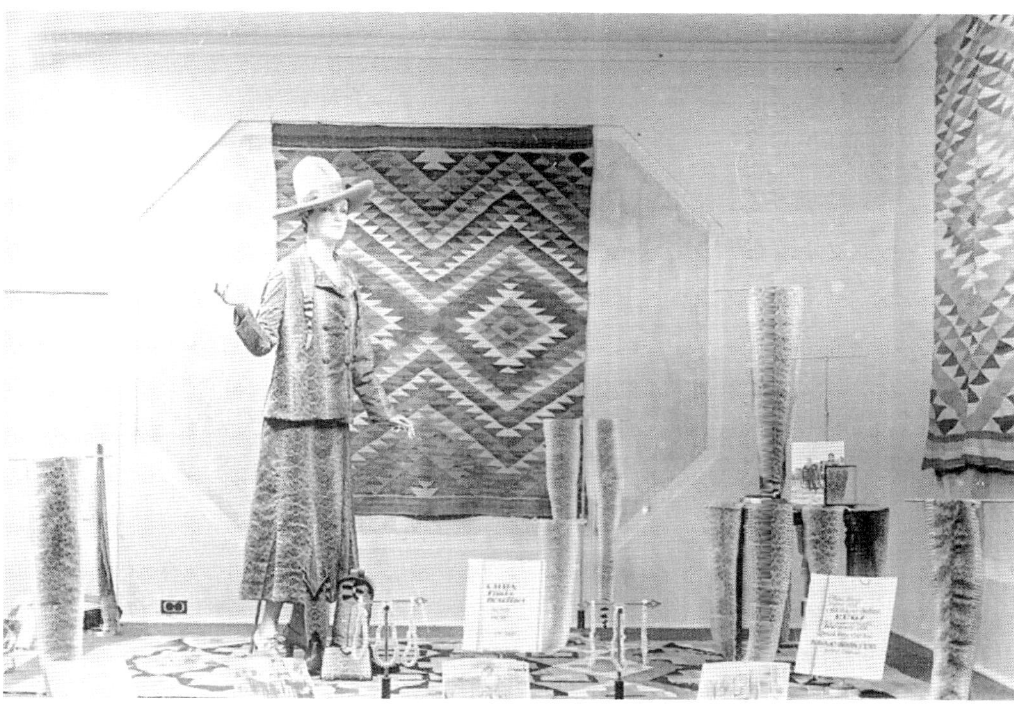

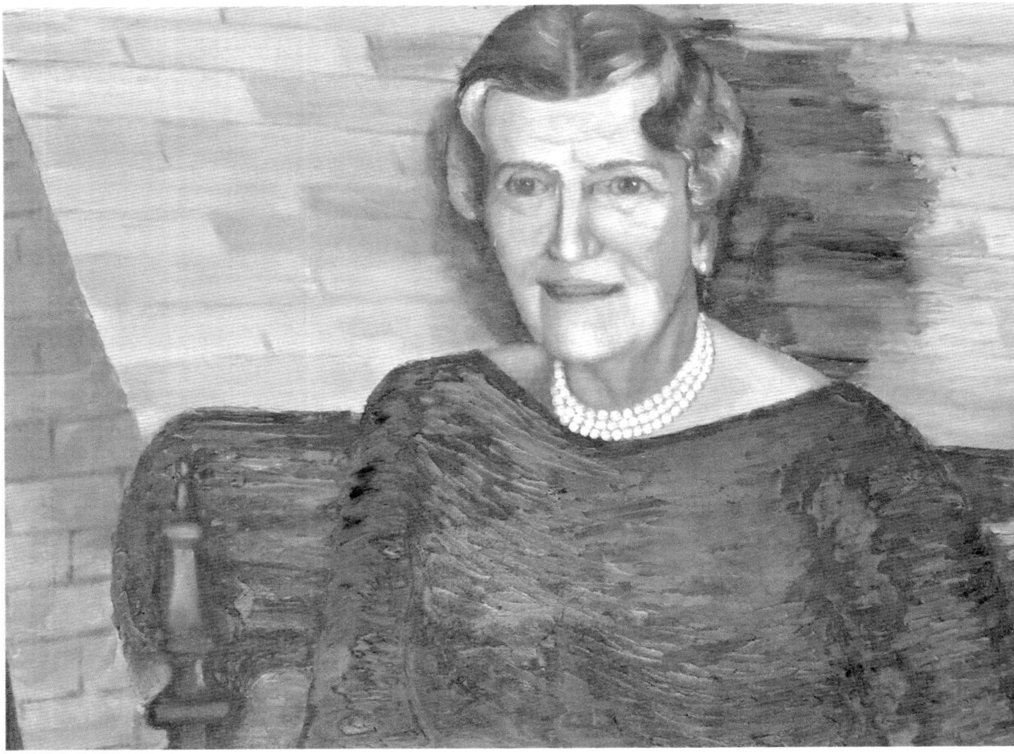

The Countess

Daisy Leiter Howard was a wealthy socialite from Chicago, whose family made their money in dry goods and real estate. On a trip to India to visit her sister Mary, who was married to the Viceroy of India, she met and fell in love with his aide de camp, the Earl of Suffolk. The Earl of Suffolk was killed in World War I. Although a widow, the countess loved European society life and rarely visited her American family. A provision of her father's will required she spend a considerable amount of time in America. She complied and moved to Arizona, building an art deco style home in the 1940s in Oro Valley. The home is now owned by the Sisters of the Immaculate Heart. The countess, a pilot, was killed in a plane crash. (Courtesy of Clark Riddin and Mike Marriott.)

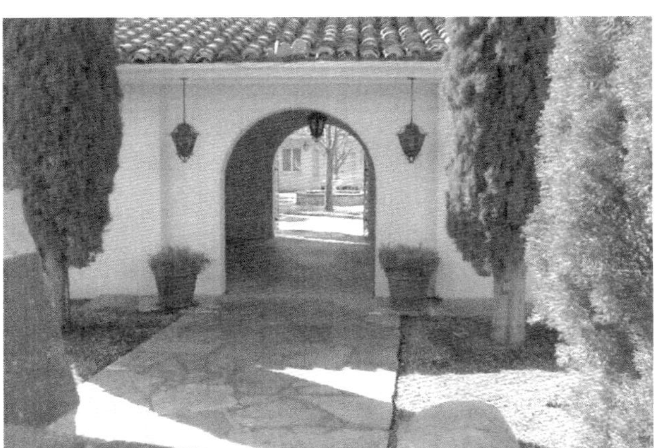

A New Royal Home

As Oro Valley expanded and the population rose, it was too much for the Countess of Suffolk. She sold her home in the Oro Valley foothills and bought land further north between the town of Oracle and the village of Catalina. While her old home was in the style of the day, an art deco model, her new home reflected the cultural inheritance of the Southwest. It was built in the Spanish Mediterranean style. It is now part of the Biosphere II. (Courtesy Mike Marriott.)

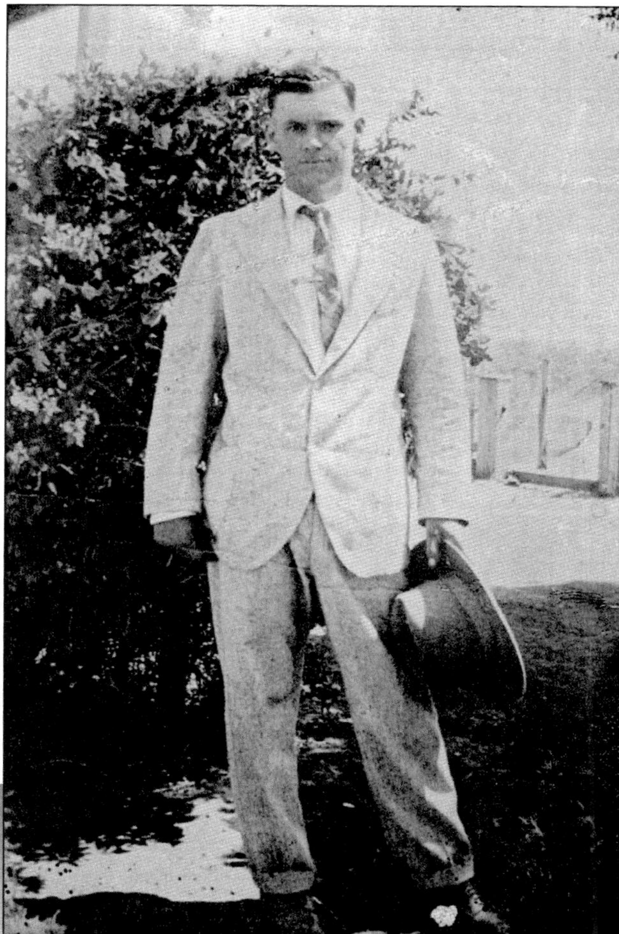

The Hunter and His Hounds
Bee Dee Daniels was a man with a passion for the outdoors, a passion honed by his work with the California and Arizona fish and wildlife agencies. In 1924, he was a grown man of 21 ready to strike out on his own. He became an internationally known hunting guide. Daniels and his hounds led the hunt for mountain lions, bobcats, and bighorn sheep in the Santa Catalina and other local mountains. Daniels trained his own dogs to follow a scent even after the animal left the ground. One of his clients, a California author, was so impressed with Daniels and his dogs, particularly Copper, that he wrote a children's book about the dog. The book was made into a film by Disney called *The Fox and the Hound* (Courtesy Alpha Adkins Evans.)

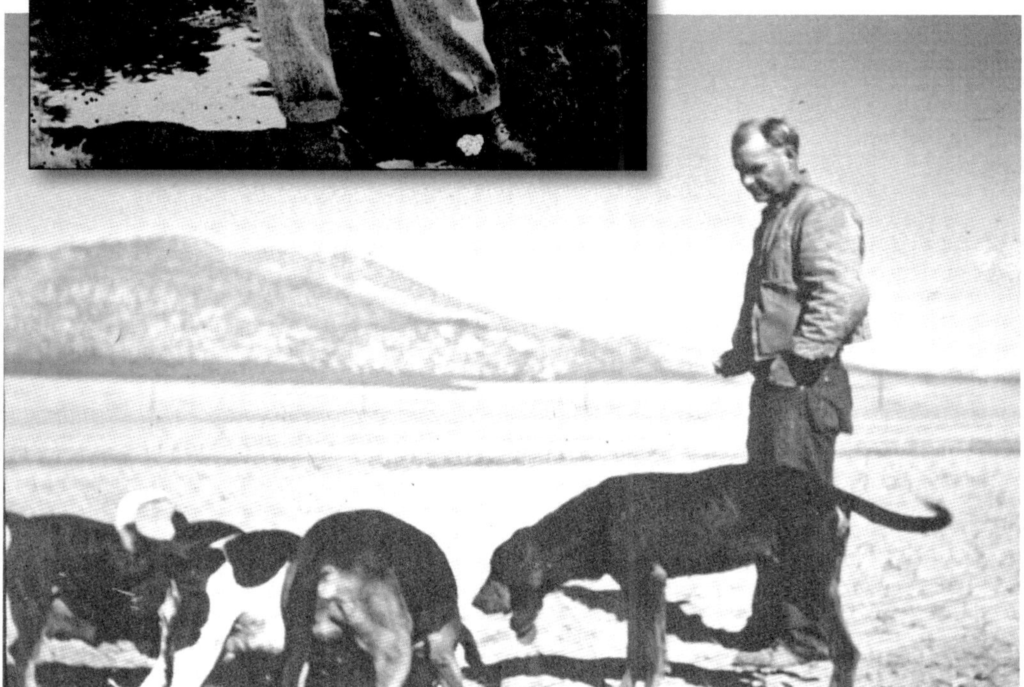

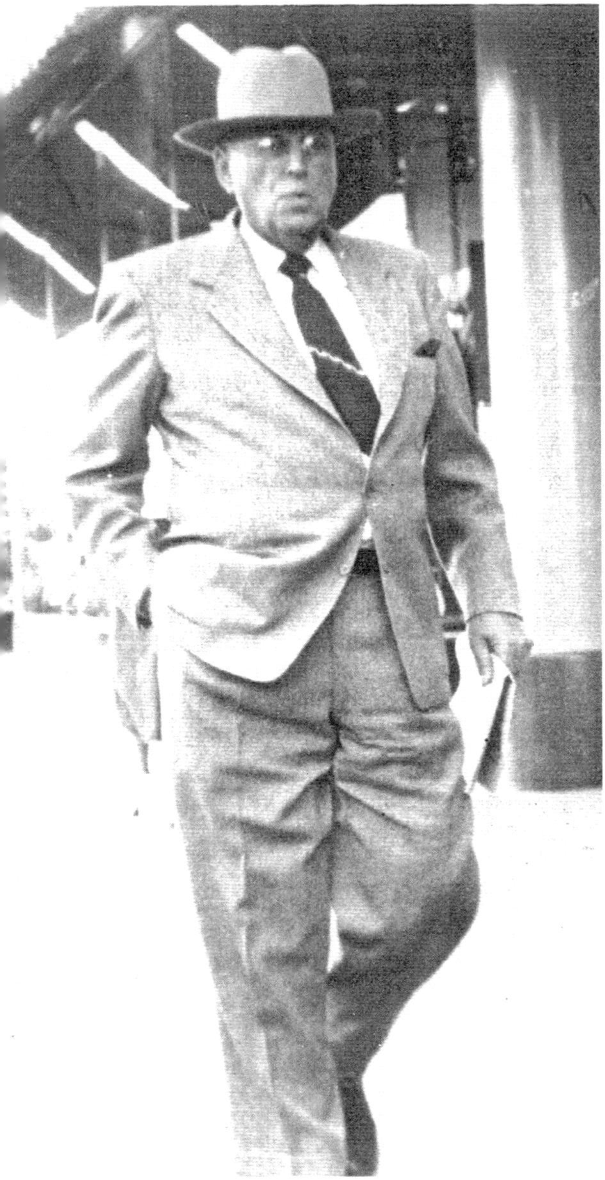

The Owl and the Hunter

Dr. William Lackner and his wife Gladys (on the right) were friends of Bee Dee Daniels. Lackner was a dentist, and he and Gladys lived in Oracle. Every day he made the 38-mile trip to his practice in Tucson from his Oracle ranch. But vacation time and special days were for hunting and guiding hunters through the local mountains. The Lackners were friends with Daniels and were his daughter Alpha's godparents. In the 1940s, Lackner and his wife met Daniel P. Mannix, who was in the area hunting with Daniels and Cooper. When Mannix wrote *The Fox and the Hound*, he patterned his owl character after Gladys Lackner. People who knew Gladys said he got it right. (Courtesy Alpha Adkins Evans.)

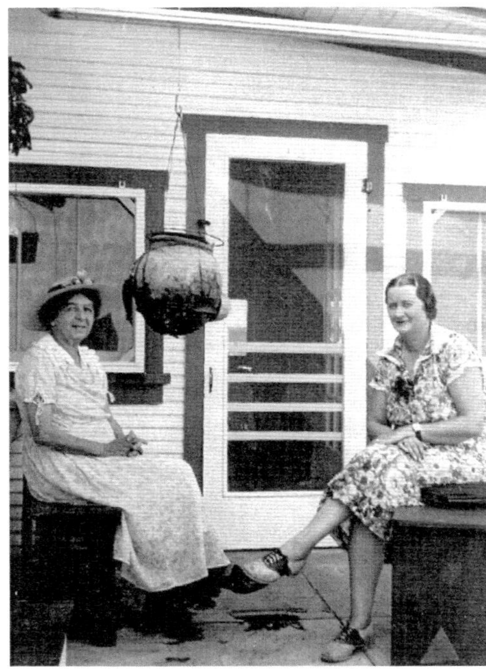

The Professor and the Rooneys (RIGHT)

The L.E. Rooney family from Oklahoma wintered every year at their Oro Valley ranch. Mr. Rooney sent his sons off to get educated at the Russell School. In this 1939 school picture (top), John Rooney is third from left, his brother Larry is on the far left in the back row, and Dr. Frank Russell is standing in the back row wearing a plaid shirt. Ten years later, in 1949, the school was still going strong but it now had a more formal approach. Doctor Russell is seated in the second row wearing a dark jacket. The Rooney ranch was sold and part of it became the Oro Valley Country Club. The Russell School also disappeared. It is private property and the former school buildings are rentals. (Top Rooney class picture courtesy John Rooney, bottom picture courtesy William Haugh.)

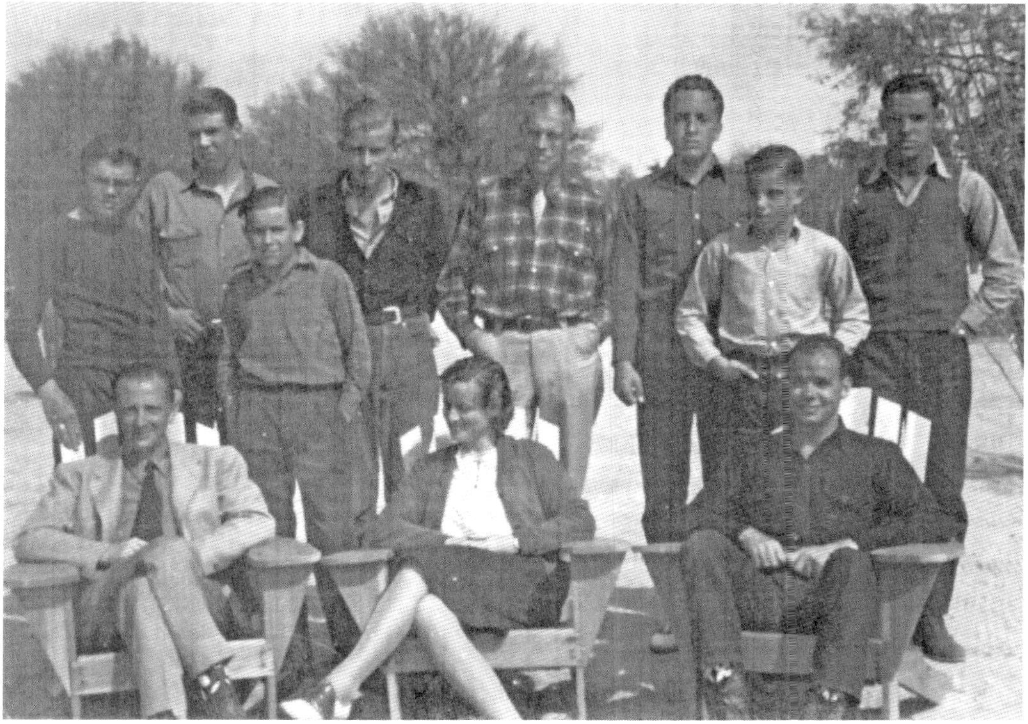

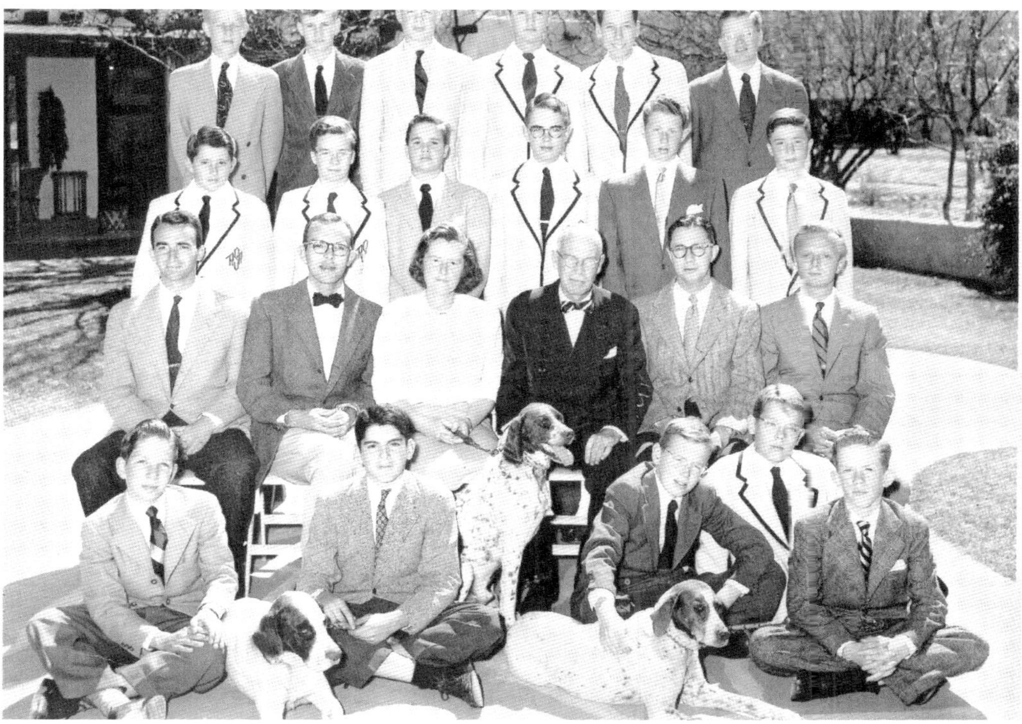

The Land Brokers

In 1957, Ester and Lloyd Golder acquired 10,000 acres of deeded and leased land in the northwest section above Tucson. The Golders had owned and managed a hotel and several properties in Chicago and decided to sell out and retire. Their plans didn't work out quite the way they had hoped. In 1958, their son, Lloyd Golder, and his family joined the senior Golders and they entered a new business arrangement. At their Rancho Vistoso home, they grew alfalfa and entertained guests, including Greta Garbo, who swam nude in their pool. Their land was wilderness, complete with frogs, snakes, and wild animals. The view of the Santa Catalina Mountains shows part of their ranchland. Mustangs came down from the nearby Tortolita Mountains for water. The Golders' house is gone, and the wild land is now the site of several shopping centers and upscale communities, including Sun City and SaddleBrooke. (Courtesy Dawn Doubek, mountains, Mike Marriott.)

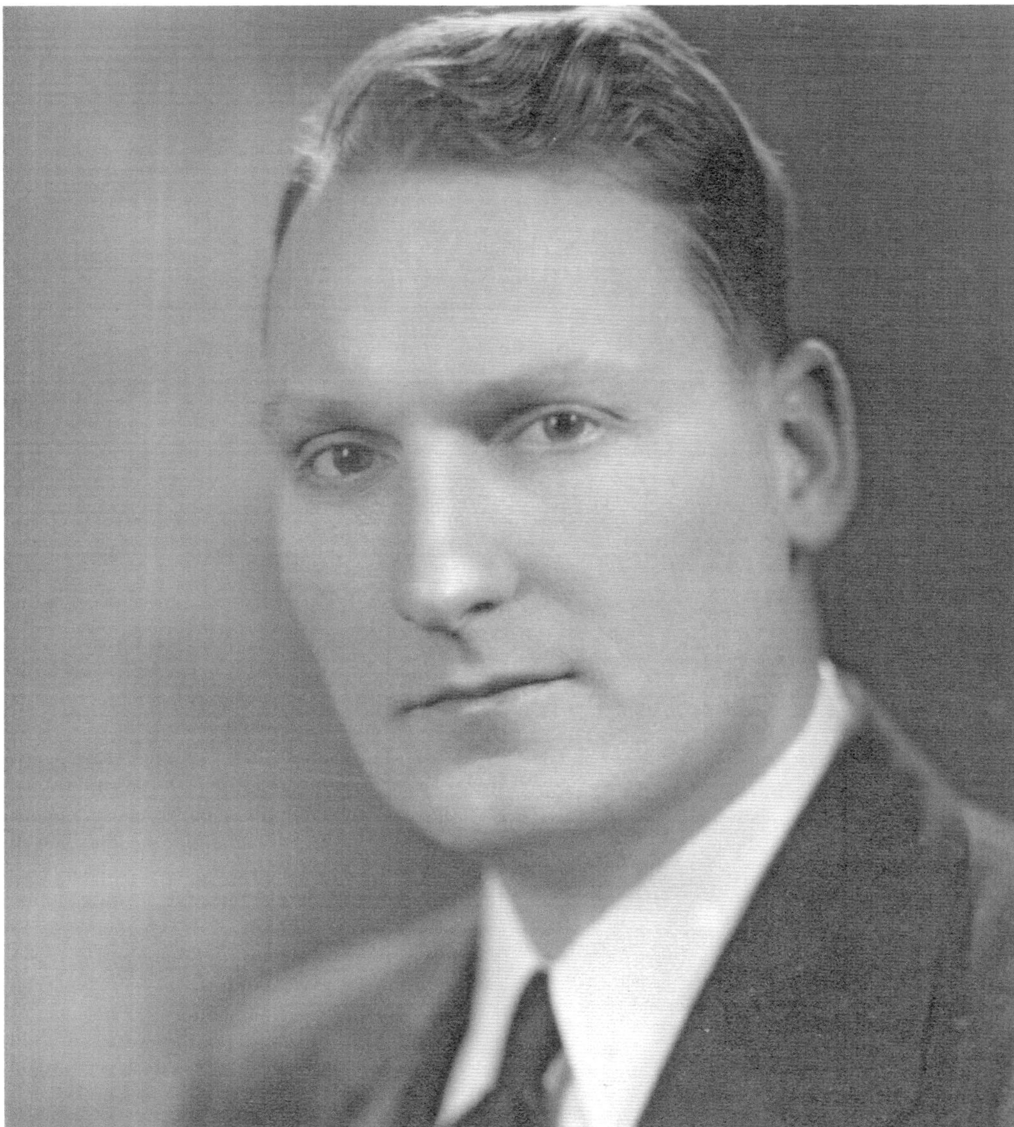

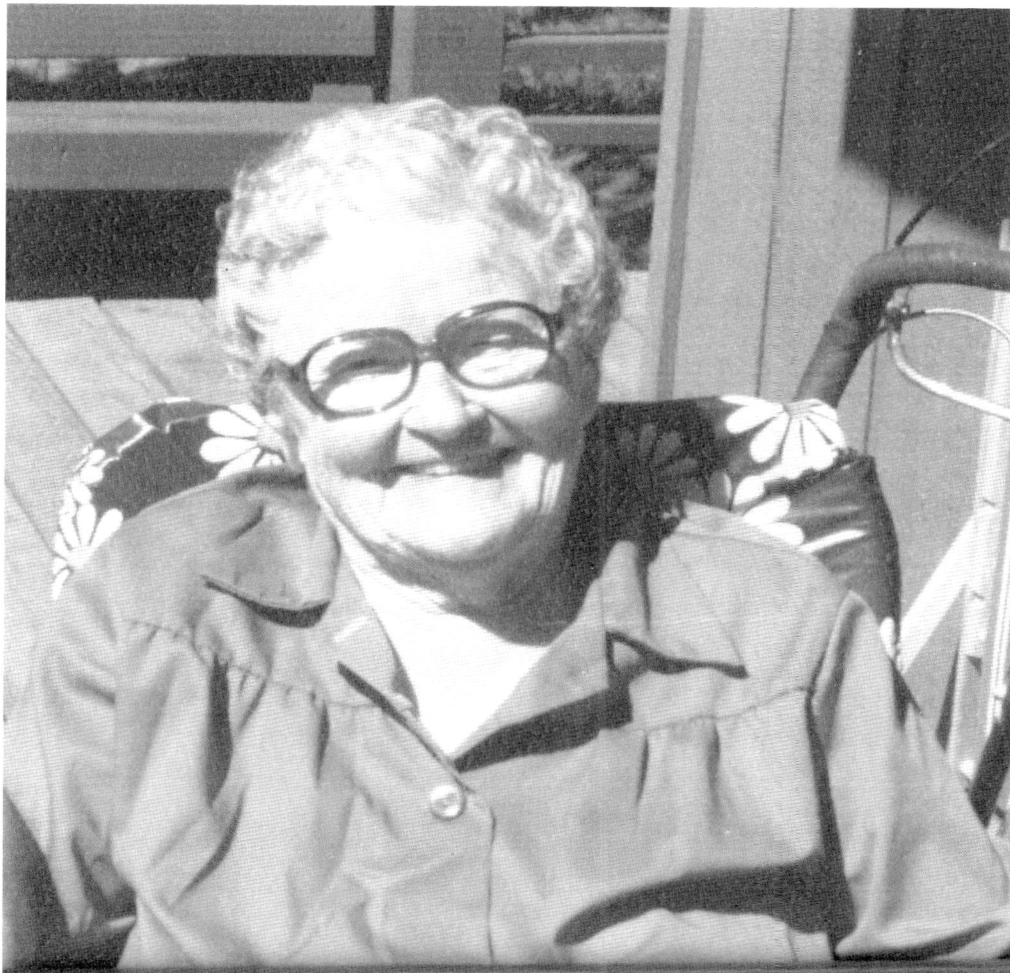

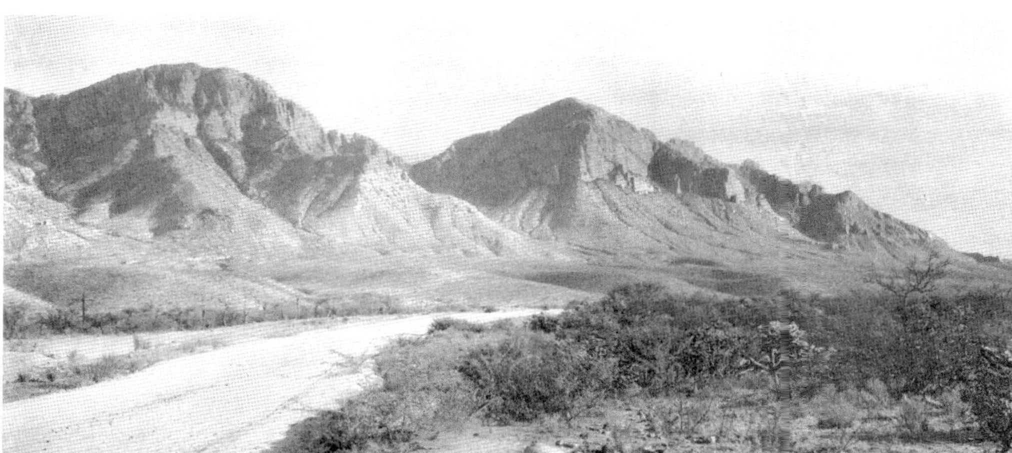

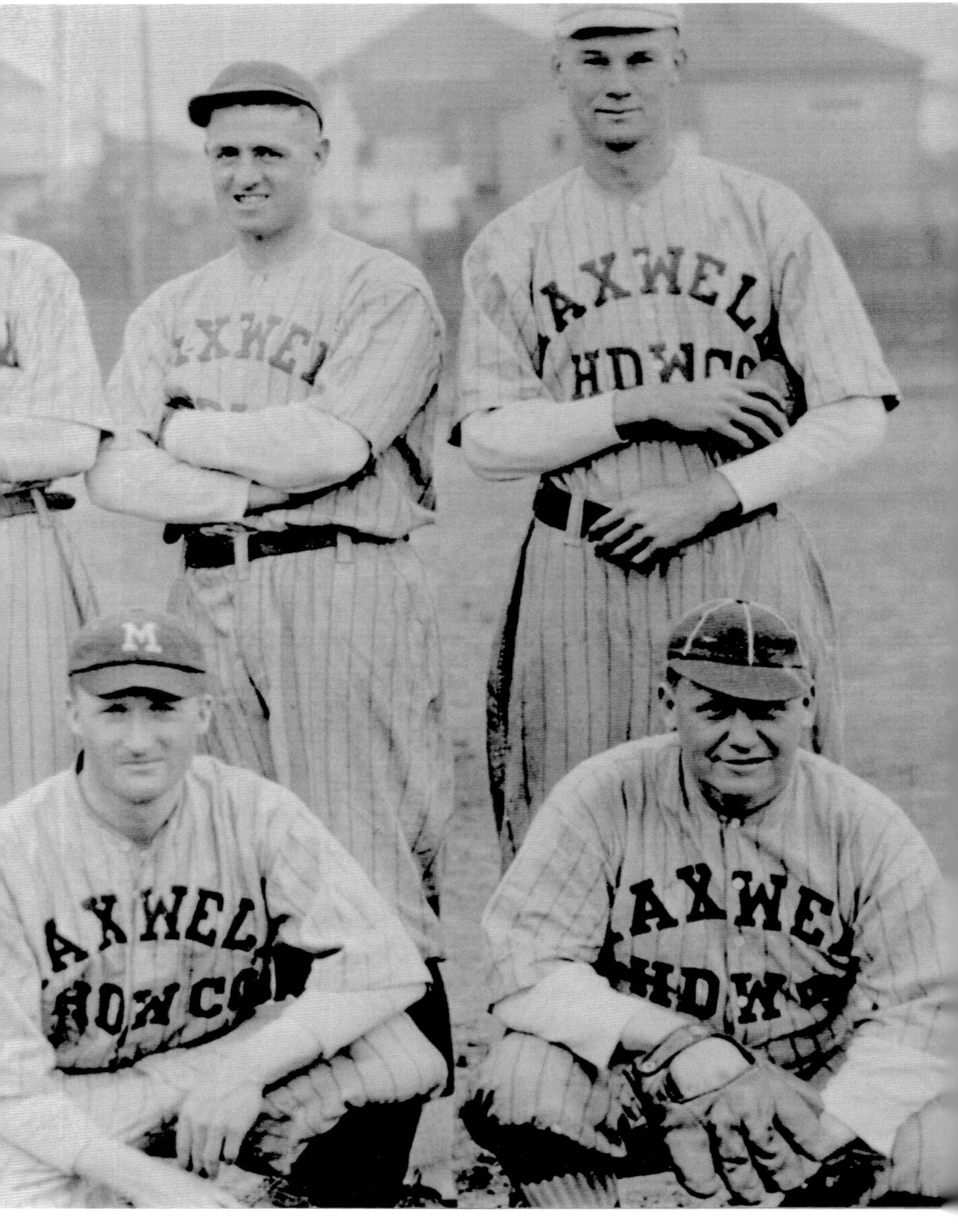

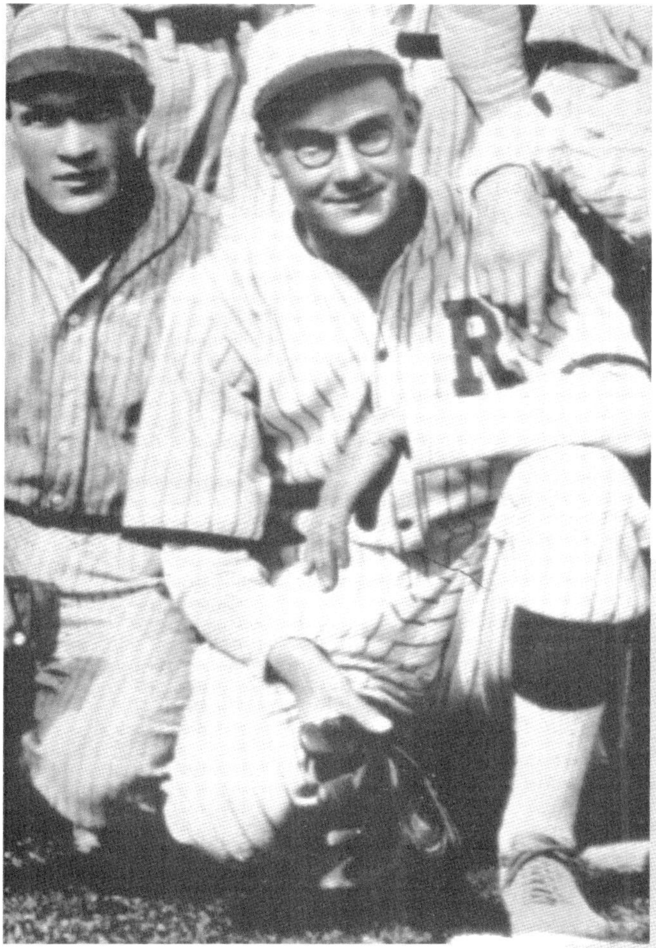

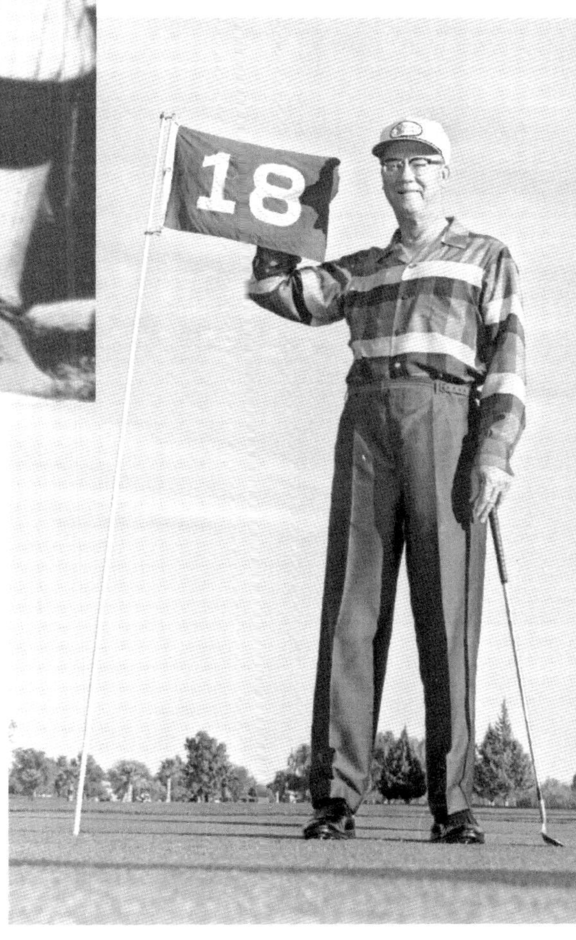

The Baseball Player
When Del Webb was 13, he played semi-professional baseball. He was a beanpole of a kid, weighing 130 pounds and standing six feet three inches. But baseball was not to be the calling of the personable Webb, who became known for his developed communities. One of his first projects was building the workers' homes for the copper mining company in San Manuel, Arizona. Another local project was the Army Air Training Base in Marana. But what he is best known for are his upscale retirement communities found throughout the United States, including the Rancho Vistoso Sun City, which was completed in 1997. (Courtesy Del Webb Sun Cities Museum.)

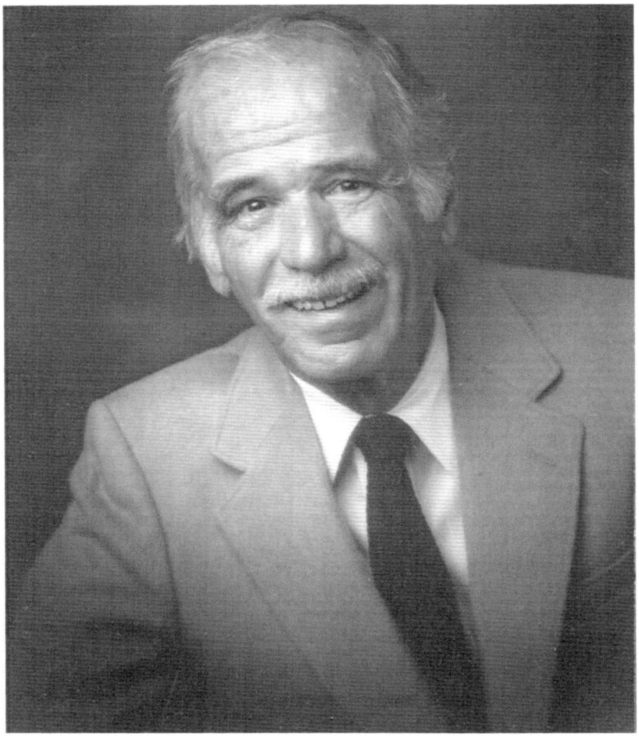

A Beautiful Fore Thought

In 1959, Nidilor G. Sakeller, a well-known architect in the Southwest, was commissioned to design a clubhouse for the newly established Oro Valley Country Club. The country club was situated on the old Rooney Ranch, north of Tucson, in a sparsely populated area. It was a challenging task. Sakeller had to work with desert land covered with cacti and surrounded by mountains. In addition, the clubhouse had to blend with the golf course, not fight it. Sakeller's design was a structure of glass and adobe offering views of the course and the magnificent mountains surrounding it. It became the most significant building in the town when Oro Valley was incorporated in 1974. (Clubhouse courtesy Oro Valley Country Club, Sakeller courtesy of the Sakeller family.)

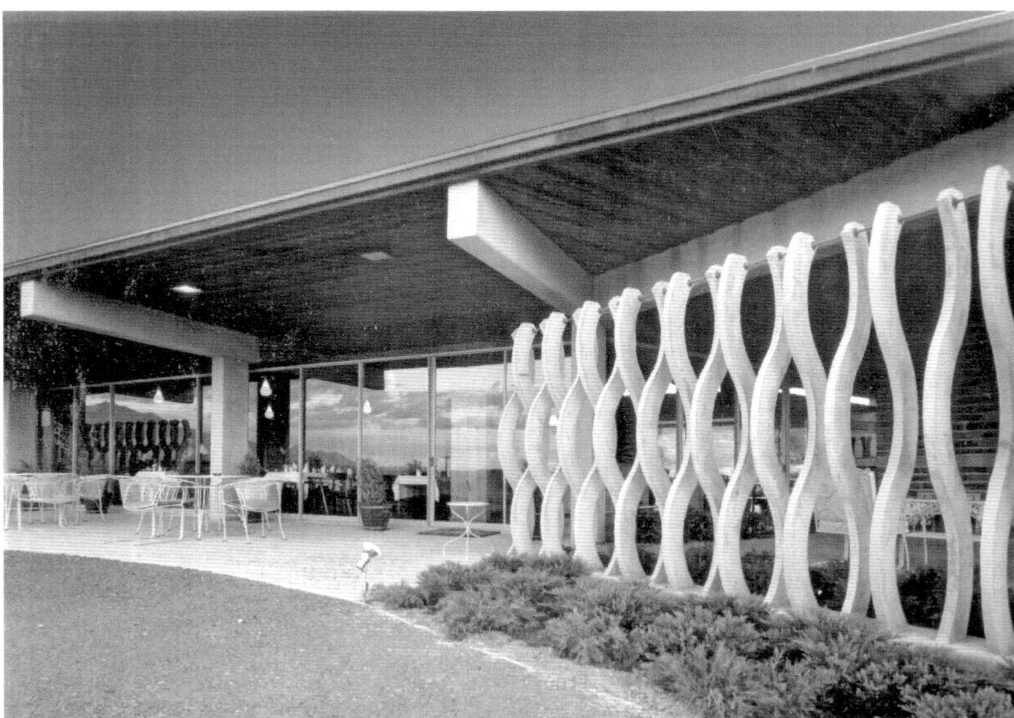

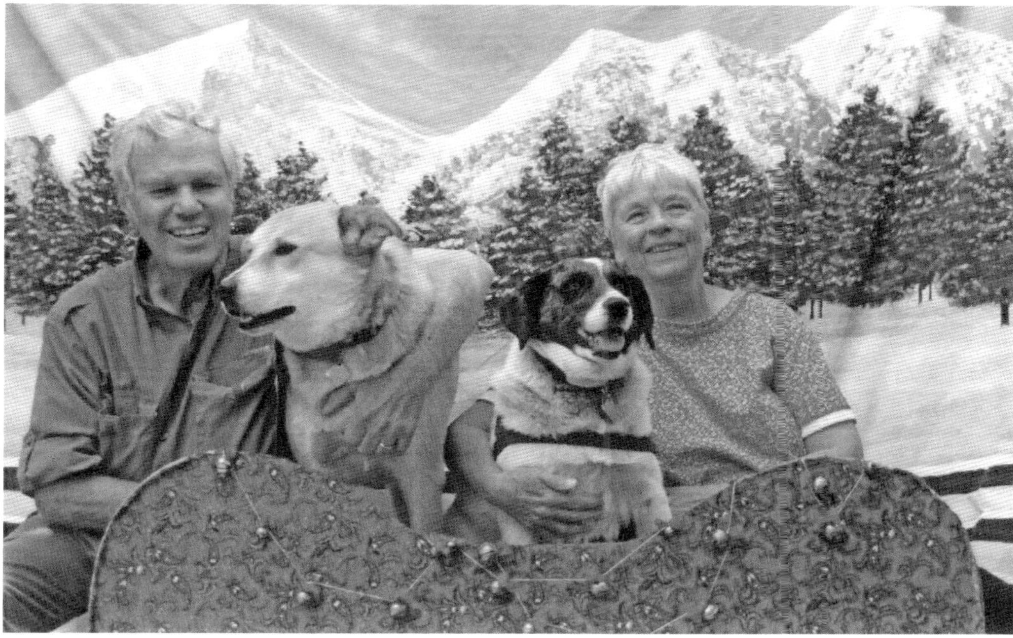

A Garden in the Desert

In the 1920s, Maurice Reid planted frost-sensitive citrus and date palms on a section northwest of Tucson. In 1937, John T. deBlois Wack bought the property and constructed a Santa Fe–style house on the land. In 1966, Richard and Jean Wilson began buying up parcels of land around the Wack property, which would become the 37 acres of Tohono Chul Park. The Wilsons fought continual battles with developers and the town of Tucson to keep the land from commercial development. For their efforts, the Wilsons received a citation from the Tucson Audubon Society in 1980 for saving the desert greenspace. Tohono Chul Park was dedicated as a 37-acre desert preserve on April 19, 1985. The Wilsons deeded the property to a nonprofit foundation. (Courtesy Tohono Chul Park and the Wilson family.)

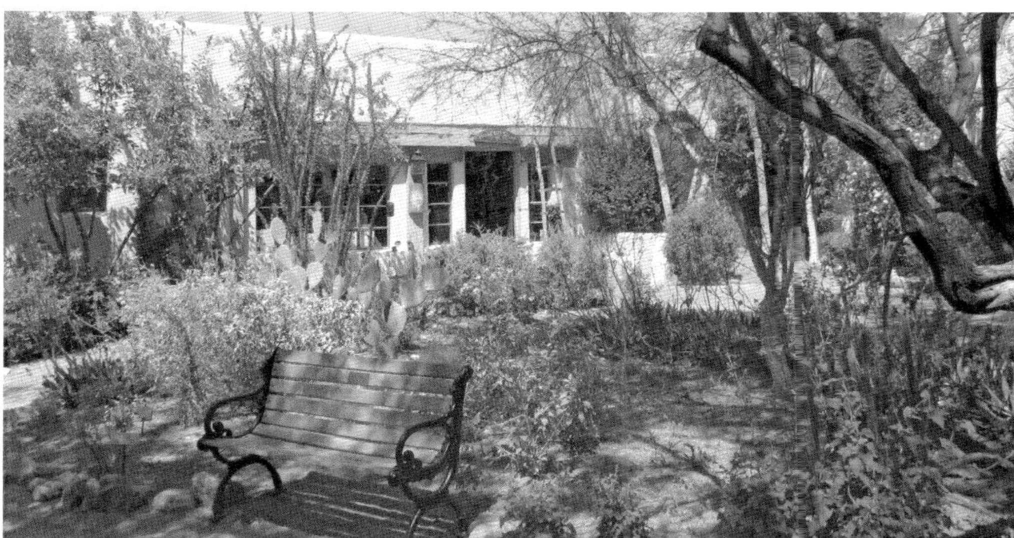

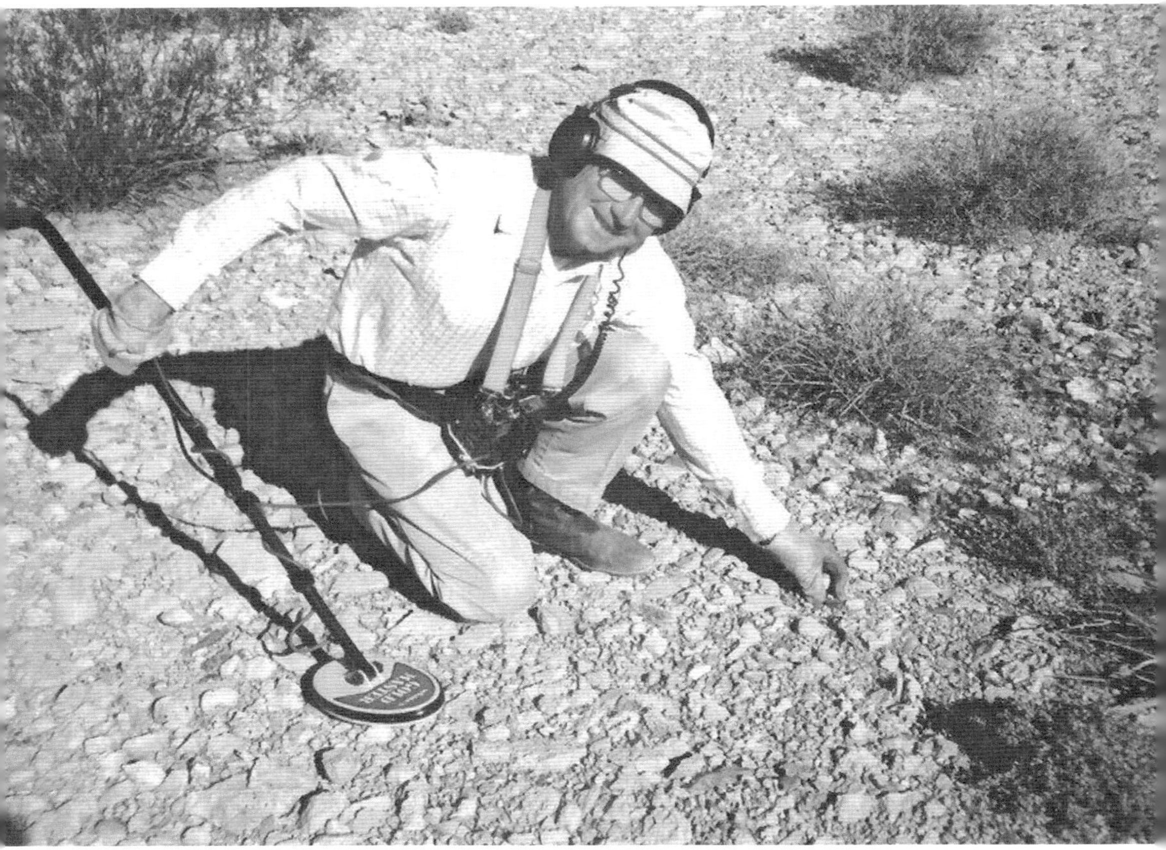

The Father of Oro Valley

When the mayor of Tucson announced the town would annex a small community just north of the city, the local residents of that community went into action to prevent their envelopment by the city. A small group of concerned citizens held several meetings in the home of Jim Kriegh and decided to fight the movement by incorporating their 2.4-square-mile area. A civil engineering professor at the University of Arizona, Kriegh used his knowledge to help survey the area that would become Oro Valley. His work in diligently checking documents and pursuing regulations was instrumental in helping Oro Valley achieve incorporation in 1974. To gain backing for the new town, the founding fathers decided to name it Oro Valley after a country club by that name in the area. It was hoped the adoption of the name would bring the support of the country club community for the new town. Although honored as the founding father of Oro Valley, Kriegh is known to the scientific community for another reason. After his wife's death in 1991, Kriegh looked for something to keep him busy, preferably an outdoor activity. He decided to try metal detecting. This introduced him to gold hunting, which led to an interest in meteorites. He discovered the Gold Basin meteorite field in northwest Arizona on November 24, 1995. Meteorites are 4.5 billion years old. Radiocarbon dating of the Gold Basin fall shows it happened 15,000 years ago, at the end of the Ice Age. The size of the strewnfield mapped by Kriegh and his team for the University of Arizona was 12 by 15 miles, but it is undoubtedly much larger. Gold Basin is not Kriegh's only meteorite find. In November 1954, he discovered the Greaterville meteorite. His interest and work with meteorites has earned him international recognition and respect from amateurs and professionals. His appreciation of history led him to found the Oro Valley Historical Society. (Courtesy Twink Monrad.)

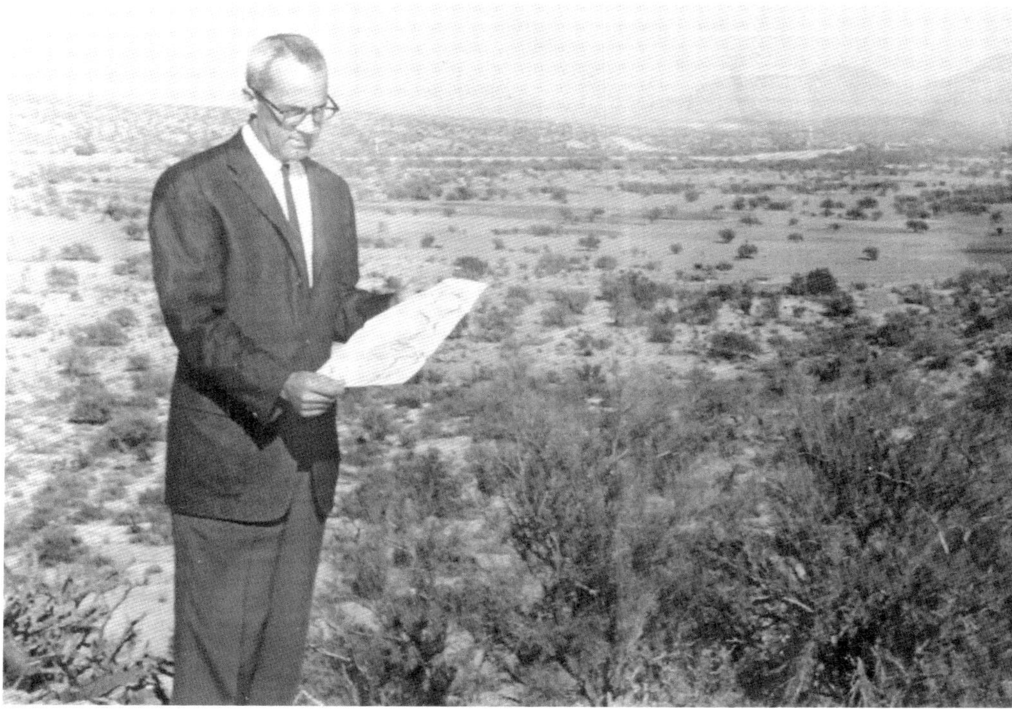

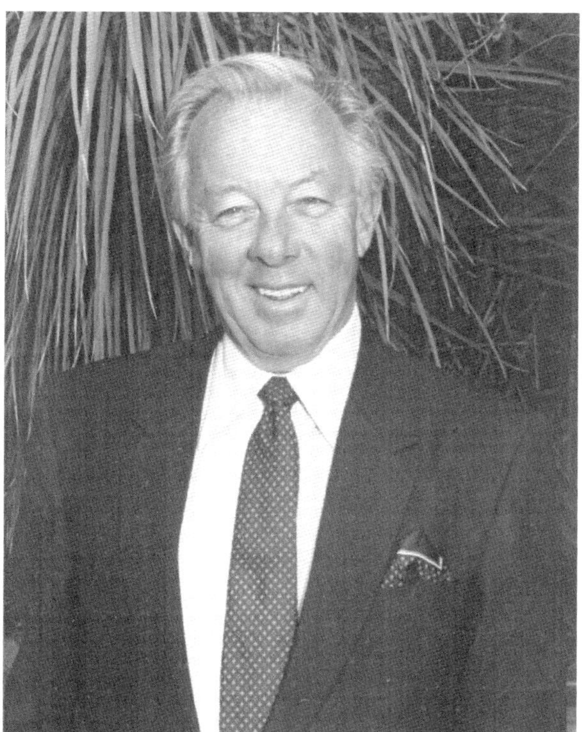

From Golf Course to Town
Louis Landon was an avid golfer and came to Tucson to play the game he loved. He firmly believed there were not enough golf courses in the area, and in 1958 he set out to correct the situation by developing a resort called Oro Valley Estates with luxury homes surrounding a country club golf course oasis. This community became part of Oro Valley. (Courtesy Oro Valley Country Club.)

The New Town's Mayor
Richard Kolt served as mayor in Oro Valley from April 1975 until May 1976. He was the town's second mayor. The first, Kenneth Holford, served only six months. As the town has grown over the years, so has the length of service of the mayor. (Courtesy Town of Oro Valley.)

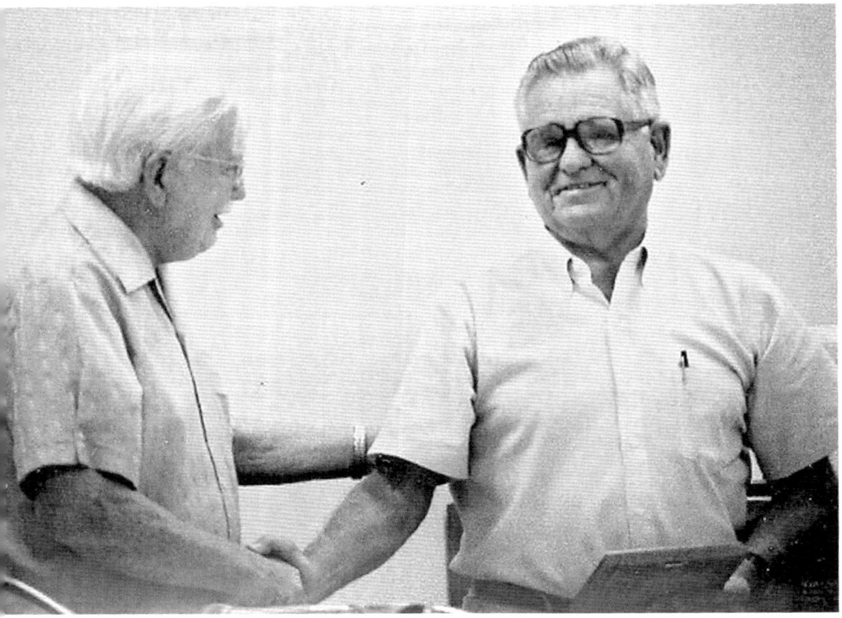

Leading A New Town
In May 1978, E.S. Steve Engle, the fourth mayor of Oro Valley, followed Lois Lamberson, Oro Valley's third mayor. He served in that office from 1978 until May 1990. His vice mayor was Henry Zipf (on the right). Zipf is the grandson of George Pusch, founder of the Steam Pump Ranch. (Courtesy Oro Valley Historical Society.)

A Driving Force
From 1998 to 2010, Mayor Paul Loomis on the right, completed an enormous number of projects and saw the town grow from 14,000 people to 40,000. He negotiated for water rights that ensure the town will have a sufficient supply of water until 2025. Loomis expanded the tax base with significant commercial development, yet managed to keep Oro Valley one of the prettiest small towns in America. (Courtesy Paul Loomis.)

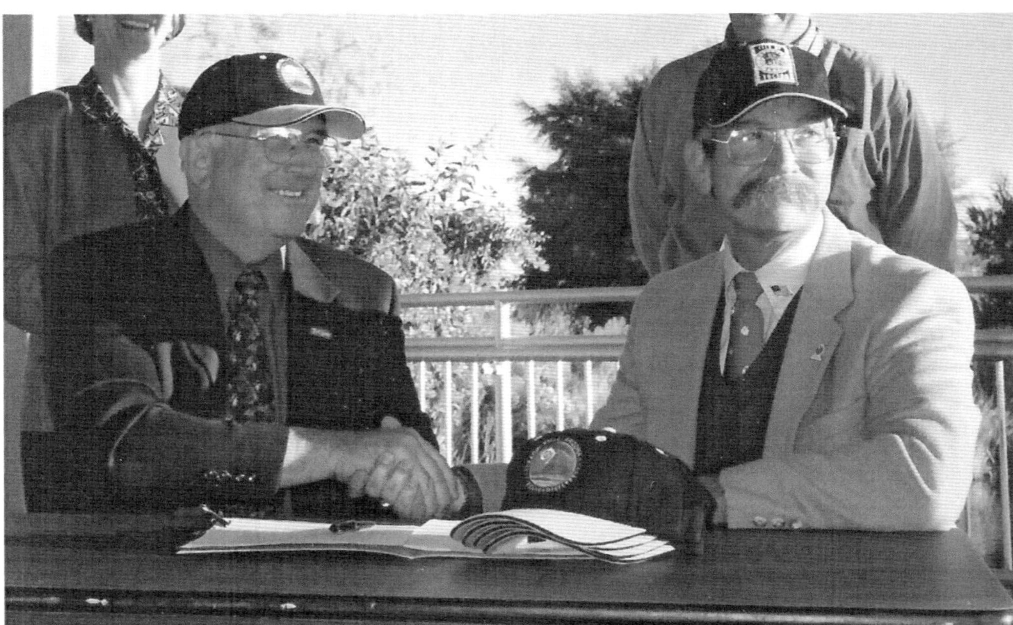

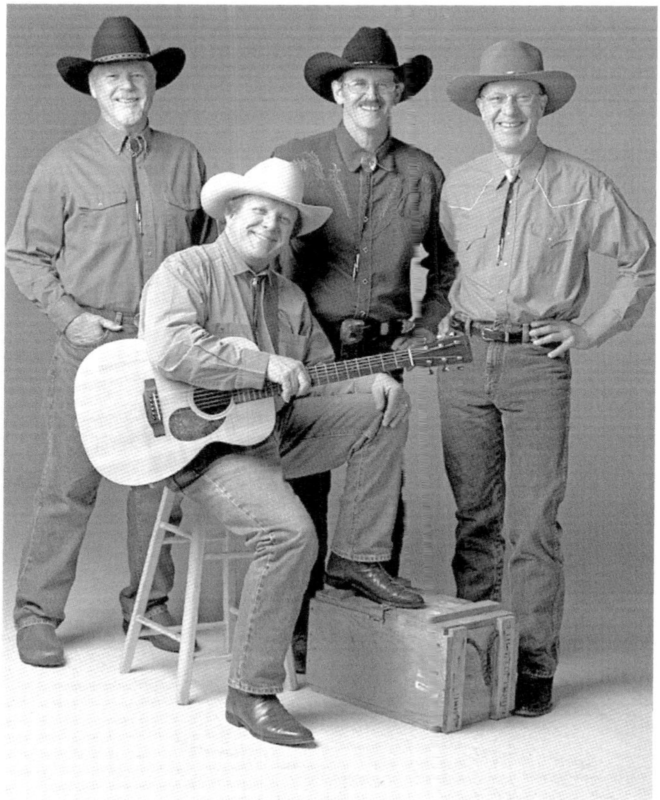

Music from the Old West
The Bill Ganz Western Band brings back the rousing and sometimes poignant music of the old West. It is their mission to protect the legacy of western music, especially songs about Arizona's western culture. Sometimes performing alone, and sometimes with the Tucson Symphony Orchestra, they evoke the spirit of America's wild frontier days while managing to be highly entertaining. (Courtesy Bill Ganz Western Band.)

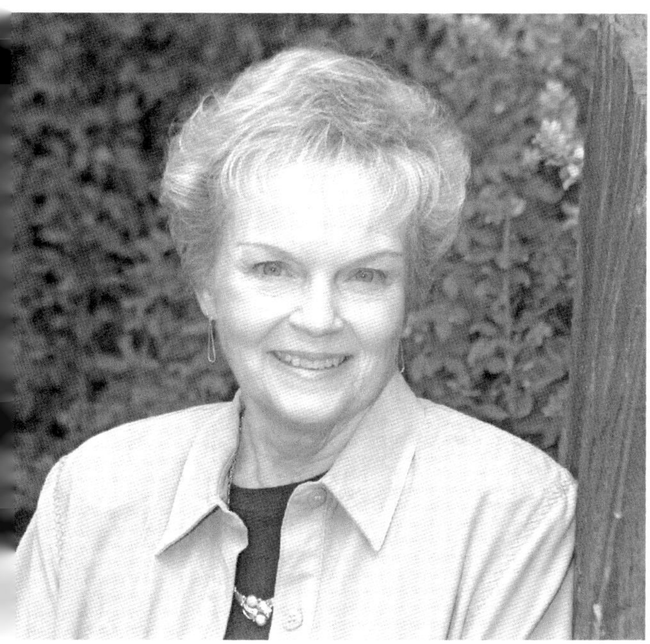

Words of the Old West
Jan Cleere's writings capture the courage and uniqueness of the old West. She is recognized as one of the major authorities on historical southwestern women. Her popular books and magazine articles have won her multiple awards for her writing. Cleere is a meticulous and dedicated researcher with an easy style that is entertaining as well as informative. (Courtesy Jan Cleere.)

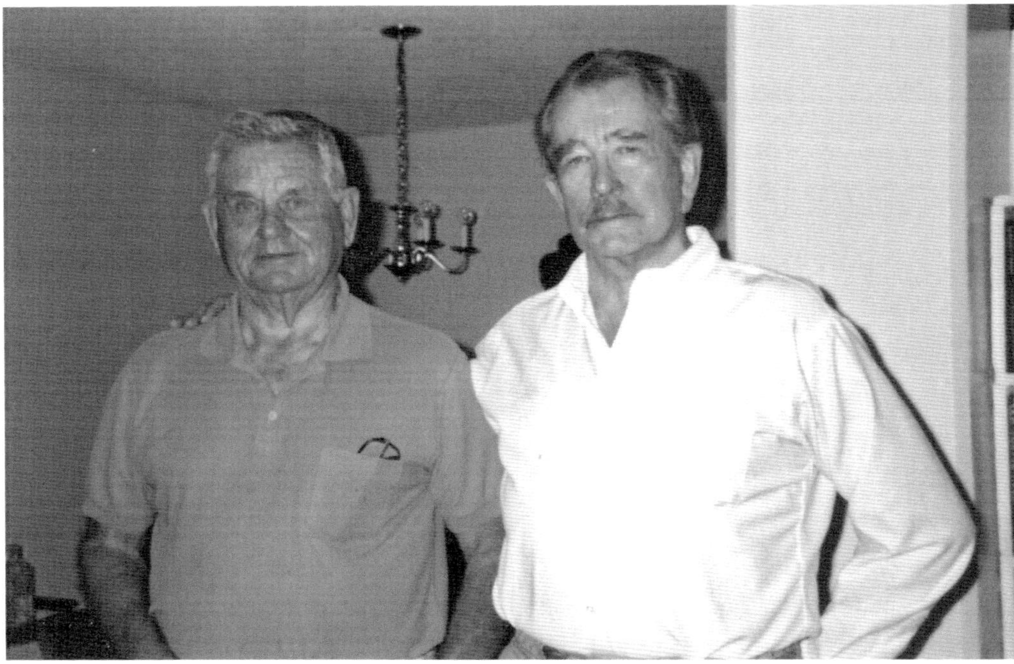

Deep Roots

Hank Zipf, on the left, and his brother Frank, have deep roots in Oro Valley. Before there was even a town, their grandfather, George Pusch, established the Steam Pump Ranch next to the Canada del Oro. Frank grew up and left the area, but Hank stayed around, becoming an attorney, then serving as vice mayor in Oro Valley. A young Hank Zipf, shown on the right next to his brother and pictured with a cousin, about 1922, thought the Steam Pump was a great place to spend childhood days. He has wonderful memories and tells priceless stories about ranching, ghosts, and his famous grandfather. His mother, Gertrude Pusch, loved the ranch and brought her children there, instilling in them a great respect for family, Arizona history, and the Steam Pump. (Courtesy Oro Valley Historical Society.)

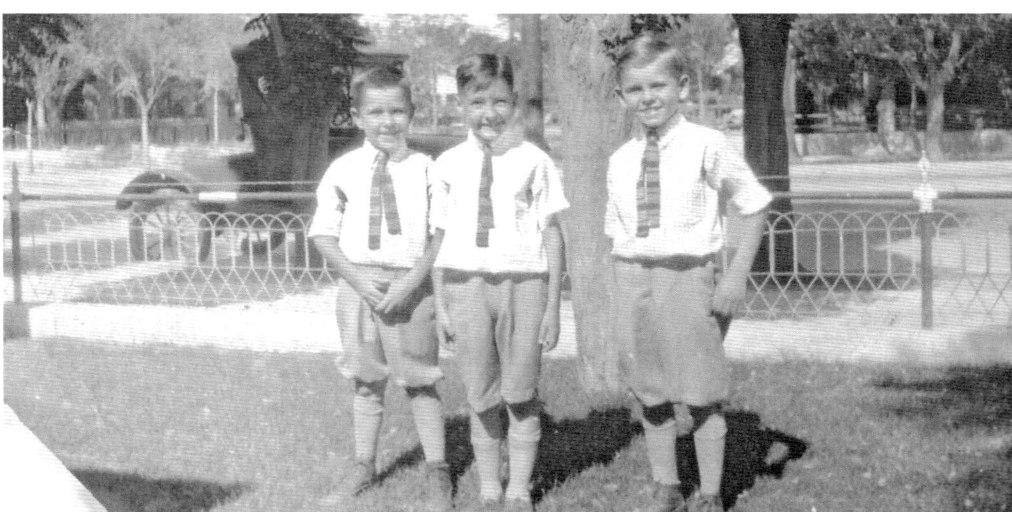

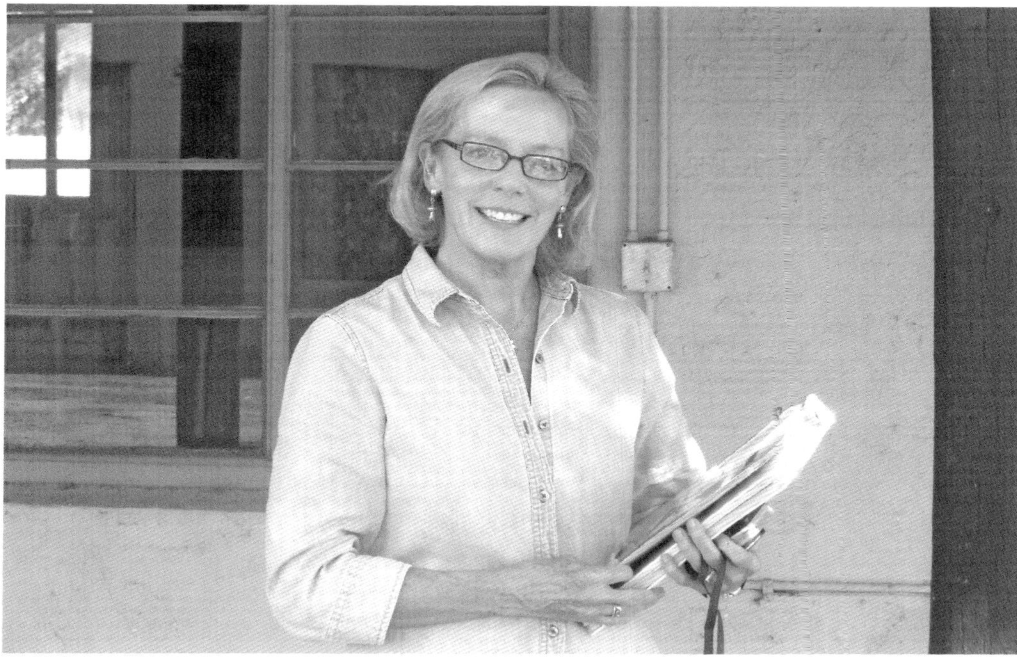

A Guardian of the Past
Archaeologist Pat Spoerl saw Oro Valley's history disappearing under developing communities. To preserve the history of Arizona, and her hometown, she helped Jim Kriegh create the Oro Valley Historical Society. Through her quiet and relentless efforts, she persuaded the town to buy the Steam Pump Ranch. Spoerl is past president of the society and still working to protect artifacts of Oro Valley's history. (Courtesy of Pat Spoerl.)

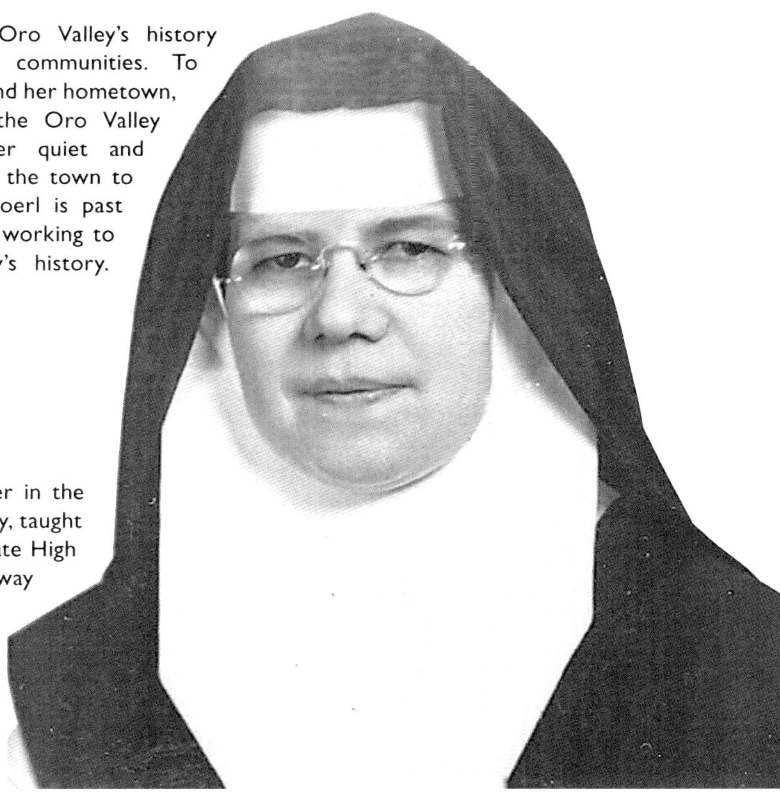

Teaching with Heart
Sister Mary Rose Zepeda, a sister in the order of Immaculate Heart of Mary, taught American history at the Immaculate High School for many years. She had a way of bringing history alive for her classes. Sister Mary Rose was well loved by her students, and her kindness and understanding helped many of them find their place in life. (Courtesy Sister Superior Luisa Sanchez.)

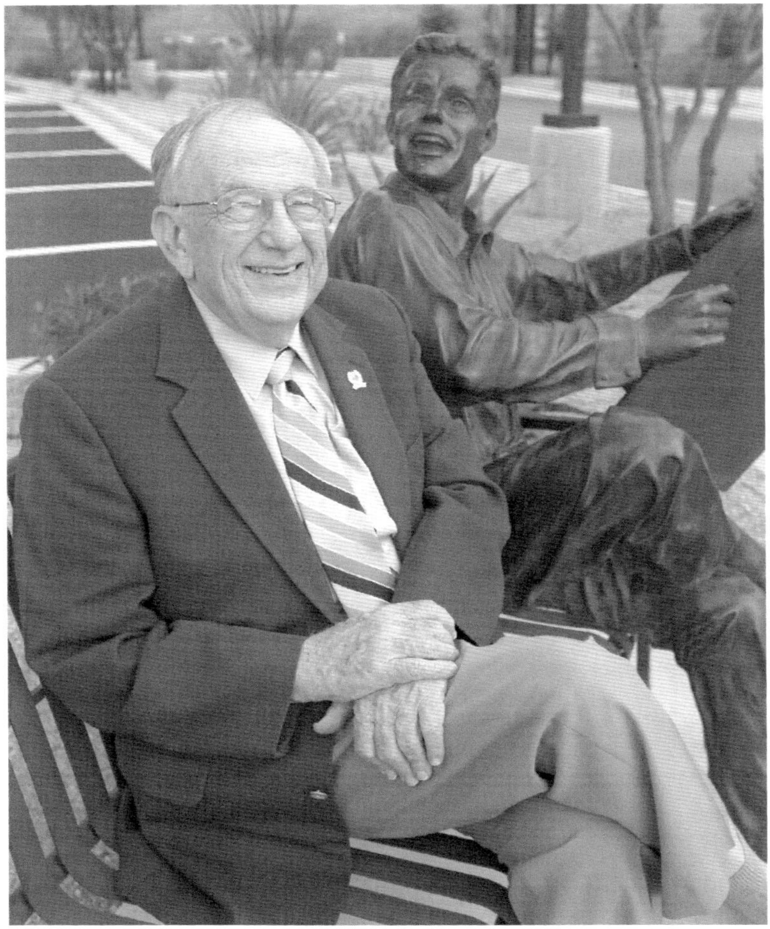

The Muse of Oro Valley

Everywhere you look in Oro Valley you see the fine touch and the driving force of Dick Eggerding. He is a tireless worker who was designated in 2003 the Citizen of the Decade by the newspaper, *The Northwest Explorer.* He chaired the Oro Valley Arts Advisory Board and co-founded the Greater Oro Valley Arts Council. Eggerding is a lover of all arts. Before retiring as an insurance executive, he sang with the St. Louis Municipal Opera and Symphony, and was a board member of the Cincinnati Art Museum. He spearheaded a program that brought the symphony to Oro Valley, and he partnered in promoting classical music training in the schools. Through his efforts, public art has become a major component in the planning and development of Oro Valley. One percent of every new construction project in the town goes to public art. The town is a delight to view. Statues and art murals are found in shopping malls, in front of and part of public buildings, on trails, and at the Oro Valley hospital. This dynamic man's fervor for public art has made the town a living gallery and makes a walk around town a visual and educational treat. There is no one style; each piece is a representation of the many styles of both classic and modern in the world of art. Some will make you smile, some will make you ponder, and they all provide a pleasant mini-course in art. Eggerding has left his signature on the town, a signature that represents the world of art and music in all forms, made available to young and old alike. (Courtesy Richard Eggerding.)

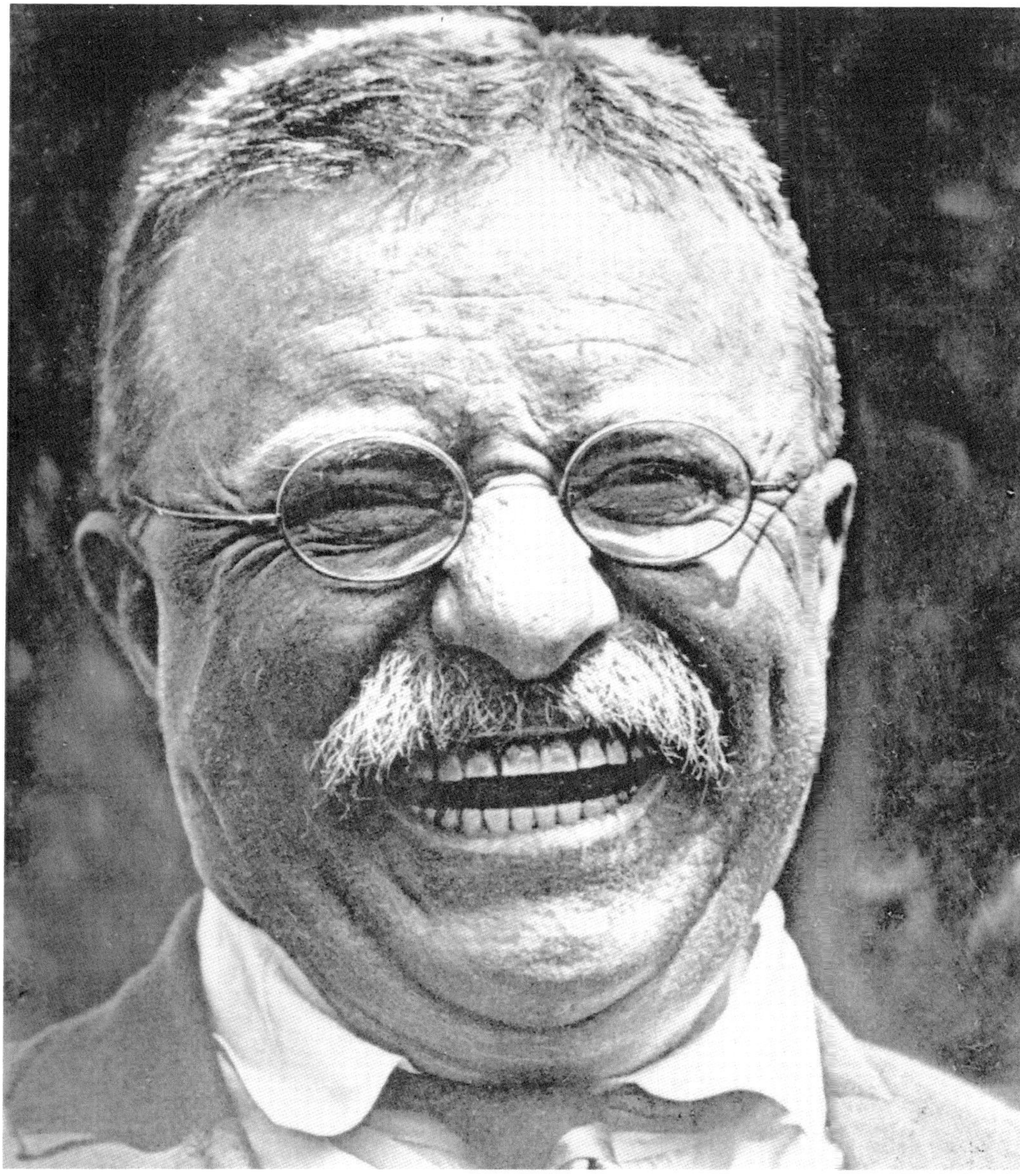

A Gift of Nature

No one influenced the look and lifestyle of Oro Valley more than Theodore Roosevelt. As president from 1901 to 1909, he signed legislation that established and protected the national parks. Bordering Oro Valley is the Coronado National Forest, which covers 1,780,000 acres and ranges in elevation from 3,000 feet to 10,720 feet. Part of Roosevelt's national parks system, it offers town residents breathtaking vistas of mountains and ridges, and challenges hikers, campers, and riders to test themselves in the canyons and hills, and on its trails. Tourists come to play in this natural treasure, and residents enjoy its many recreational benefits. The Coronado National Forest enhances the look of the town, and beckons all to enjoy its offerings, teaching young and old to appreciate the gift of nature. (Courtesy author's collection.)

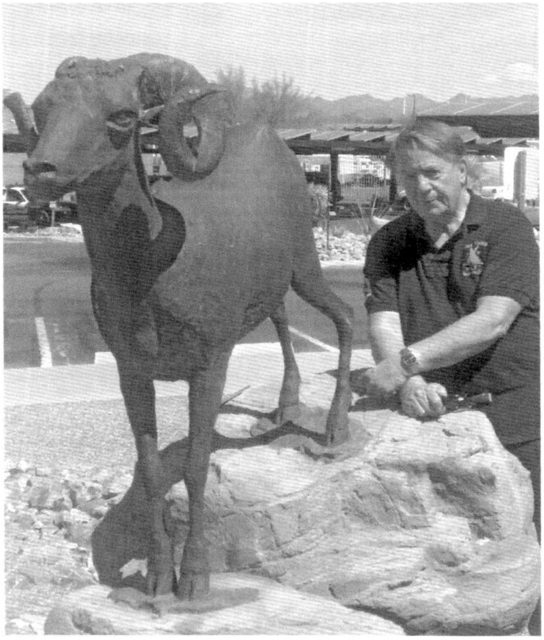

A Sight to Behold

The unique and distinctive look of Oro Valley owes much to its public art program. Scattered around the town are original works of art, all in view of the passing public. Some are whimsical, some traditional, and others thought provoking. The artistic works of Matthew Moutafis, the town's most prolific artist, can be seen on the streets and by public and commercial buildings. Moutafis created and executed the town's symbol, a powerful bighorn sheep that stands outside of the town hall. In his gecko piece, he shows his whimsical side. He has had a major impact on the visual artistic profile of the community and has lived in the area for over 35 years. Proud of his hometown, he has taken an active role in the community, chairing numerous boards and commissions. (Courtesy Matthew Moutafis.)

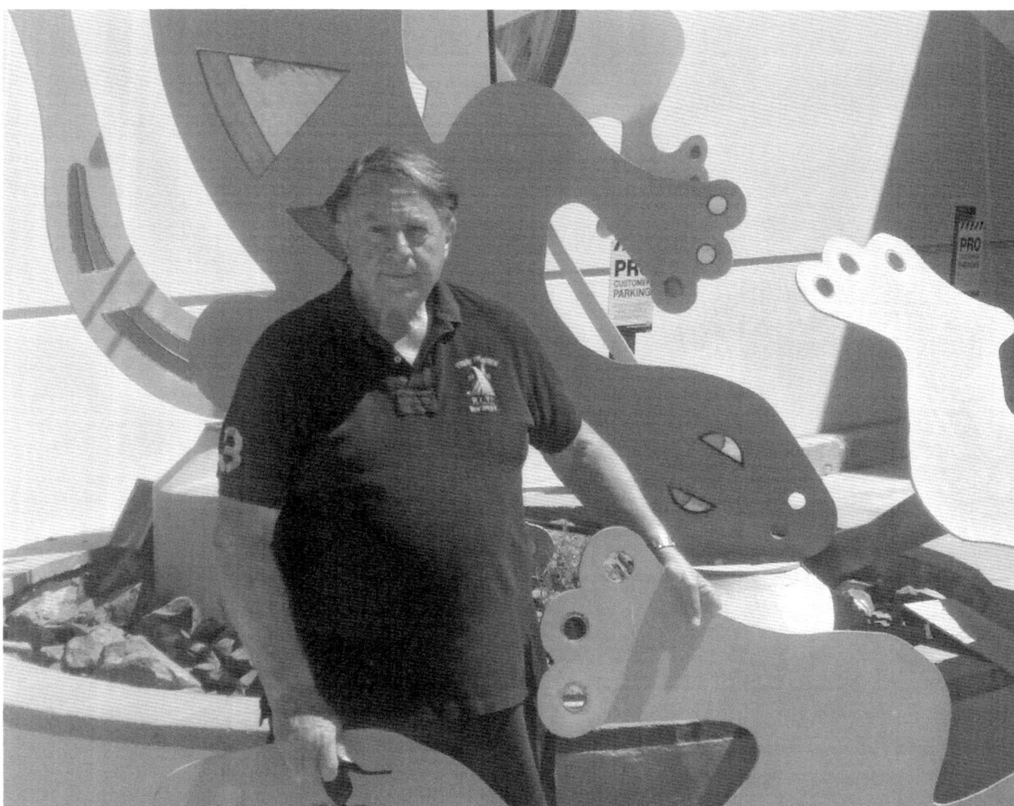

CHAPTER THREE

Catalina: Hard Work and Heart

The smallest of the three areas profiled in this book, Catalina, isn't even a town, but rather a village nestled at the foot of the northern end of the Santa Catalina Mountains. Its total land area is only 13.9 square miles. Originally, it was a site for Apaches like Eskiminiza and his Aravaipa tribe, who hunted, and mounted attacks on travelers and supply trains. It was here that Elias Aboud, who was headed for Oracle with supplies, was set upon and saved by the timely appearance of some of Pancho Villa's men.

In 1883, Mariano Samaniego established his ranch in this wilderness. He named it the Canada del Oro Ranch because its waters came gushing down from the mountains right onto his land, ran south almost the entire length of his holdings, then turned west and entered Oro Valley. The flow was so robust at times that it created a small lake and certain sections remained marshy all year.

When Samaniego died, he willed his land to his nephews, Higinio and Epiphano Aguirre. After years of droughts, followed by floods, the Aguirres gave up their Canada del Oro Ranch and moved their ranching enterprise over to their family ranch in the Marana area. There the weather seemed to be more favorable to ranching. On the roundup the last day of their operation, 500 head of cattle came stampeding down the side of the Santa Catalina Mountains, prodded on their journey by cowboys and dogs nipping at them.

That was not the end of ranching in Catalina. Some of the Samaniego land had been sold over the years. Between 1899 and 1917, William Sutherland and his wife Matilda acquired some of the old Samaniego land and added to it, creating the MS ranch. It wasn't nature that caused the Sutherlands to give up their land, but disastrous circumstances. William Sutherland died, leaving the ranch to his two sons, Frank O. and William Ray Sutherland. Frank died of a ruptured appendix, and William Ray sold the ranch to Sheriff John Nelson in the early 1900s. Nelson's Rail N ranch thrived until he died in an aircraft crash in the Santa Catalina Mountains. He and the pilot were searching for a missing hunter.

Myron Nelson was now in charge of the Nelson ranches, which covered both sides of the Tucson to Florence Road. This University of Arizona graduate knew the ranching business well. He grew up on the ranch and spent all his free time there while at the university. When Myron Nelson sold the ranch land that was first established by Samaniego, it was broken up into pieces, although none of the ranches could be called small.

The Charouleau brothers owned several sections in extremely rough terrain. Now called Charouleau Gap, that mountainside land is owned by the state and is an all-terrain vehicle trail. Sections of the original ranching land became the Brave Bull, owned by Mrs. Nicholas. Mrs. Nicholas sold out to the Golder family.

It was the ruggedness of the Catalina land, struck through on one side by the dominating Santa Catalina Mountains reaching a peak of over 9,000 feet, and cut by the temperamental, but generous waters of the Canada del Oro, that originally drew the ranchers. It is here in the rough Sonora Desert country that the wrangling Rivera family left a legacy of hard work and cowboying. It also drew another breed: individuals who wanted to get away and live in a rural area where they could dictate their own lifestyle.

E.B. Garner recognized an opportunity, and in 1948 bought property in Catalina and subdivided the lots. A lot of people couldn't understand why he wanted land in the wilderness. However, as Tucson grew from town to city, more and more people recognized the advantages of living "out" from the city where the views were spectacular, and life had the pace of a rural community. Robert Murphy and James McLoughlin helped make living safer when they established the Catalina Fire Department in 1977.

There were others who recognized the potential of Catalina. Although the land had its limitations due to the mountain ranges in the area, the Santa Catalina and the Tortolita, the Canada del Oro held promise, if it could be tamed. Lloyd Golder Jr. tried. He built a dam and visualized a water resort area complete with boating. Unfortunately, the dam was breached for safety reasons and Golder's lake dreams were washed away. But the mountains were still there, and Edward Robson saw an ideal location for an upscale adult resort community. His SaddleBrooke community changed the whole complexity of the small village of Catalina. The golf course and the tennis courts went in, and the retirees arrived from all over the country, and even some from other places in the world. The draw was not only the upscale community, but also the timeless mountains.

It wasn't long before these former business and professional men and women began looking for ways to fill their time and put to good use their life skills. Dorothy Stephano's daughter, who was teaching in the San Manuel/Mammoth area, remarked on how poorly some of her students were dressed. Some had no shoes, and some had no coats for cold weather. Stephano and her friends started Community Outreach. Their Kids' and Teens' Closet supplied over 36,000 school outfits in 2010. Today, they also offer tutoring and scholarships to students from the surrounding communities, and have expanded their clothing program to the San Carlos Indian Reservation.

Al Trice helped set up the Catalina Community Service food bank and clothing store. He also took an active interest in the community, serving on the Catalina Village Council, which was founded by Vicki Cox Golder. Harlan Nygaard established a Rotary Club, and Richard Varian and William Anderson were founding members of the Elks Lodge.

The Catalina location drew people with a wide variety of interests. James Cloer, a naturalist, continues his love of wild animals by giving lectures on the local wildlife at schools and Catalina State Park. James Sanderfer started the Cyclemasters cycling club, now with over 200 members. The peaceful setting of Catalina also attracted those who had seen more than their share of life. Joseph Owens was at Pearl Harbor on December 7, 1941, Rear Admiral (Retired) Lew Chatham flew with the Blue Angels, Maren Seidler was an Olympic athlete, William Rowe worked with troubled boys at the state detention center, and Lew Thorsness received the Medal of Honor.

Although Catalina is today the site of upscale communities, it still retains a flavor of its heritage, with the spreads of ranchers Donald Martin and Joe Goff surrounding the area. Catalina is a village that holds tight to its western values of hard work and heart. Its Legendary Locals have made that possible.

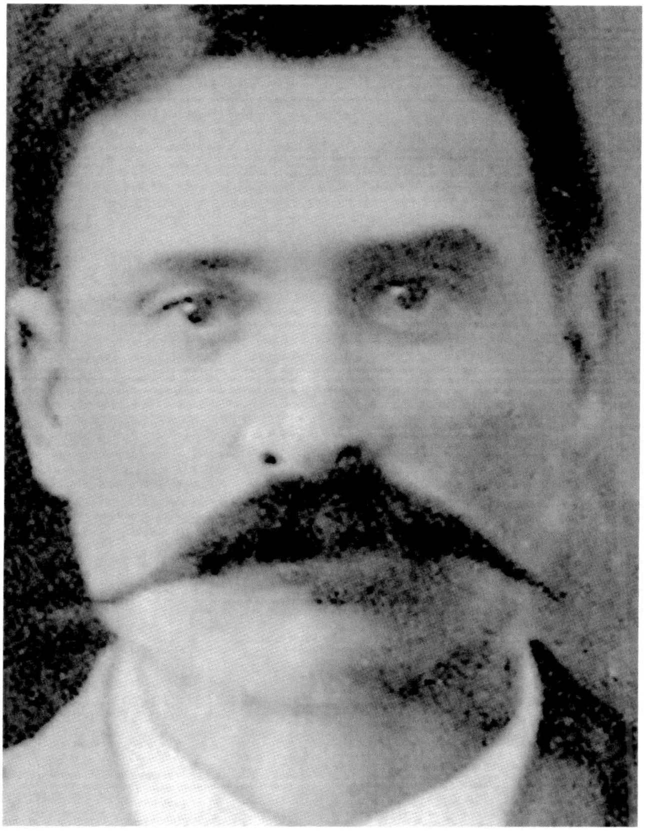

The Frontier Trader

In the late 1890s, the owner of the Puerto Manilla saloon and general goods store was on his way back from buying supplies in Tucson with a wagon train load of goods. As he and his brother made their way to the end of the Santa Catalina Mountains, they were set upon by Apaches. Elias Aboud, an emigrant from Lebanon, was a courageous man and an exceptionally strong one, yet he was overpowered. The Abouds had little hope of surviving this attack, although they fought back with everything they had. Just when things seemed impossible, help arrived from a band of Pancho Villa's followers who were on their way to visit relatives in Globe. The Abouds and their supplies were rescued. Villa's men continued on their way, and the Abouds headed home. (Courtesy Aboud family.)

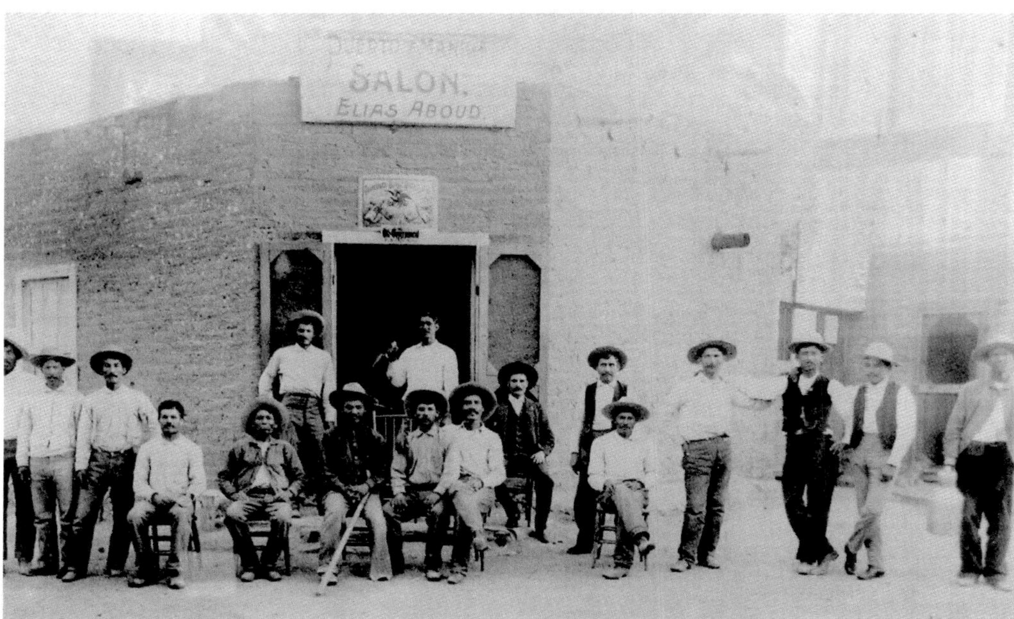

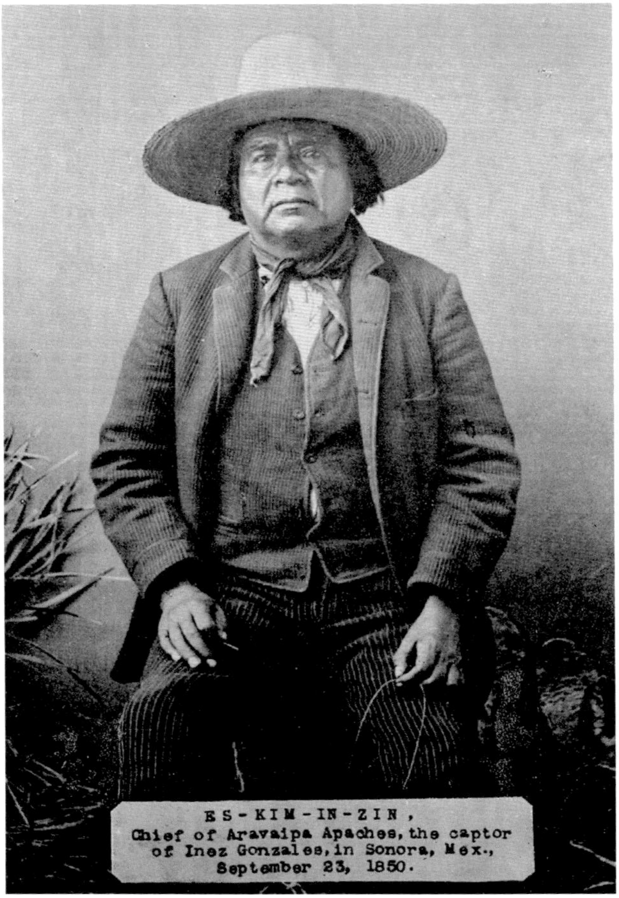

The Apache Chief

Long before settlers arrived in the lands of the Catalina Mountains, Apaches hunted the ridges and canyons. They waged war on the other Indian tribes in the area, including the Tohono O'odhams and the Yaquis. As settlers arrived, attacks on supply trains and wagon trains were frequent and there was not a Tucson resident who had not lost a friend and/or a relative to the Apaches, in particular Chief Eskiminzim and his Aravaipa tribe. The prime route of attack was along the base of the Santa Catalina Mountains as it heads northwest, the site of the present community of Catalina. As settlers continued to arrive, and communities sprung up on his hunting grounds, Eskiminzim realized the futility of continuing the battle. He asked for asylum from the commanding officer at the small Camp Grant. The road to Camp Grant was partly through the Canada del Oro in Catalina. The commanding officer did not have it in his power to grant Eskiminzim's request, but did allow the tribe to stay just outside the military camp, believing that would give them sufficient protection. Unfortunately, the citizens of Tucson had had enough of the Apaches. On April 30, 1871, a small band of vigilantes attacked the Camp Grant Indian site. Over 100 Apaches were killed, but only eight of them were men. The other braves were out hunting. President Ulysses S. Grant was furious. He ordered Arizona governor A.P.K. Safford to find and bring the perpetrators to trial. The ensuing five-day trial ended in 19 minutes of deliberation by the jury and all defendants were acquitted. This attack, and the resulting trial, is known as "The Shame of Tucson." It broke the spirit of the Aravaipa Apaches and Chief Eskiminzim. (Chief courtesy Arizona Historical Society #30378, Apache attack area, top, Camp Grant area bottom, courtesy Mike Marriott.)

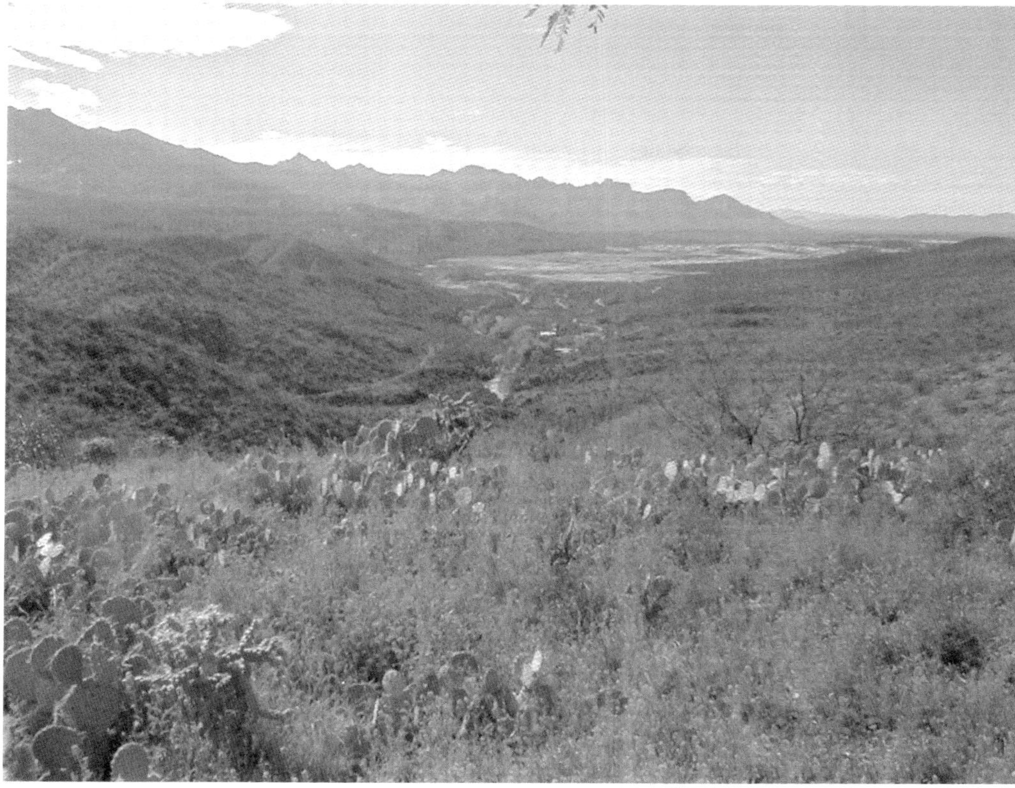

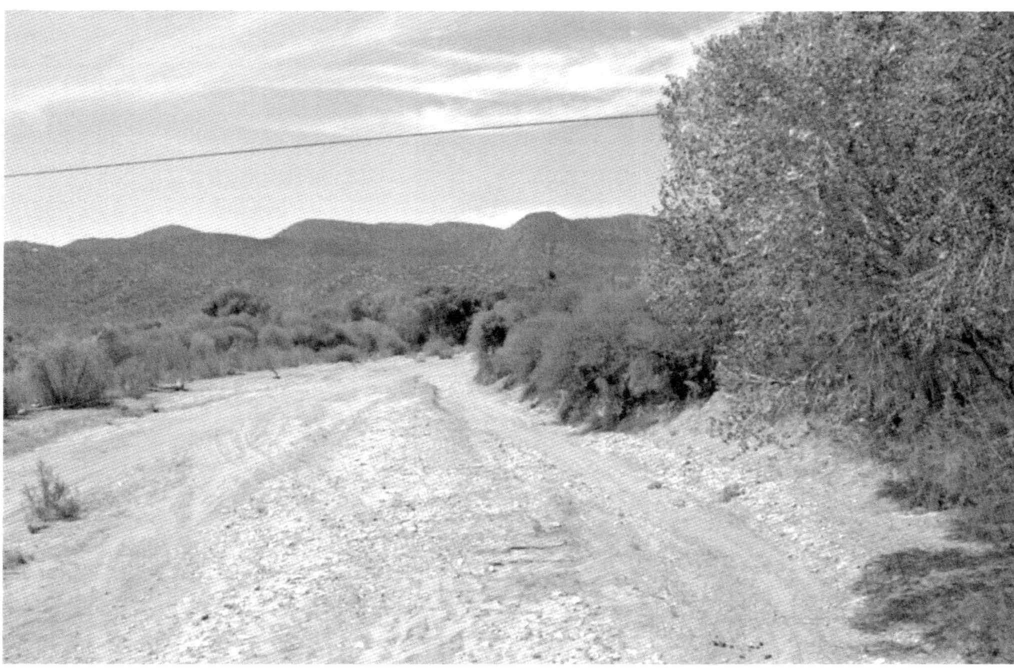

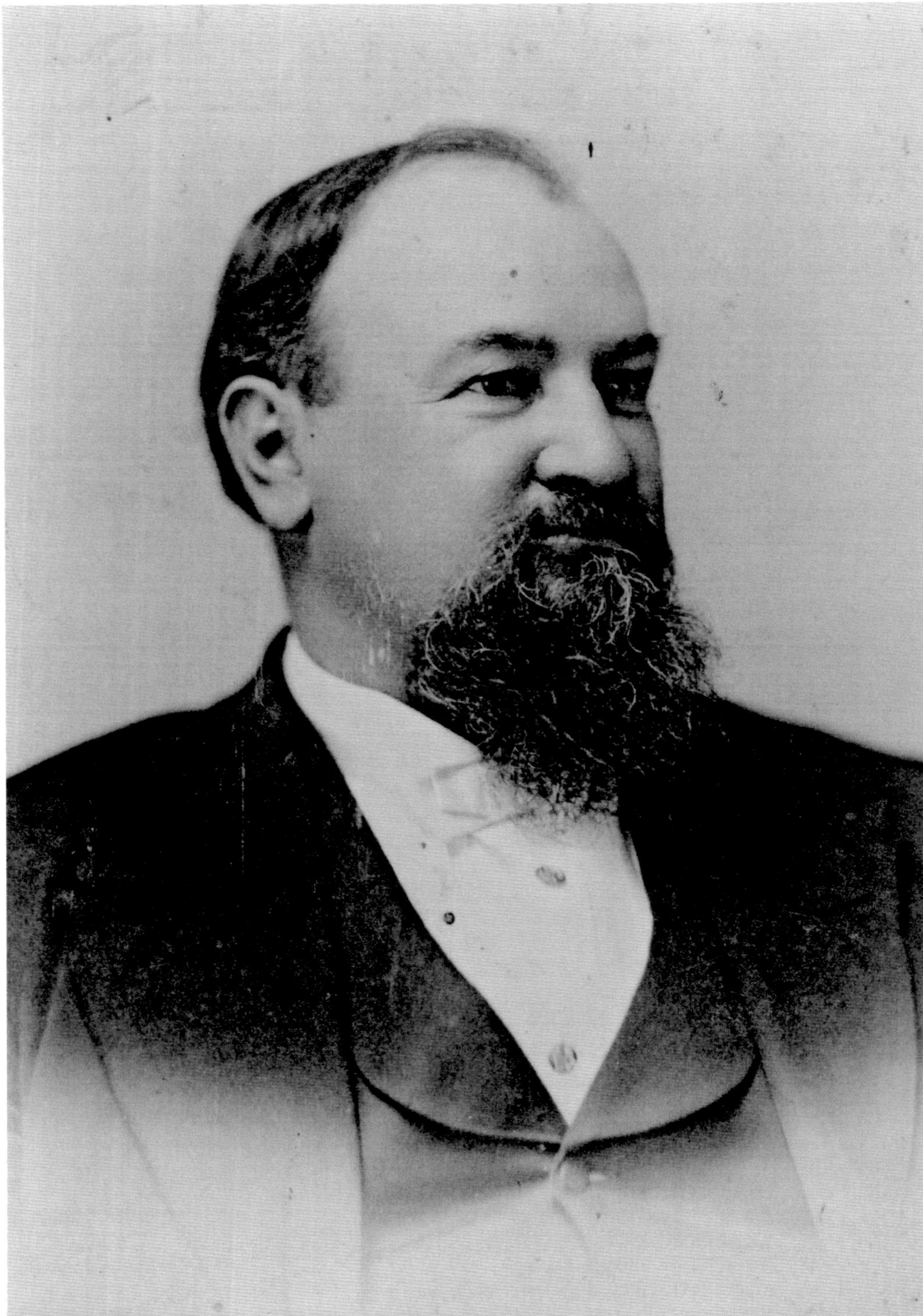

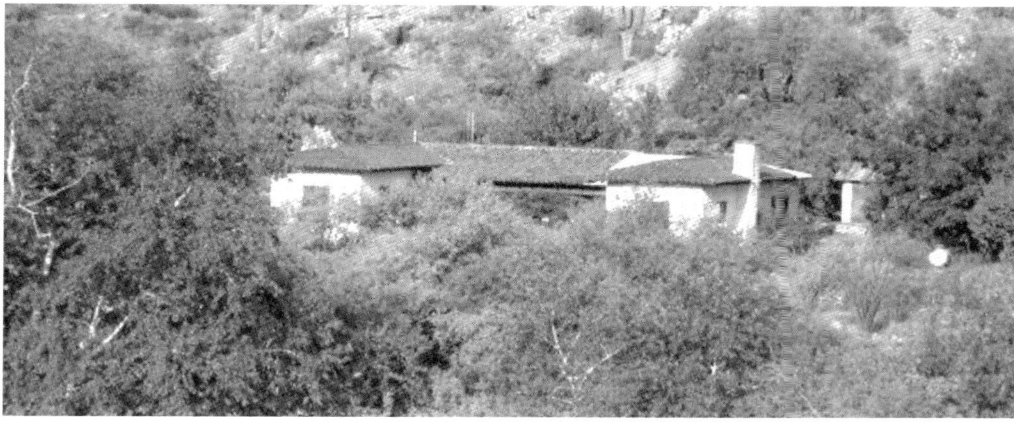

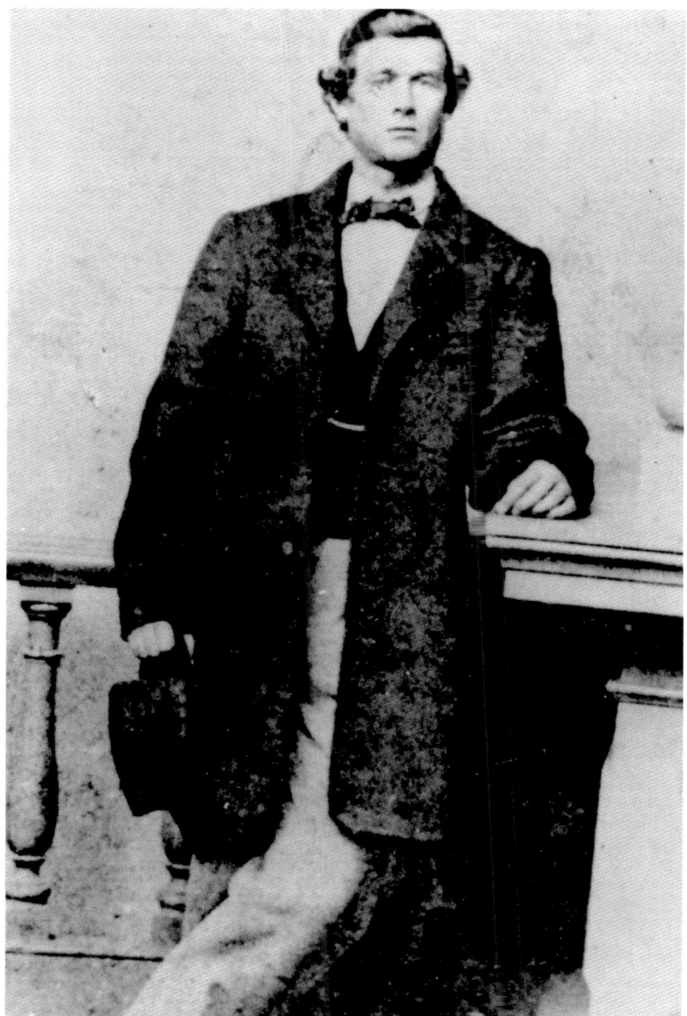

A Pioneering Civic Leader
In 1862, Mariano Samaniego graduated from the University of St. Louis with honors. He put that good education to work when he moved to the Arizona Territory. He established the Canada del Oro Ranch near where the waterway comes down from the mountains. He was the first assessor of Pima County and served on the board of supervisors for 10 years. He served four terms on the city council and represented Pima County in four assemblies, leaving his foreman Maximo Molina in charge of his ranch. When Samaniego died, the ranch went to the Aguirre family and Epiphano and his brother Higinio worked the ranch until a series of droughts, then floods, forced them to sell. The Molina house still stands. (Courtesy of the Arizona Historical Society, Epiphano, standing, #44455, Samaniego #1628. Maximo's house courtesy Dawn Doubek.)

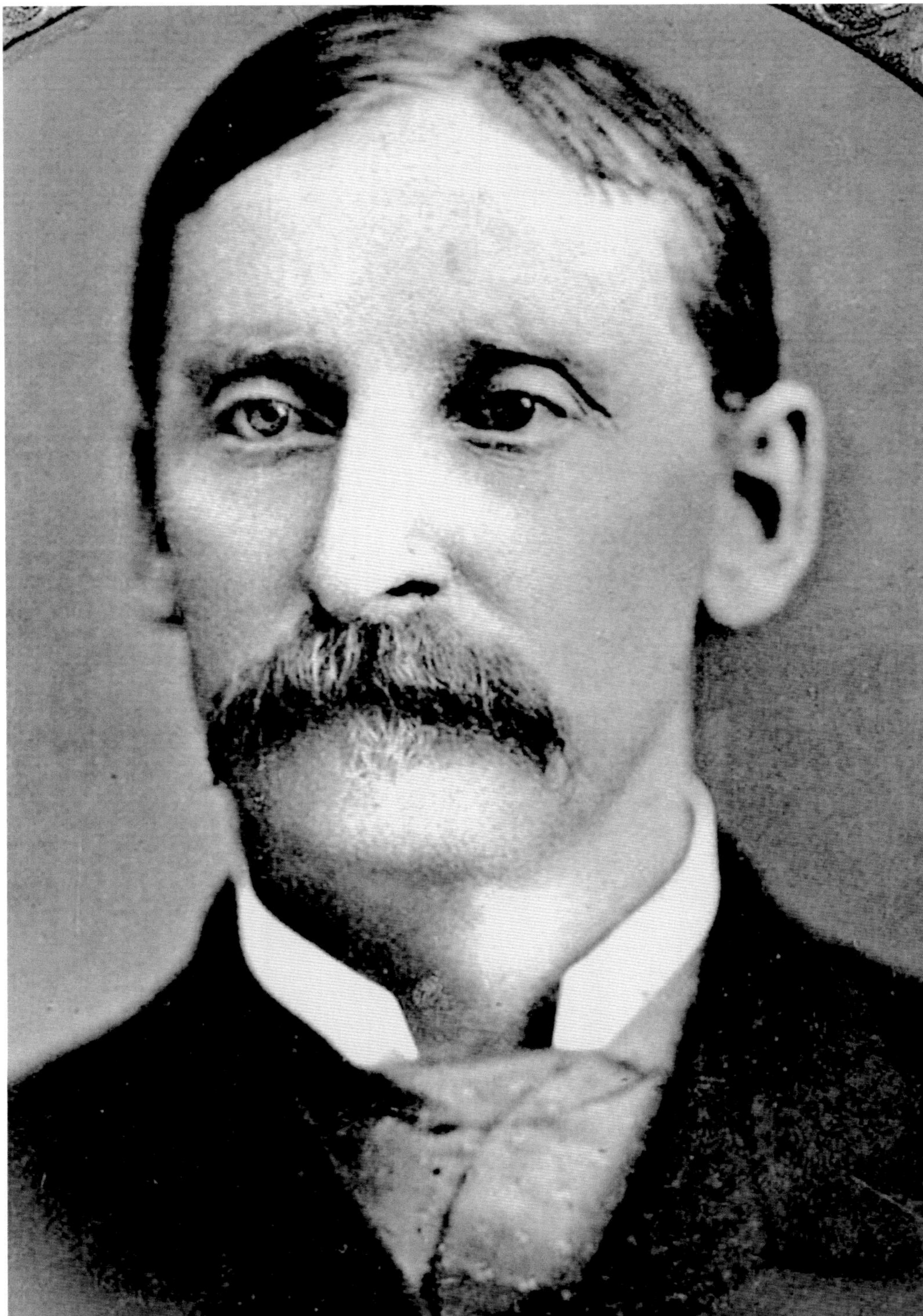

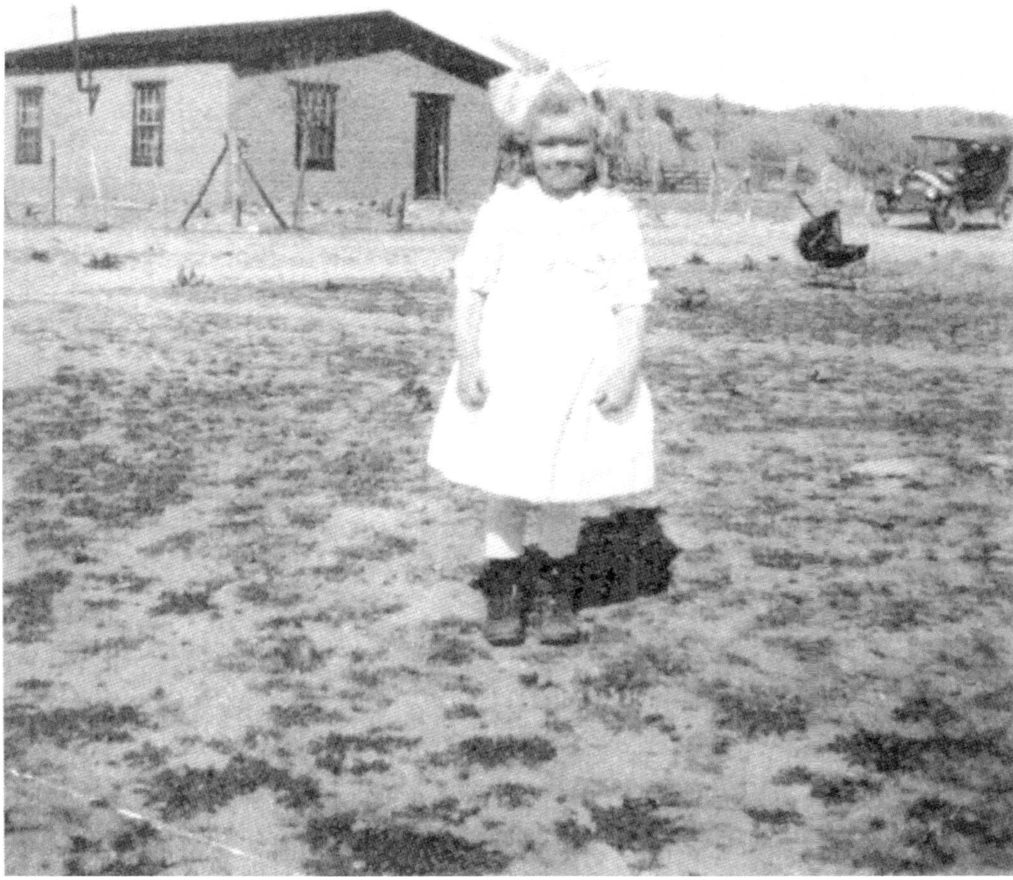

The Gentleman Rancher

William H. Sutherland was part owner of the Arizona Stage, which supplied services from Casa Grande to Florence, Silver King, Globe, and Tucson. In 1882, he sold his interest in the stagecoach company and he and his wife Matilda purchased a portion of the old Samaniego land. He built an adobe house, 28 feet long and 18 feet wide, and set about establishing his cattle headquarters. His granddaughter Muriel is shown standing in front of the ranch house. Between 1913 and 1917, the Sutherlands increased their holdings, filing separately for homestead rights. Matilda was a businesswoman in her own right and owned a millinery shop in Tucson. William died in 1927. The family had a powerful influence on the area and their name lives on in the Sutherland Wash. (Courtesy of William Ray Sutherland Family.)

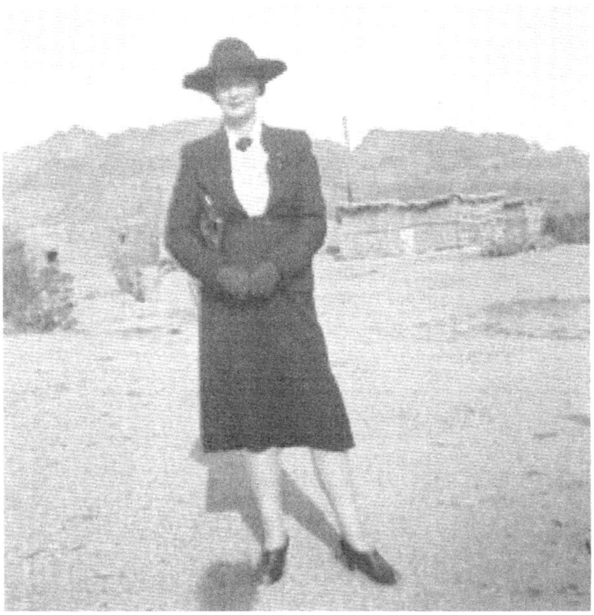

The Washer Woman

There was not a tougher frontier woman than Elsie Sutherland . On a trip into Tucson from the MS ranch, she interrupted the journey and pulled over to the side of the road. Settled under a mesquite tree, she then gave birth to her daughter. Sutherland did things the right way. Doing laundry on their desert ranch in 1915 was no excuse not to be fashionable. She made the clothes for all four of her children. A bolt of cloth went a long way in dressing small boys and girls. The sameness of design did not bother the children. She often dressed Muriel and her sister in pristine white, complete with hair bow. (Courtesy William Ray Sutherland family.)

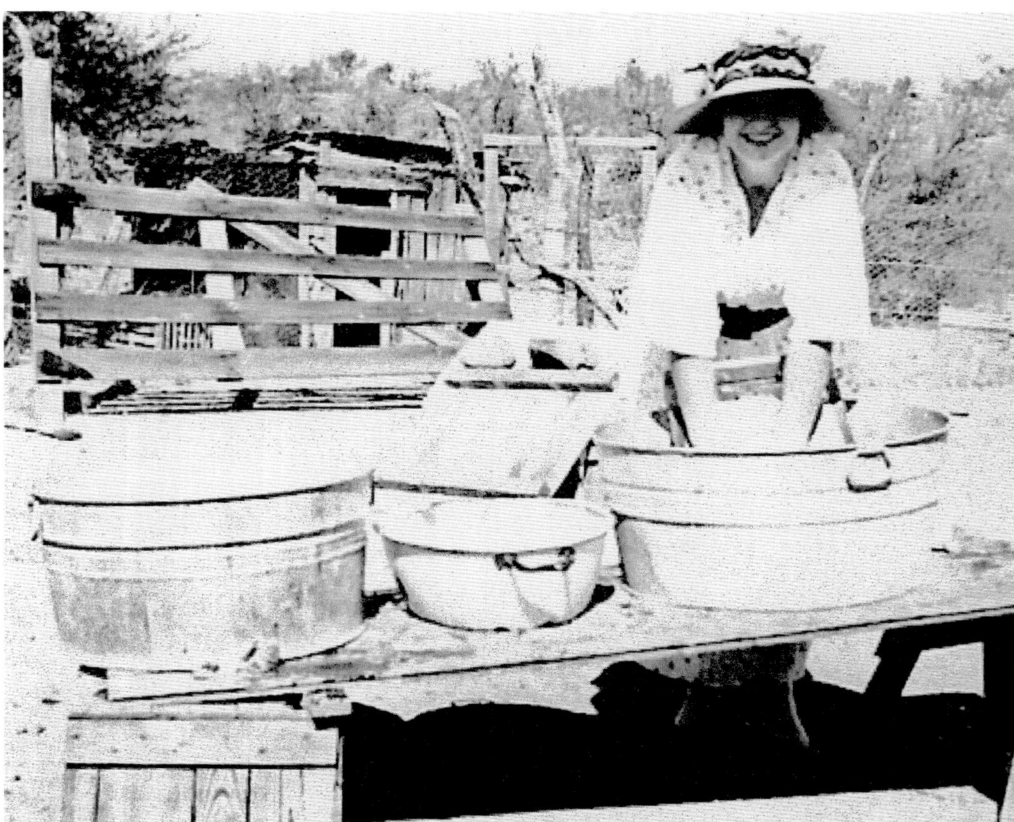

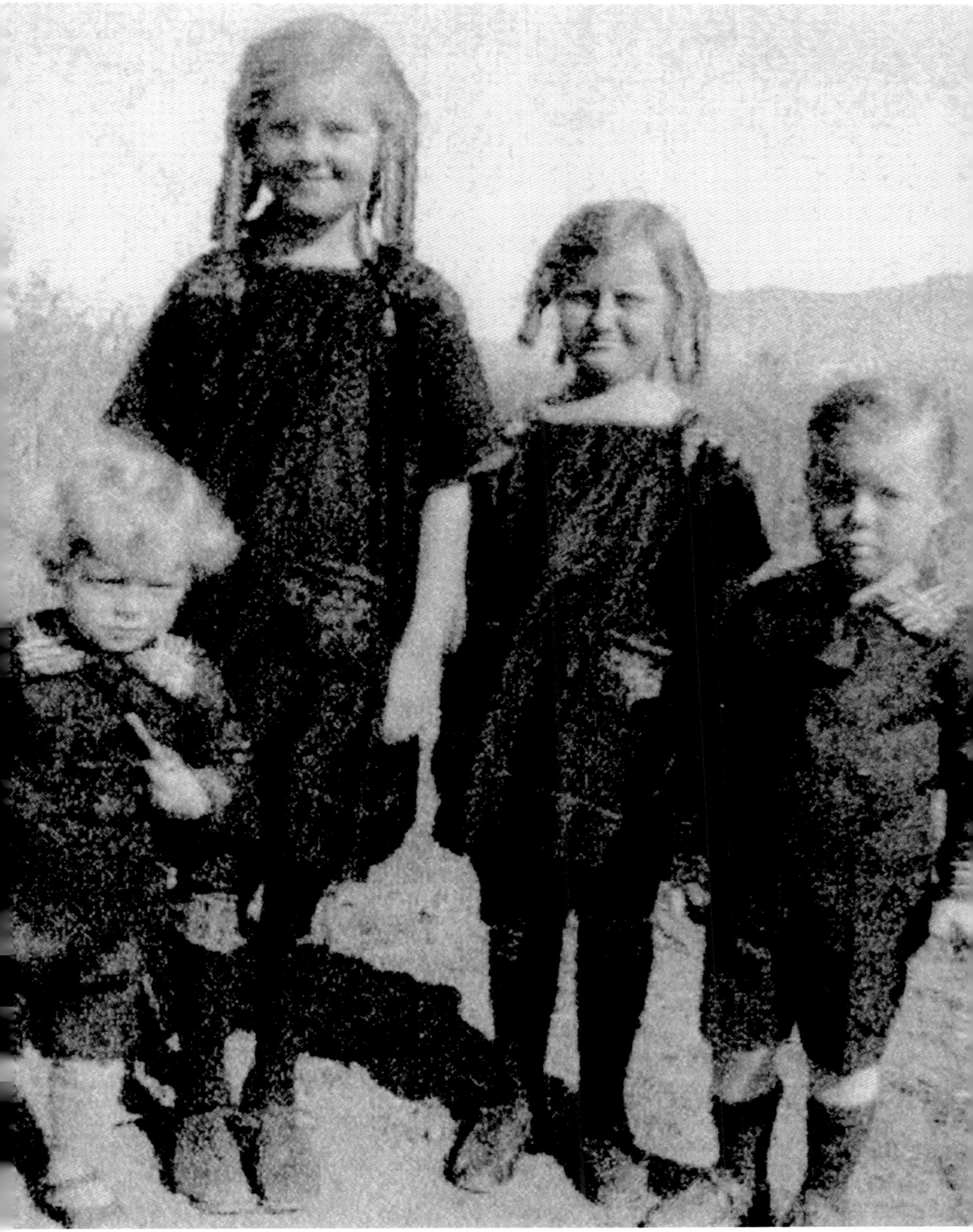

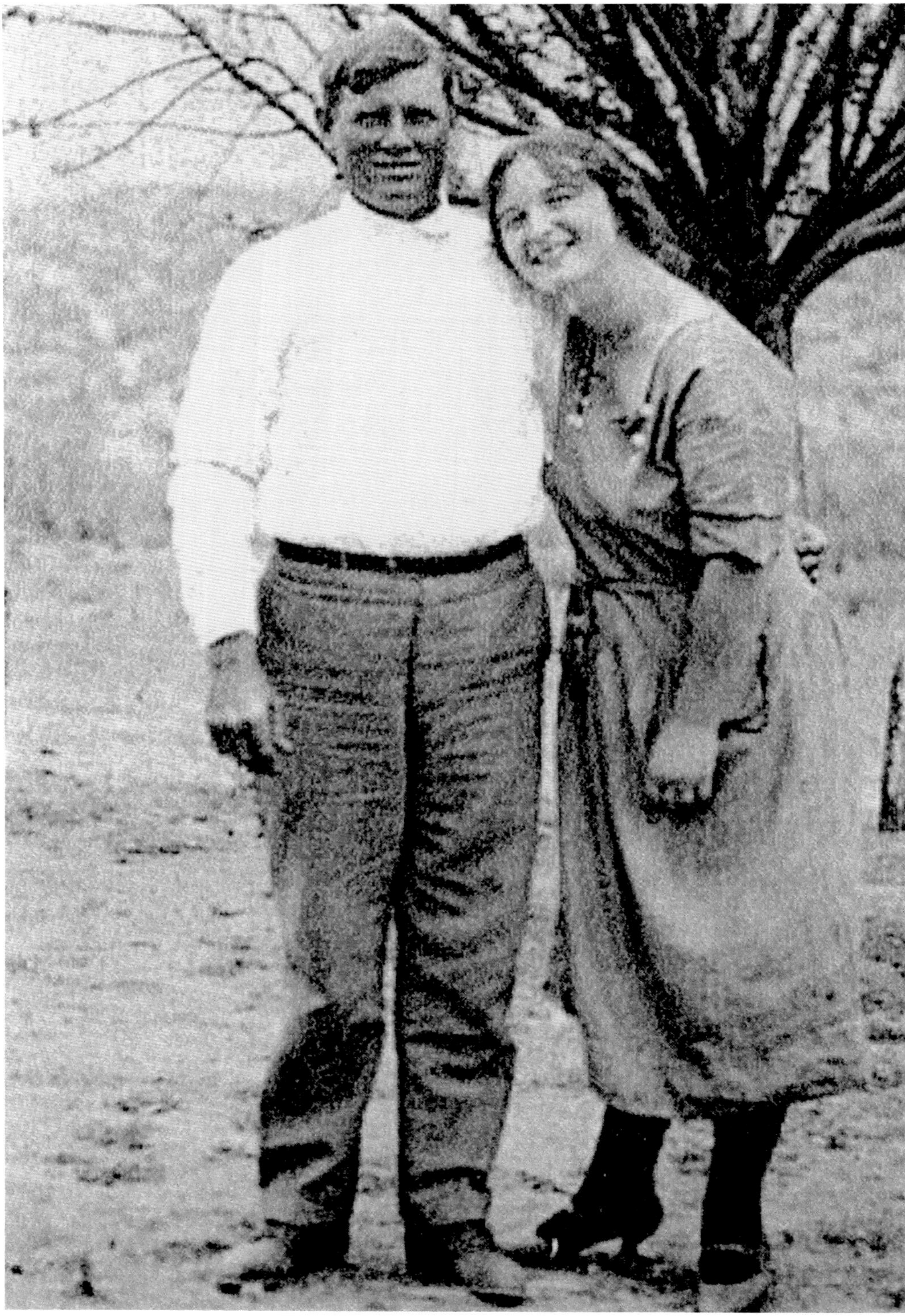

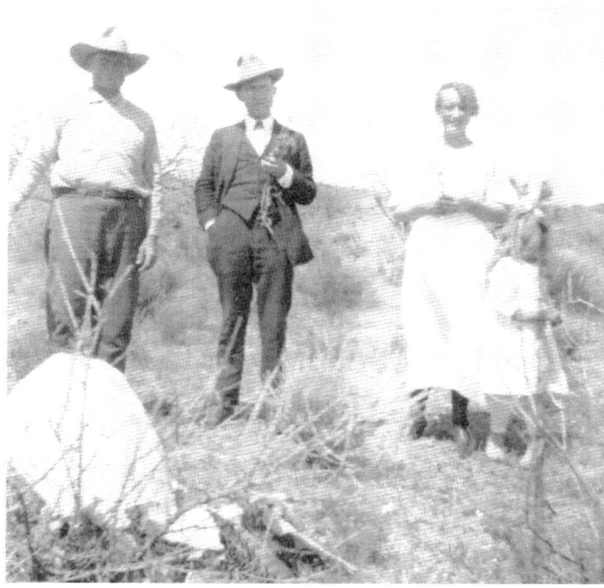

Continuing a Legacy
When William Ray Sutherland inherited the MS Ranch along with his brother, Frank, he kept the family ranching tradition going. On April 30, 1918, he and his oldest daughter, Muriel, mounted up for a trip around the ranch. Sutherland was proud of the MS and with great pleasure would invite guests to visit his ranch, where they were always welcomed by Sutherland Sutherland Sutherland's wife Elsie and also by his daughter Muriel. Ray Sutherland lost his brother in 1917 when he died in Tucson from a ruptured appendix. Sutherland eventually sold the ranch to the John Nelson family. The family had an impact on the area and now a wash bears their name. (Courtesy William Ray Sutherland family.)

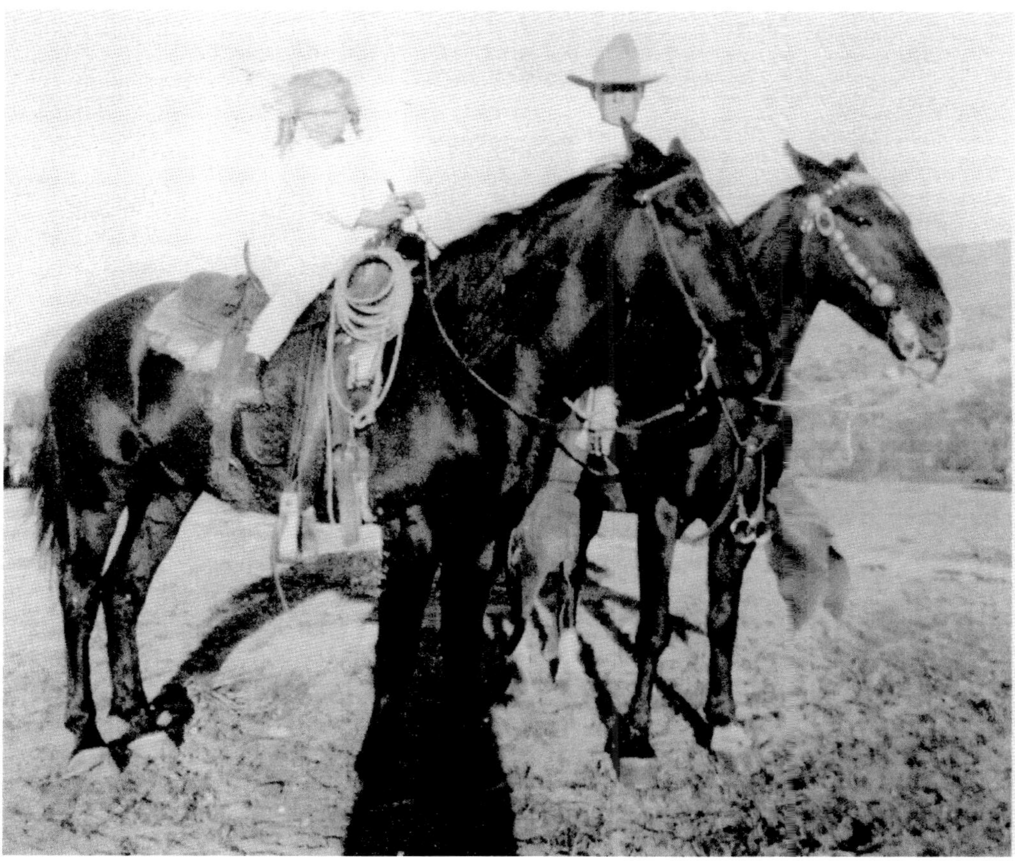

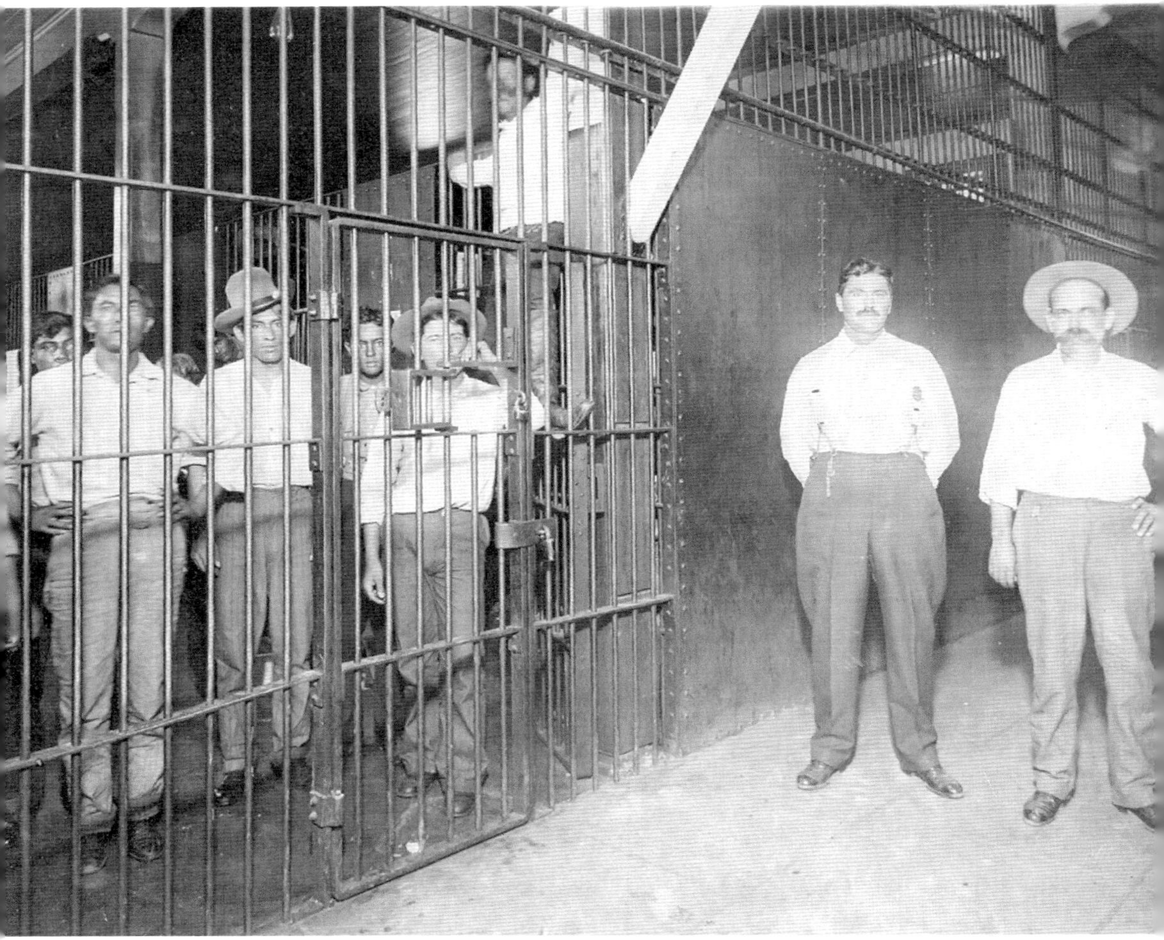

The Sheriff Rancher

John Nelson was born in Sweden and arrived in Arizona in 1889. A few years later, he partnered with Frank Sutherland in the MS and Last Chance Ranches. While he was sheriff in Tucson in 1913, a saloon argument left one man dead and the killer ran for Mexico. Nelson pursued him but returned empty-handed when the Mexican authorities refused to cooperate. Known as a tough sheriff, he pursued criminals relentlessly and managed to have a full jail in 1918. Standing second from right, outside the jail he attended to the villains. After statehood, his responsibilities grew. He is shown standing in the center of his office in 1914 surrounded by his staff. In 1920, he and his children enjoyed the water in this natural pool on the ranch right where the Canada del Oro gushed down from the mountains. (Courtesy John and Myron Nelson family.)

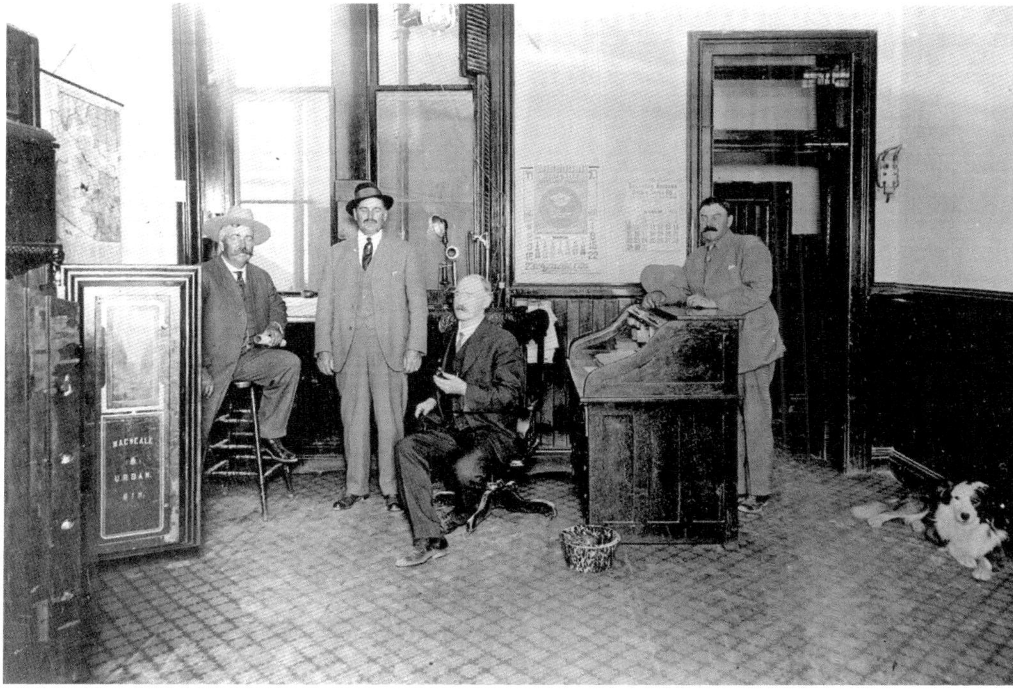
MACNEALE
&
URBAN
CIN.

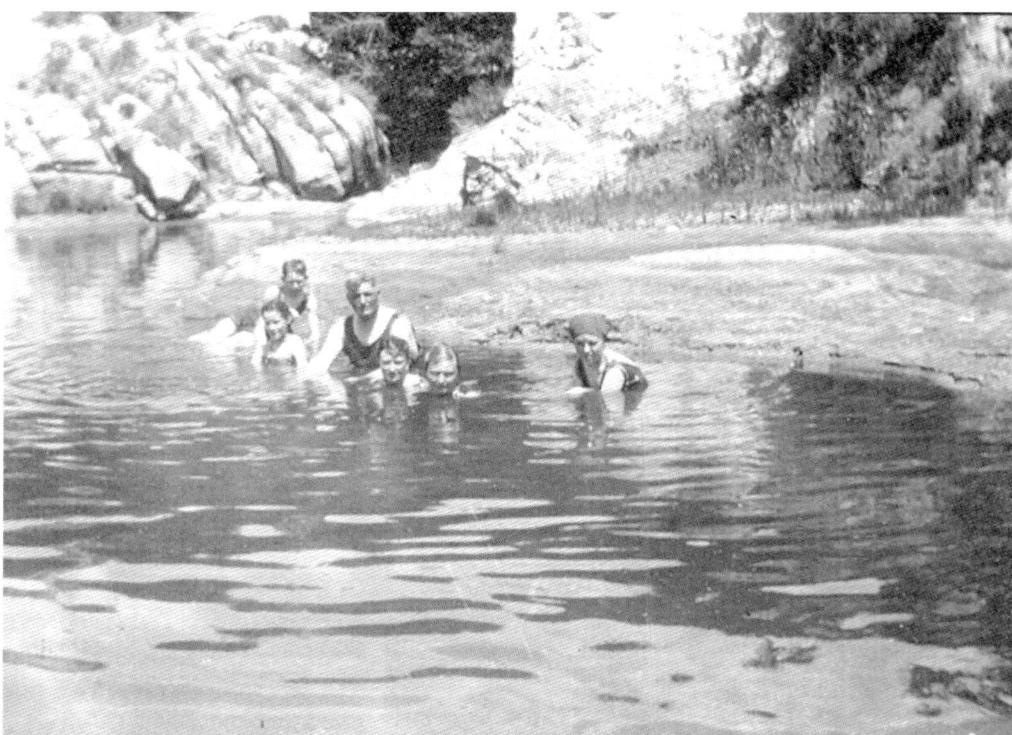

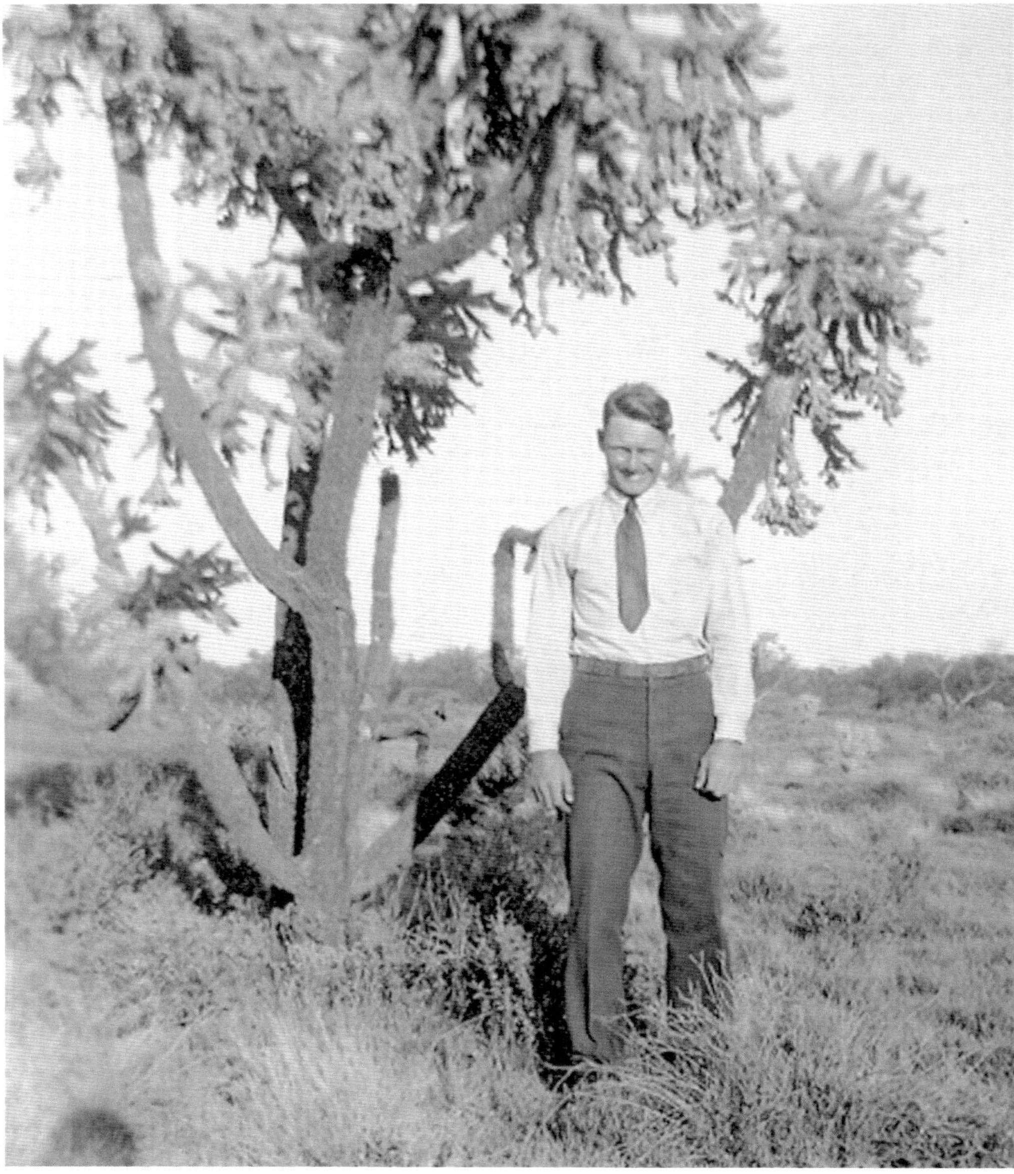

Ranching Nelson Style

Nelson's son Myron attended the University of Arizona, where he played baseball but continued to work at the ranch whenever he could. When he left the university, he returned to his roots, the ranch. When Myron married, John Nelson gave the newlyweds the adobe MS ranch house. John Nelson was killed in a plane crash while searching for a lost hunter in the Santa Catalina Mountains. Myron carried on with the ranch and became a very successful rancher, owning both the MS and the Rail N ranches where he ran over 1,000 head of cattle. Mountain lions were a threat to the cattle, and every good rancher had to be able to protect his stock. When Myron Nelson grew too old for the rigors of ranching, he decided to sell the ranch to Roberta Johnson Nicholas of the Johnson and Johnson Company. (Courtesy John and Myron Nelson family.)

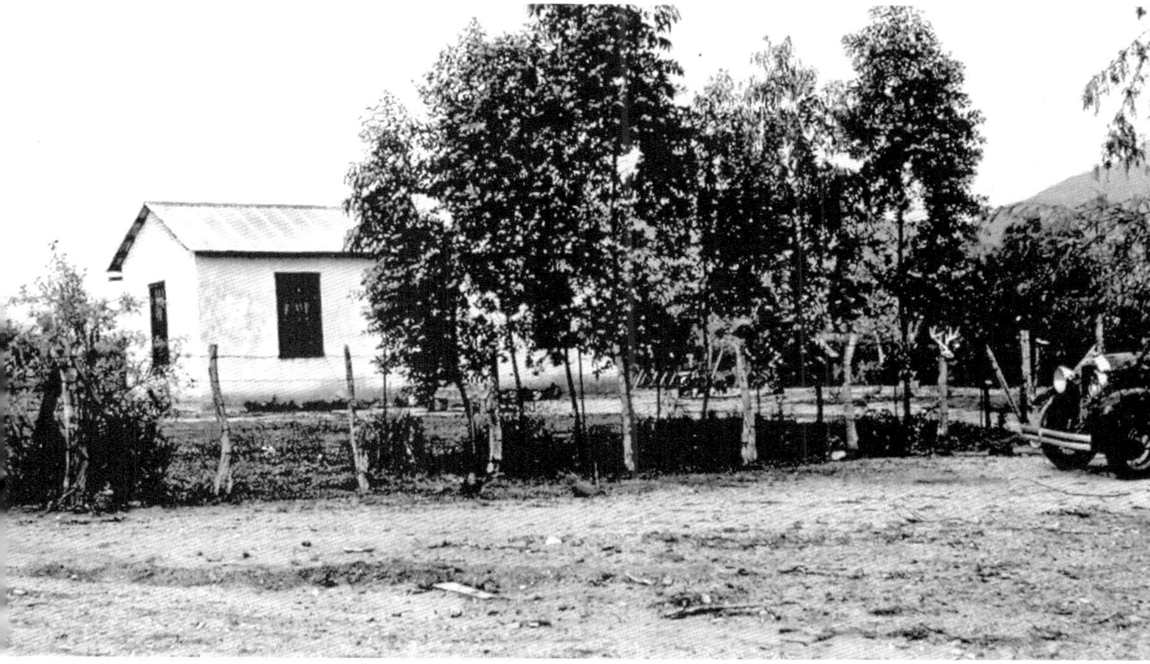

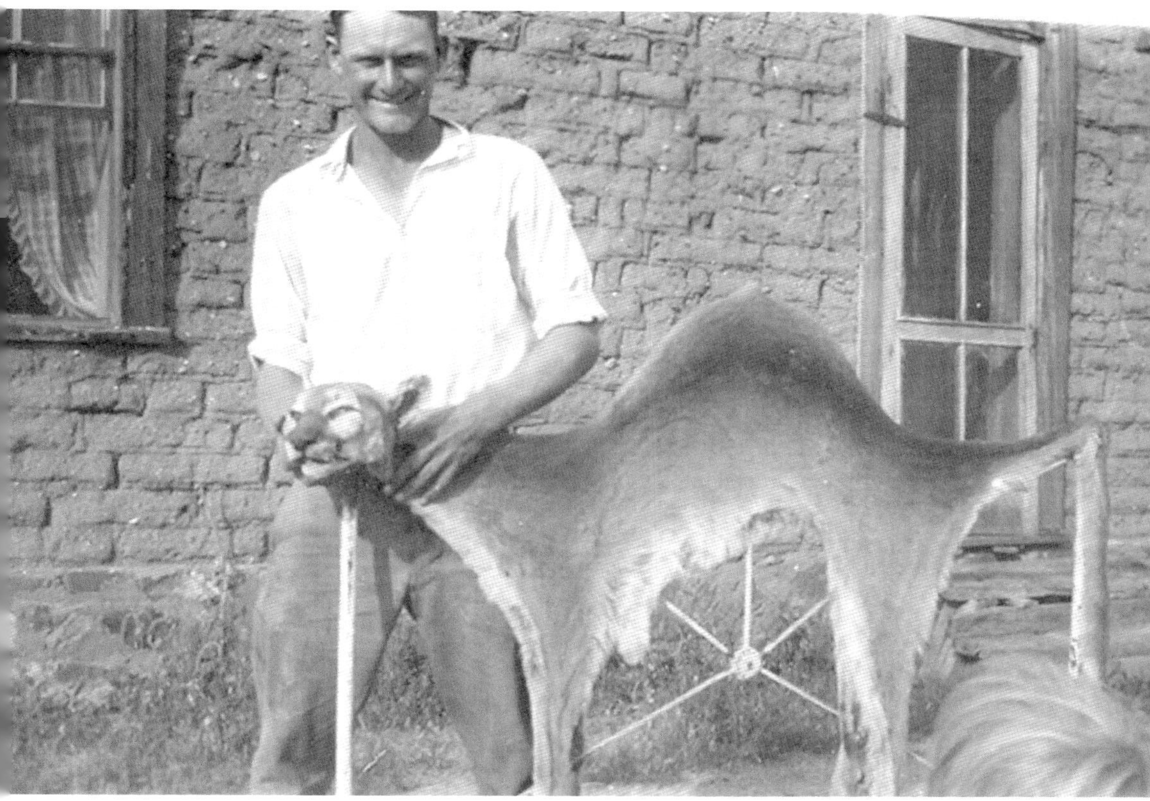

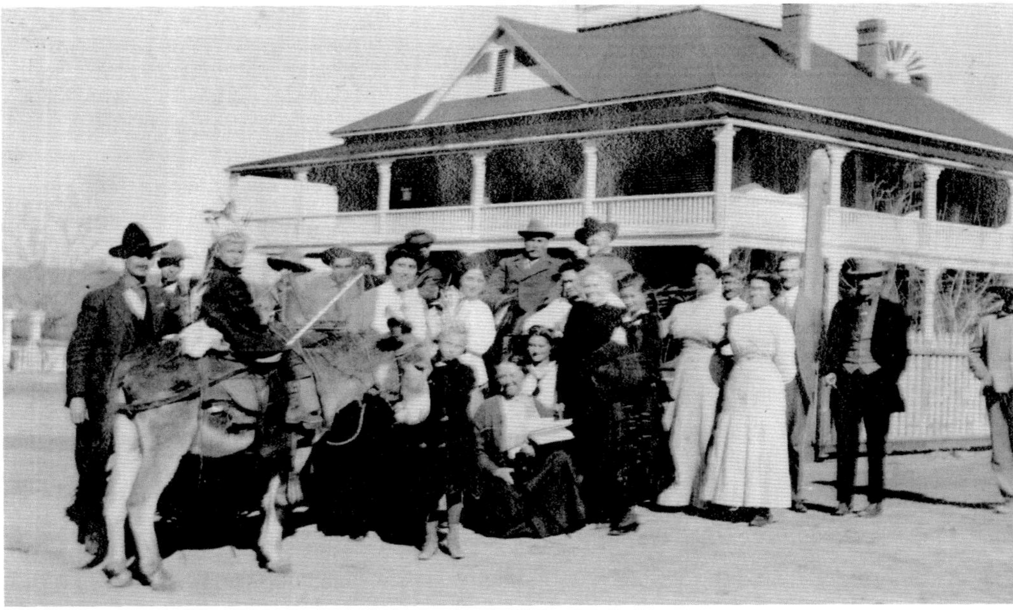

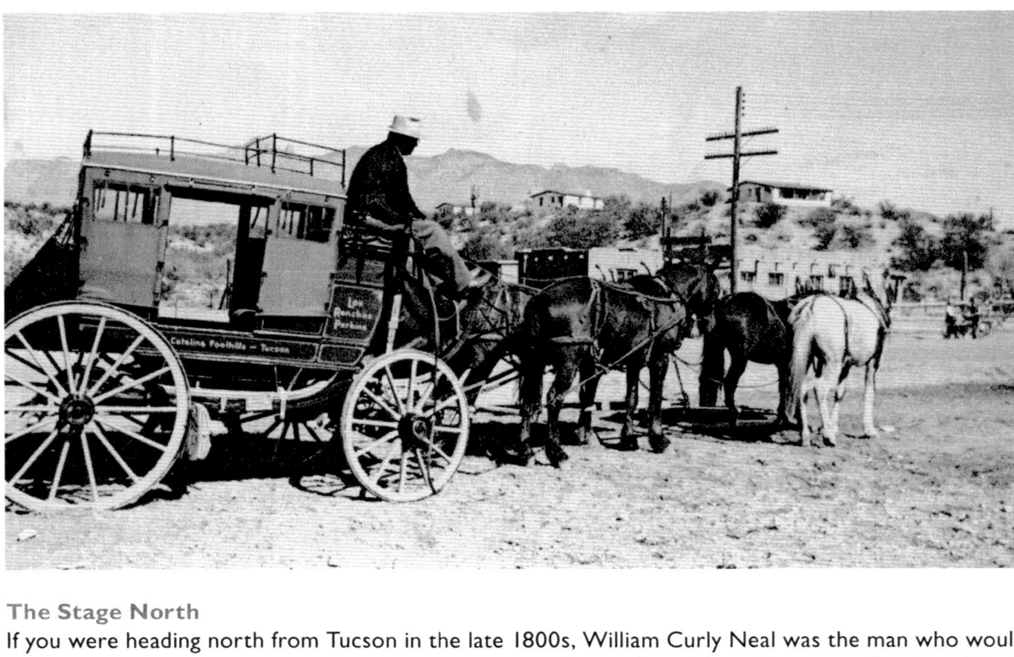

The Stage North

If you were heading north from Tucson in the late 1800s, William Curly Neal was the man who would get you there. His coach ran passengers, packages, supplies, and mail from Tucson to Oracle and back on a route along the base of the Santa Catalina Mountains that followed the Canada del Oro part of the way. There were plenty of passengers for Neal, including William F. "Buffalo Bill" Cody, most heading for Curly's luxurious Mountain View Hotel. Neal, who was part Cherokee and part black, is shown in front of his hotel, standing in the back row next to Cody. He died in 1936 in a freak accident when his own car ran over him as he was checking the engine. (Courtesy Arizona Historical Society Hotel #28063, stagecoach #52039.)

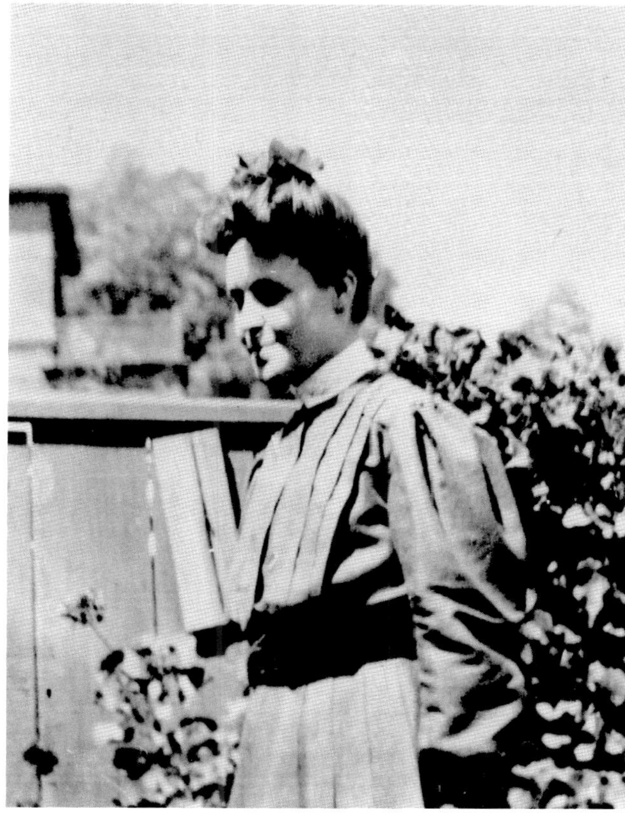

The Basque Ranchers

In 1873, Pierre (Pedro) and his brother Juan Charouleau got the call from their Aunt Ana Charouleau to come to the American West and take care of her ranch in the Santa Catalina Mountains. When Aunt Ana had enough of the Wild West, she returned to France deeding all her western property to the two brothers. Part of that property was in Tucson, where Juan had a bar and where he spent a considerable portion of his time. At one point, the Charouleaus were the biggest property owners in Tucson. In 1896, Juan died from a burst blood vessel in his brain. Pedro was an adventurous man and traveled the world, locating three gold mines in the Yukon. The brothers are long gone, but the area still bears their name in a challenging four-wheel course up the mountains called Charouleau Gap. (Ana courtesy Arizona Historical Society #65980, Gap sign, Mike Marriott.)

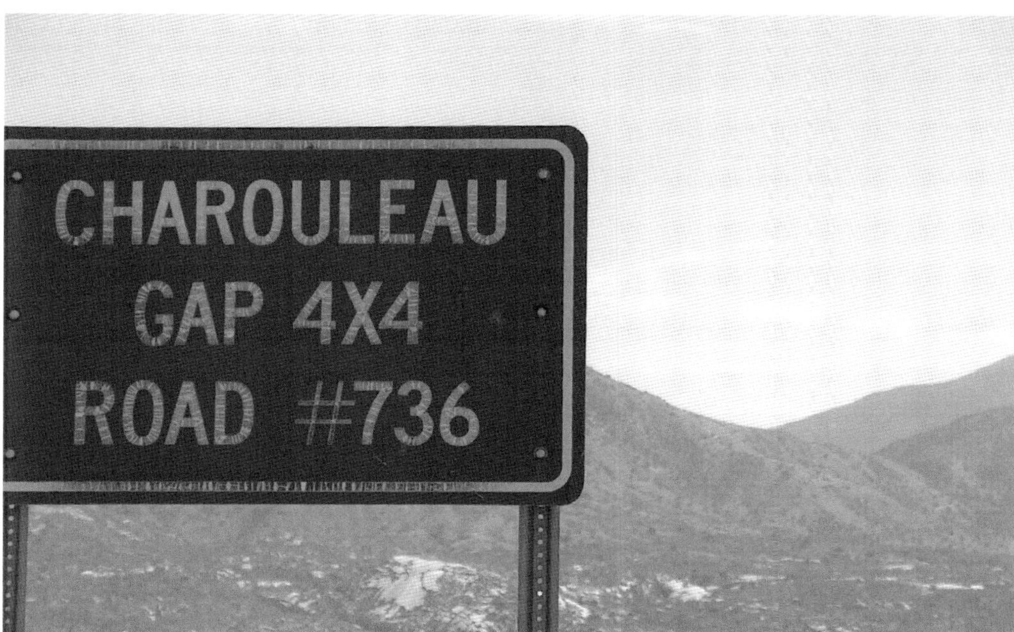

The Cowboy Movie Star

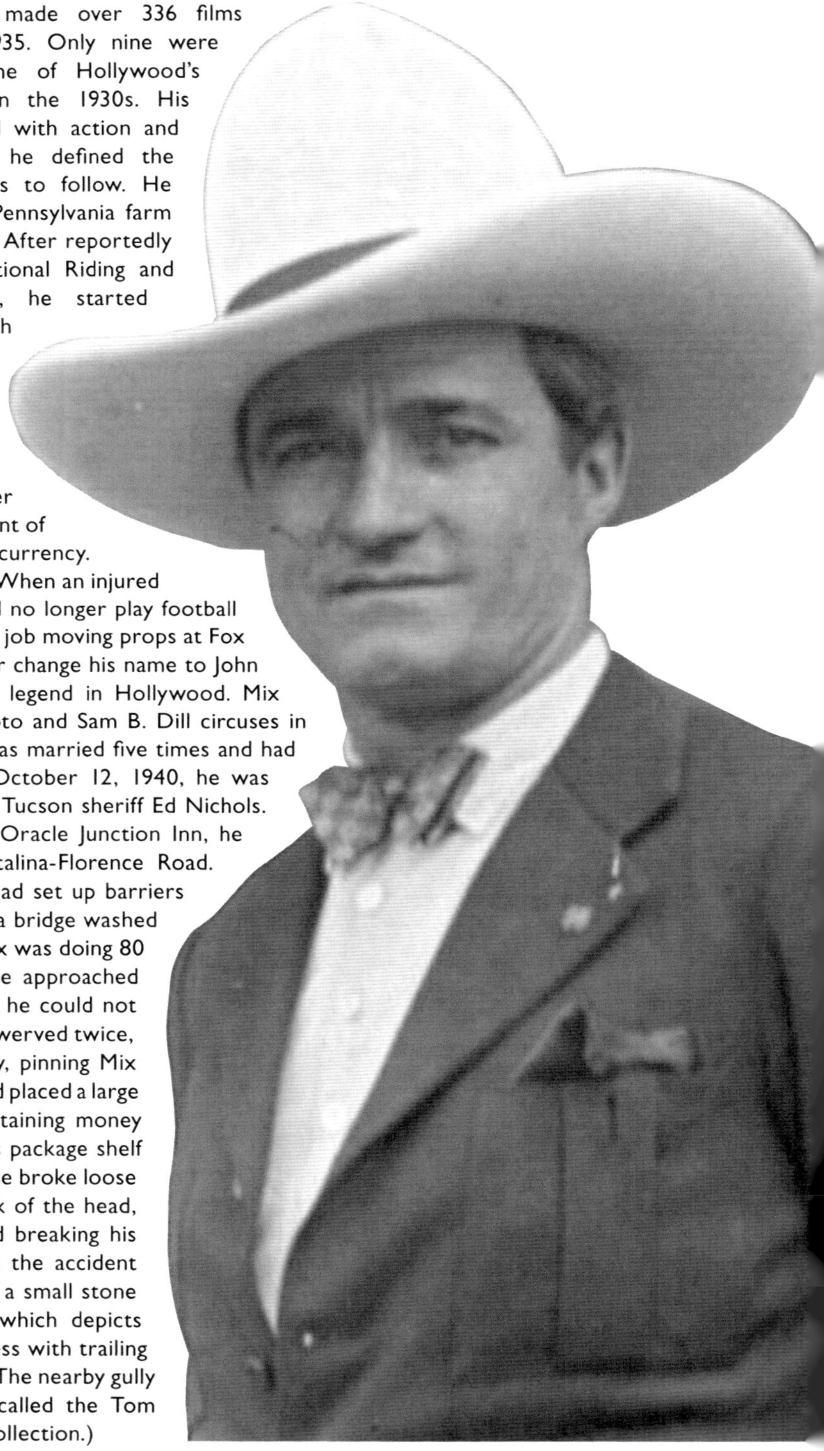

Thomas "Tom" Mix made over 336 films between 1910 and 1935. Only nine were "talkies." He was one of Hollywood's most popular stars in the 1930s. His westerns were packed with action and daredevil stunts, and he defined the genre for all westerns to follow. He learned to ride on a Pennsylvania farm near his Debois home. After reportedly winning the 1909 National Riding and Rodeo Championship, he started his film career with the Selig Polyscope Company and also worked for the Fox Film Company and Universal Studios. In his career, he made over $6 million, the equivalent of $400 million in today's currency. He did his own stunts. When an injured Marion Morrison could no longer play football for USC, Mix got him a job moving props at Fox Studios. He would later change his name to John Wayne and become a legend in Hollywood. Mix starred in the Sells-Floto and Sam B. Dill circuses in the early 1930s. Mix was married five times and had several children. On October 12, 1940, he was returning from visiting Tucson sheriff Ed Nichols. After stopping at the Oracle Junction Inn, he headed down the Catalina-Florence Road. A construction crew had set up barriers while they worked on a bridge washed out by a flash flood. Mix was doing 80 miles an hour when he approached the working crew, and he could not brake in time. His car swerved twice, then rolled into a gully, pinning Mix beneath the car. Mix had placed a large aluminum suitcase containing money and jewels on the car's package shelf behind him. The suitcase broke loose and hit him in the back of the head, shattering his skull and breaking his neck. The spot where the accident occurred is marked by a small stone and metal memorial, which depicts his horse, Tony, riderless with trailing reins, his head bowed. The nearby gully where he crashed is called the Tom Mix Wash. (Author's collection.)

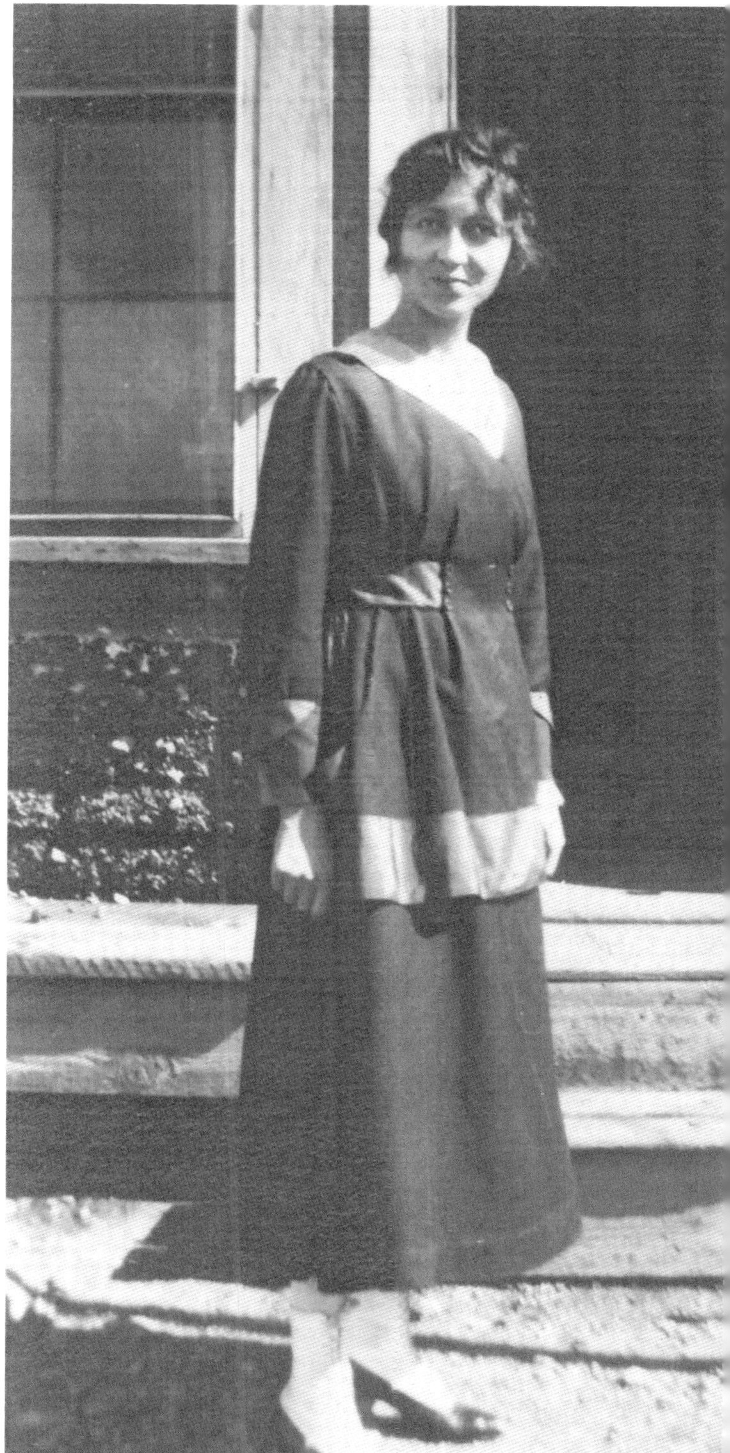

The Most Amazing Schoolteacher
When Eulalia "Sister" Bourne started teaching school in Arizona, they had a law forbidding Spanish from being spoken on school grounds. Bourne thought that was the most ridiculous law she ever heard. All but one of her students spoke Spanish and no English. With the help of her Spanish-speaking students, she set about learning their language. Every day after the lessons were over, the students spent five minutes teaching their teacher their language. Her job with the Tucson school district allowed her to attend the University of Arizona. In 1930, she received a BA in English with a minor in Spanish. Bourne homestead in Peppersauce Canyon and built her own adobe house at her new ranch. Later, she traded her ranch for land in the foothills of the Galiuro Mountains, which are north of the town of Catalina. On this ranch, she did her own roping and branding. She was the author of three autobiographies and a children's book, *The Blue Colt*. In 1979, she gave all the royalties from her books to the University of Arizona Eulalia Bourne Scholarship Fund. Her awards were many. In 1973–74 The Arizona Press women named her Woman of the Year. In 1975, she received the University of Arizona Alumni Association Distinguished Citizen Award. For 40 years, she taught school in rural areas. As a teacher and author, she was a big influence on the children of the Catalina area, giving them not only an education but a sense of pride in their heritage. (Courtesy Arizona Historical Society #65980.)

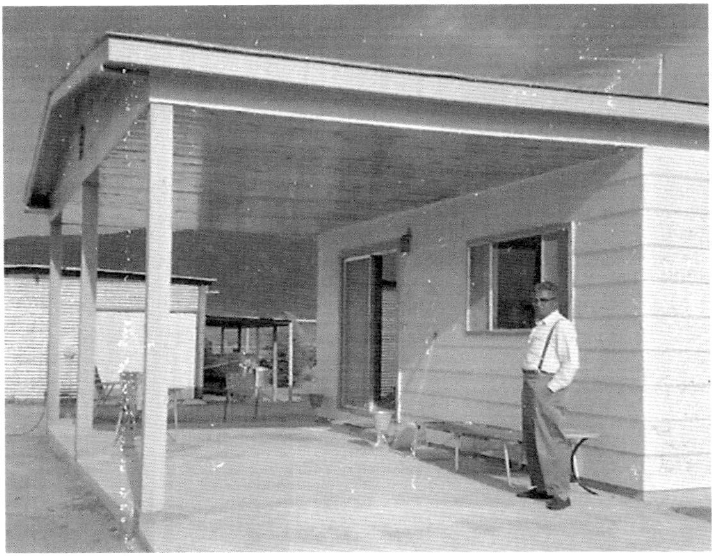

Starting a Village

In 1948, when E.B. Garner bought land between Oracle and Tucson, people thought he was crazy. There was nothing there. The Garners owned a grocery store in Oracle but lived in Tucson. E.B. purchased land between the towns and built the first Catalina community. New residents wanted to call the village Garnerville, but E.B. named it Catalina for the mountains. (Courtesy Wanda Wilson.)

The Bow Hunter

Among the multitude of awards for Pete Knagge's bow hunting ability were the 1979, 1981, and 1987 Wildlife Trophy Awards. He hunted in the wild lands of Arizona, including the Galiuro Mountains, Santa Catalina Mountains, Sand Tank Mountains, and Charouleau Gap. But the burden of his time fighting in Vietnam was too much for Knagge, who committed suicide in 2003. (Courtesy Joann Knagge.)

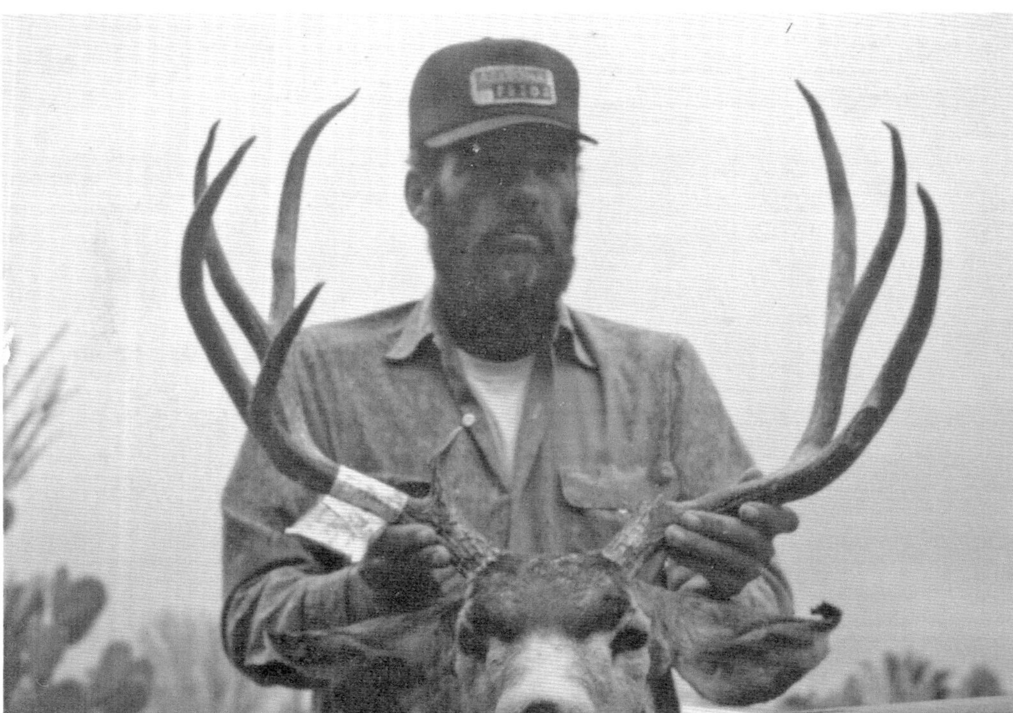

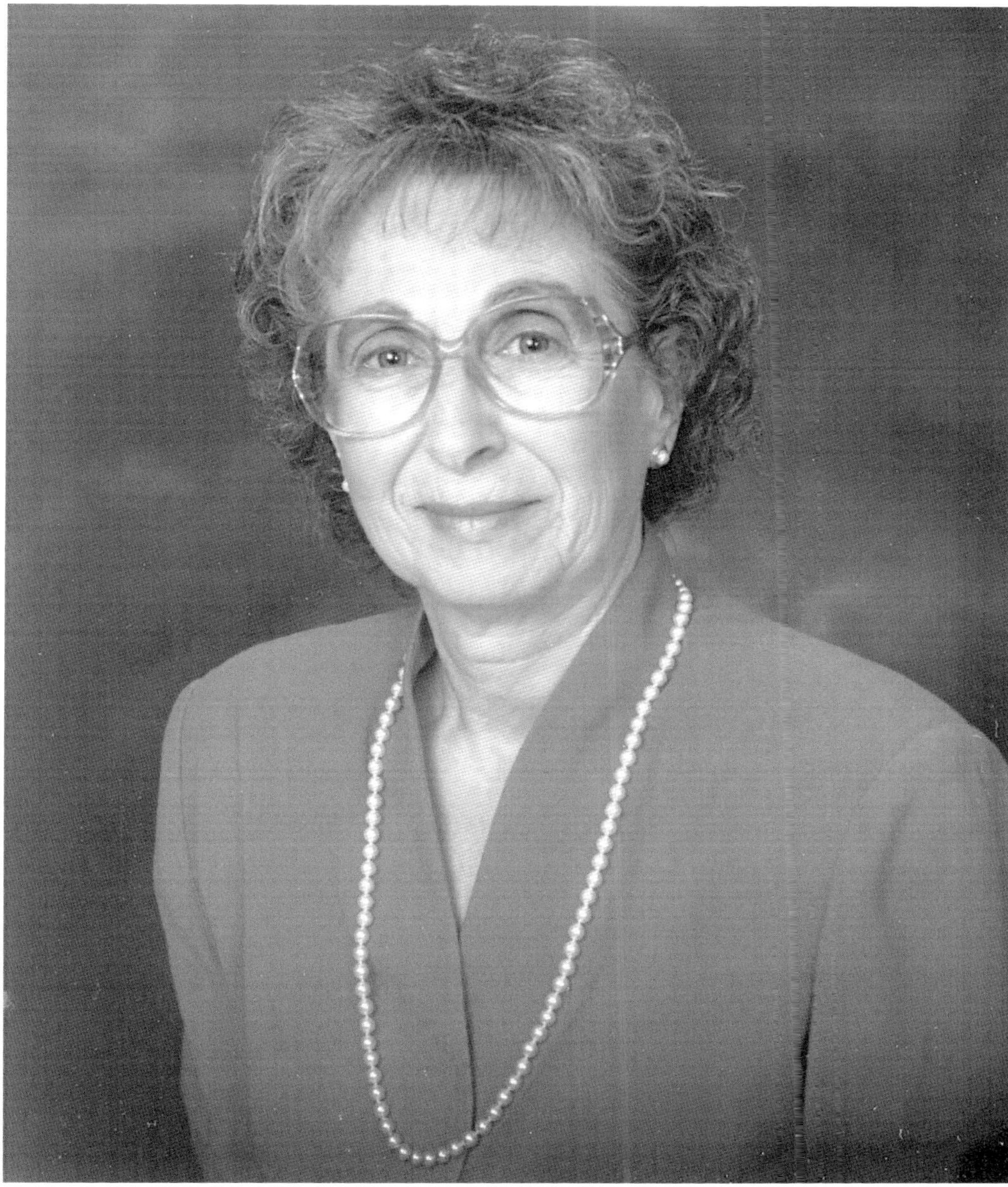

Voice of the People
When Cathryn Newman left her job as executive secretary at TRW in California, she planned on an easy retirement in SaddleBrooke. She filled her time by volunteering at the library and on the community's newsletter, the *Saddlebag Notes*. The newsletter ran about 16 photocopied pages and turned out to be a full-time investment for her and her husband Mark. Cathryn was the editor and Mark was advertising manager. Between them, they took the newsletter to a newspaper format, which is now published once a month by Tucson Newspapers and runs over 52 pages. It is still a community newspaper and features news of SaddleBrooke residents and the local area. Cathryn started the popular Billboard section, which features articles for sale. (Courtesy *Saddlebag Notes*.)

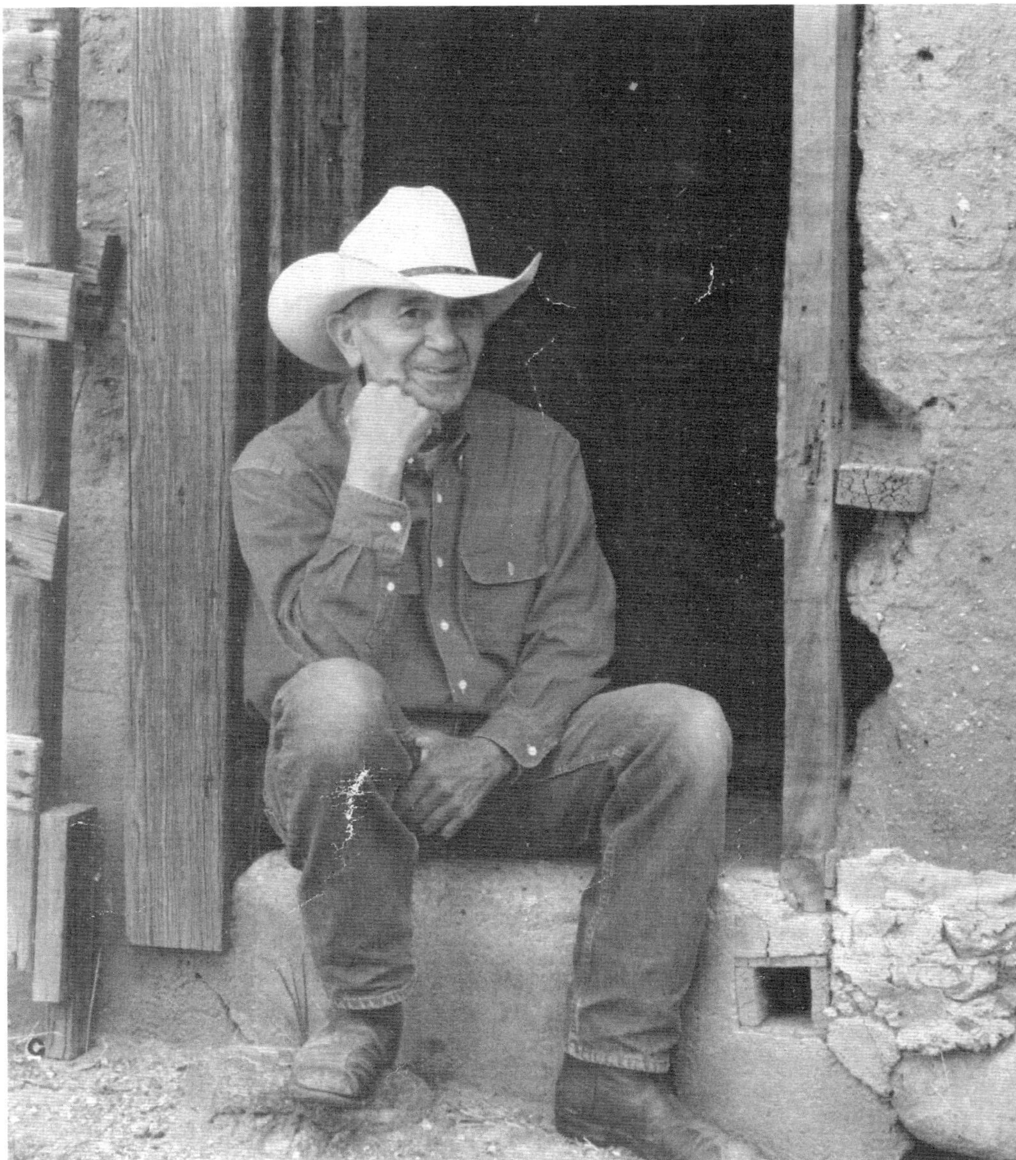

A Family of Cowboys

Cowboying for the Rivera family was a family affair. Carlos Sr. worked on the Rancho Vistoso and the Steam Pump Ranch. He taught his five sons the skills needed to handle cattle and ranch life, and they followed in his footsteps. Carlos and his sons wrangled at the Rail N and Golder Ranch. As small boys, the younger Riveras learned how to rope and ride. As men, they did everything from hauling barbed wire up the mountains on their backs to roundups. Clarence took his skills to another level competing as a rodeo team roper. In 1972, when Hollywood was making a movie in the Tucson area, Carlos Sr. was cast in the part of an Indian (below right). Above right picture shows the Rivera brothers, from left to right Clem, Clyde, Carlos Jr., Clarence, and Cecil. (Courtesy Liz Rivera, Indian picture Baggins Oro Valley.)

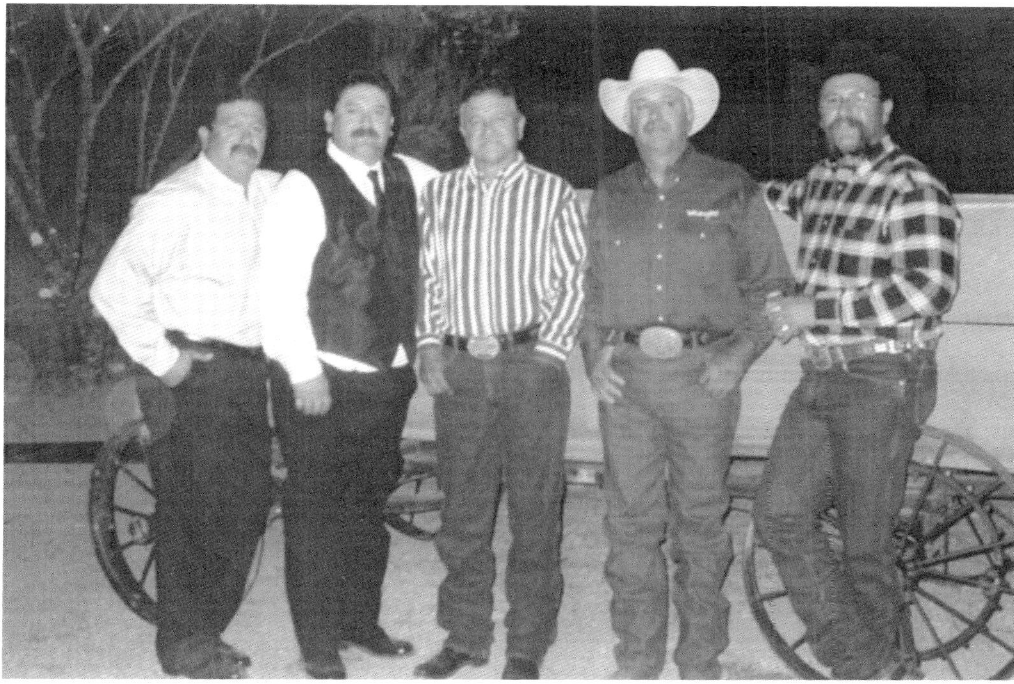

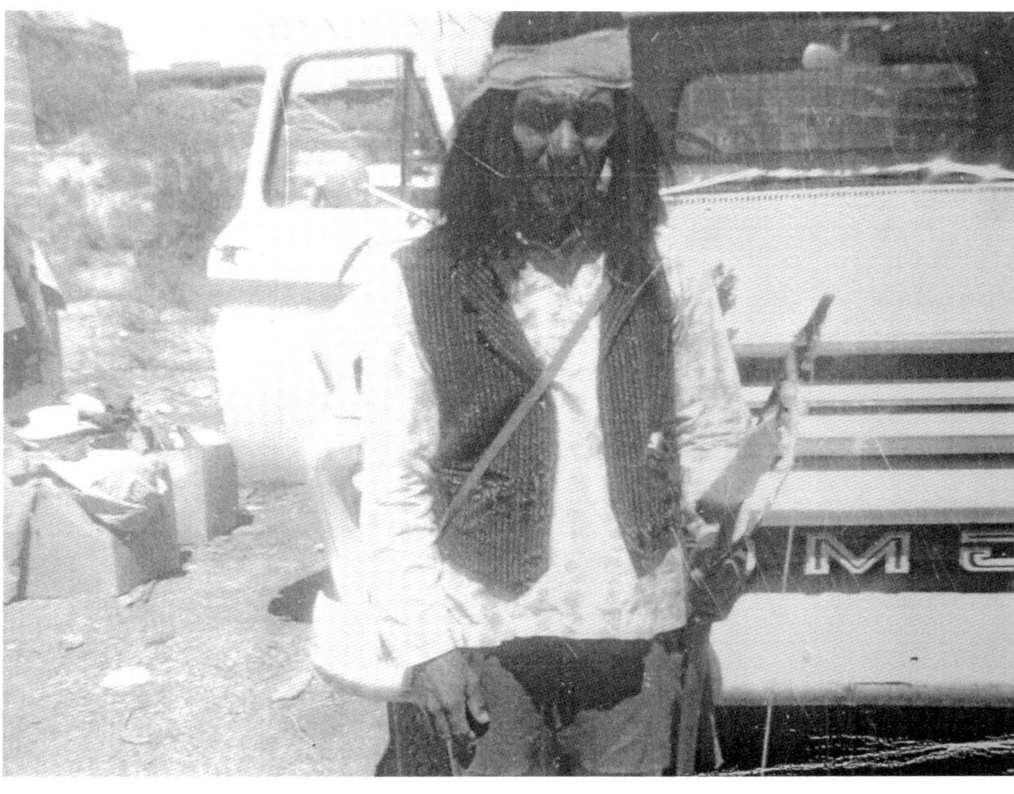

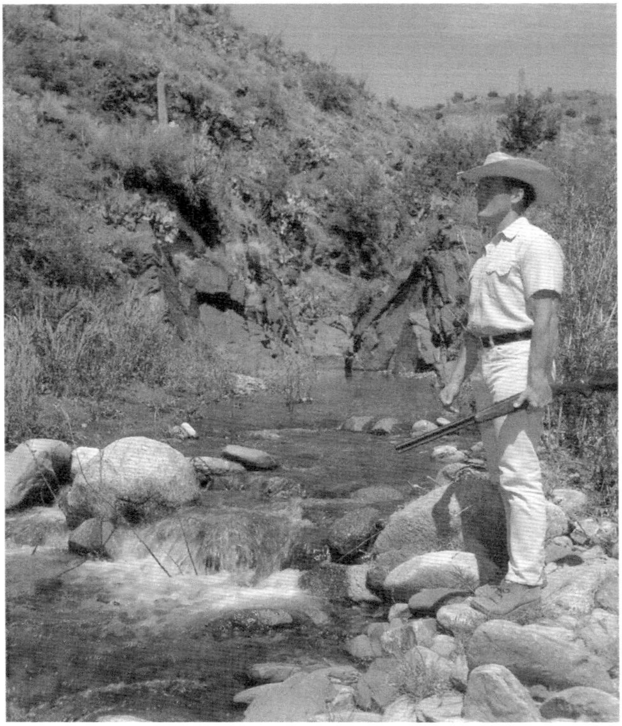

The Man with a Dream

When Lloyd Golder Jr. joined his parents in Arizona in 1958, he took one look at the land and saw not only its beauty, but its infinite possibilities. He visualized the Canada del Oro spilling into a lake surrounded by villas. He wanted to create a water-themed resort community complete with boating, water-skiing, and swimming. He set about bringing his dream to life by constructing a dam to form a lake by capturing the Canada del Oro flow. But his lakeside community dreams disappeared when the dam was breached. Not one to dwell on failure, he partnered with Ed Robson to develop a luxury up-market community for retirees. Today, SaddleBrooke is the home of over 5,000 people and has its own golf courses, tennis courts, restaurants, and lake. (Golder courtesy Dawn Doubek, lake Mike Marriott.)

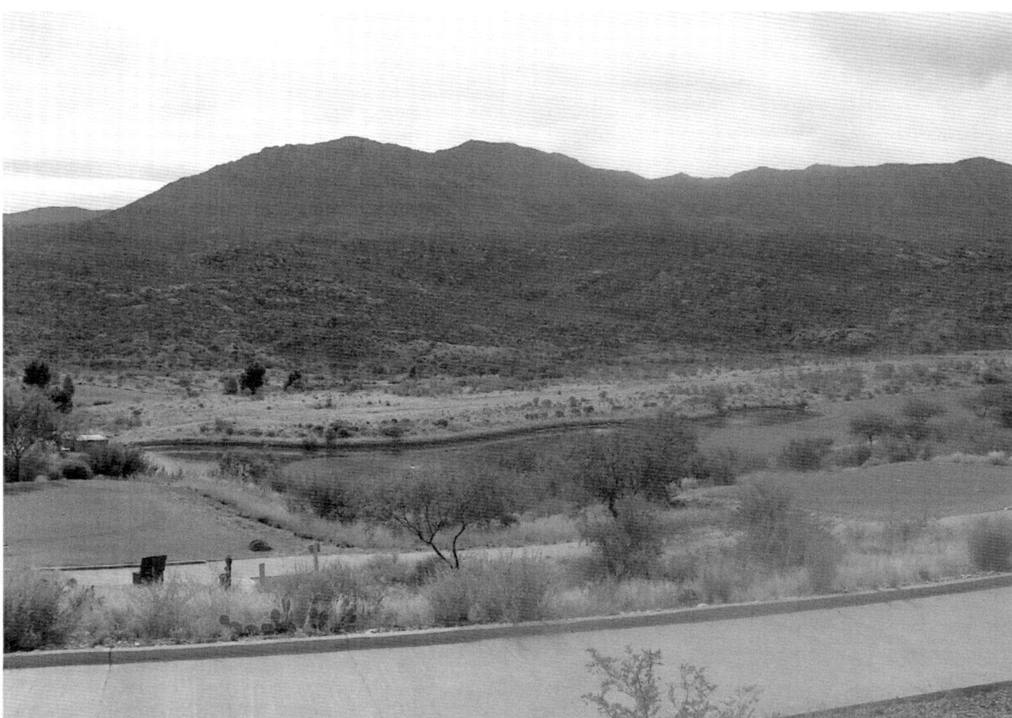

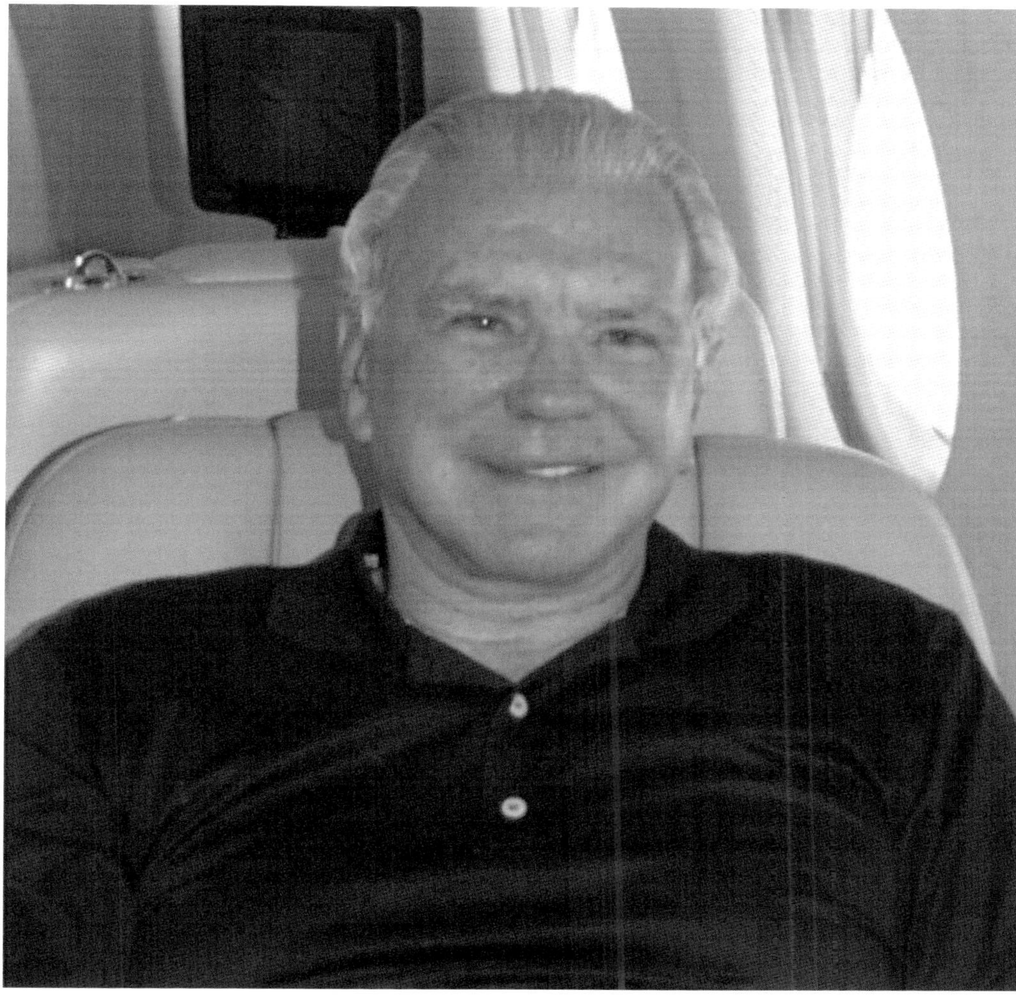

Creating a Community
When Edward J. Robson received his Navy Wings as a Marine Corps helicopter pilot in October 1957, he had no idea that he would become a nationally honored business leader. After he left the Marine Corps, he went to work first as a salesman for Coldwell Banker, then for the Del Webb Corporation as director of corporate sales. After leaving Del Webb, he started his own company. One of his first community developments was the Pinewood Golf Community in Flagstaff. In 1972, he developed Sun Lakes in Arizona, which is the largest privately held adult resort retirement community in the country. Robson Communities has created eight communities to date including SaddleBrooke in Catalina, which sprawls over 2,100 acres. No one has done more to change the character of Catalina than Robson. He turned a sleepy village of hardworking people into one of upscale homes and luxury living. Today, former business leaders, retired professionals, and PhDs work with the ranchers and village residents to create a community of history and heart. Robson set the example. In 1993, he was selected by Arizona State University as Entrepreneur of the Year. He has generously donated time and money to the Arizona Historical Society, University of Arizona, Arizona Humane Society, and the American Cancer Society, among others. Robson is the recipient of the 1998 Ellis Island Medal of Honor. (Courtesy Robson Communities.)

A Village Fire Station
In 1977, when Bob Murray came to Jim McLaughlin with the idea of a volunteer fire department, it didn't take McLaughlin long to agree. One problem: they had no place to put the station. McLaughlin took care of that. He donated a piece of property on Hawser Road, then continued his support by serving on the board of directors. (Courtesy Jim McLaughlin.)

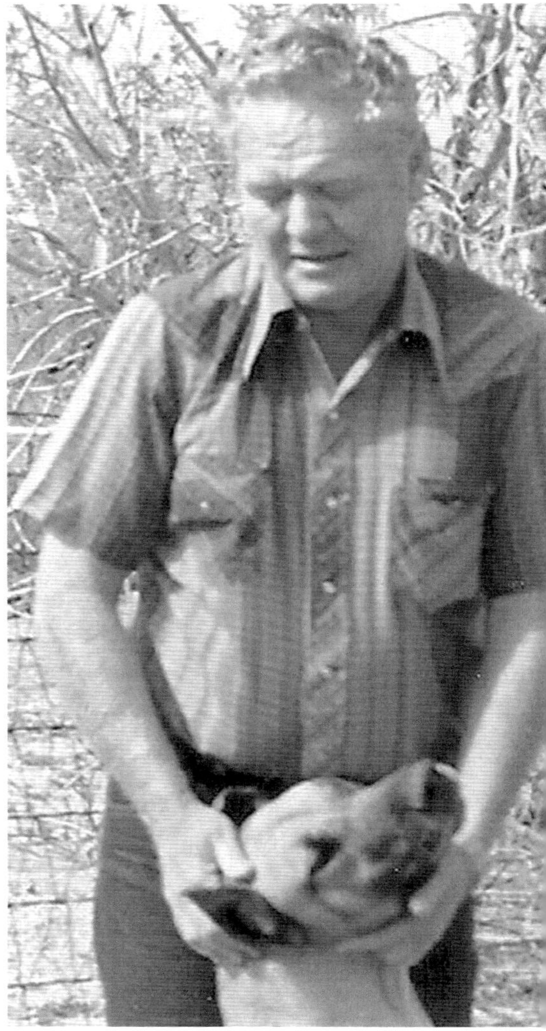

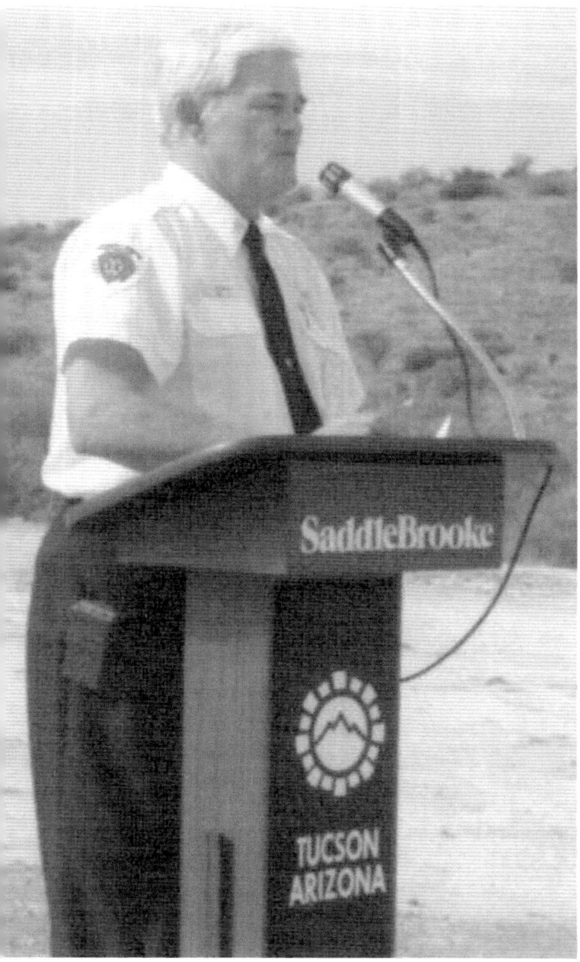

The Fire Chief
On November 8, 1977, Catalina residents voted to form the Golder Ranch Fire District. It was certified on November 15 of that year by the Pima County Board of Supervisors. Bob Murray served as the district's first fire chief. (Courtesy Golder Ranch Fire District.)

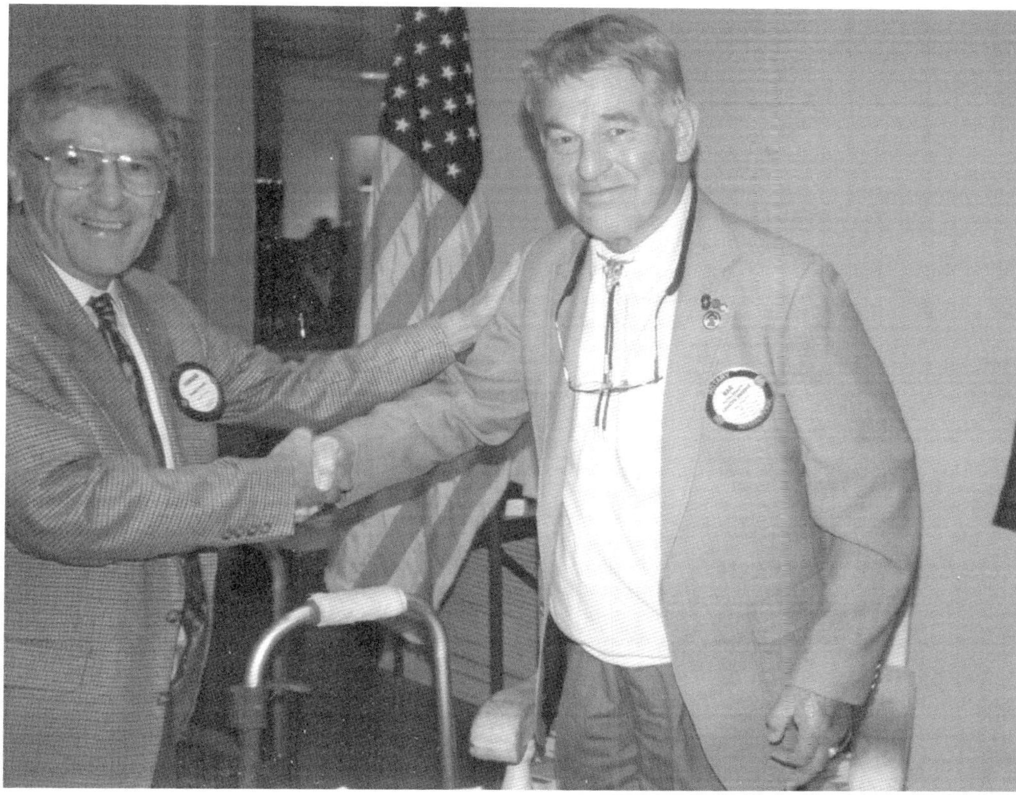

The Leading Rotarian (ABOVE)
Harlan Nygaard (right) was determined to give SaddleBrooke a Rotary Club. It was a difficult challenge, especially for a physically handicapped man. Using his political acumen gained from his years of experience as a Rotarian, he won the battle and the SaddleBrooke Rotary Club was established in 1997, the first Rotary Club in the nation to be established primarily for retirees. (Courtesy SaddleBrooke Rotary.)

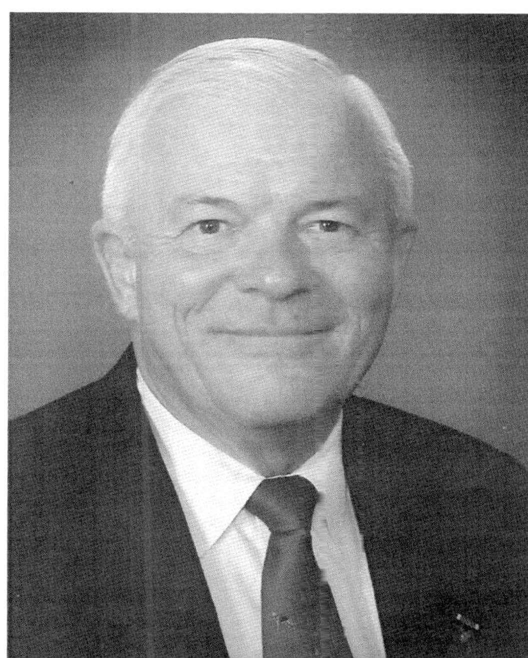

The Senator
In 2008, Al Melvin was elected to the Arizona State Senate representing Pinal County. Melvin is a retired businessman, college professor, and former Eagle Scout. He holds the rank of captain (retired) in the US Navy Reserve. As a resident of a community of retirees, he stays in tune with the concerns of senior citizens, and small-town community needs. (Courtesy Al Melvin.)

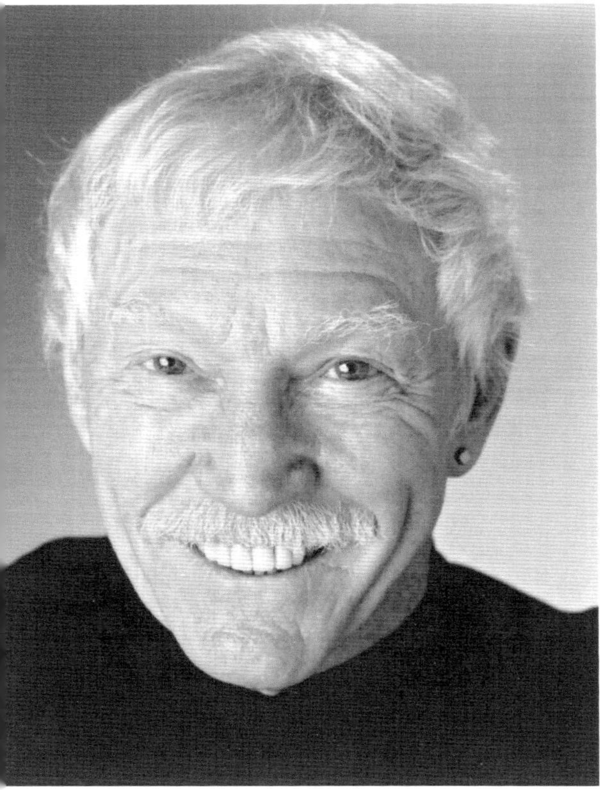

The Multitalented Man

Richard Hoyt, the actor, singer, dancer, author, and artist, had a PhD in psychology. As a professional actor, he was once the ringmaster for Ringling Brothers and secured a role in the William Shatner film *Groom Lake*. As a youth, he was jailed for going AWOL from the Navy, and shared this with troubled boys hoping to help them turn their lives around. (Courtesy Almarene Snead.)

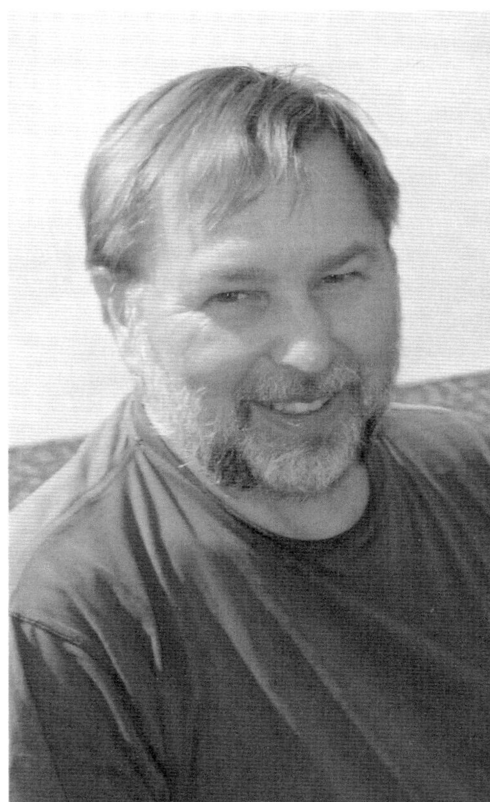

The Soul of a Poet

Fred Taylor sees Arizona with the eye of an artist, tempered by his love for the state where he was born and raised. His paintings catch the color of the West, and in poetic words he gives homage to the western way of life. In his *Wild Horses*, he eulogizes the disappearing mountain mustangs. (Courtesy of Fred Taylor.)

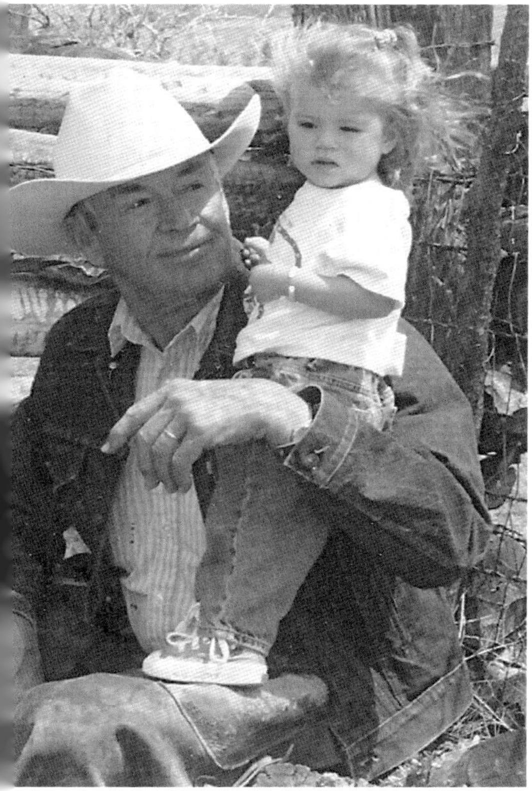

From Teeth to Cattle

Born in Phoenix, Don Martin is a native son with a distinguished family. His uncle Will Barnes was a Medal of Honor recipient. He set out studying dentistry, but didn't like working with "bad breath." At Arizona State University he switched his major to ranching. Martin is a Rodeo Championship Roper and owns several ranches in the area, which he and his sons manage, including the Rail X. (Courtesy Don Martin.)

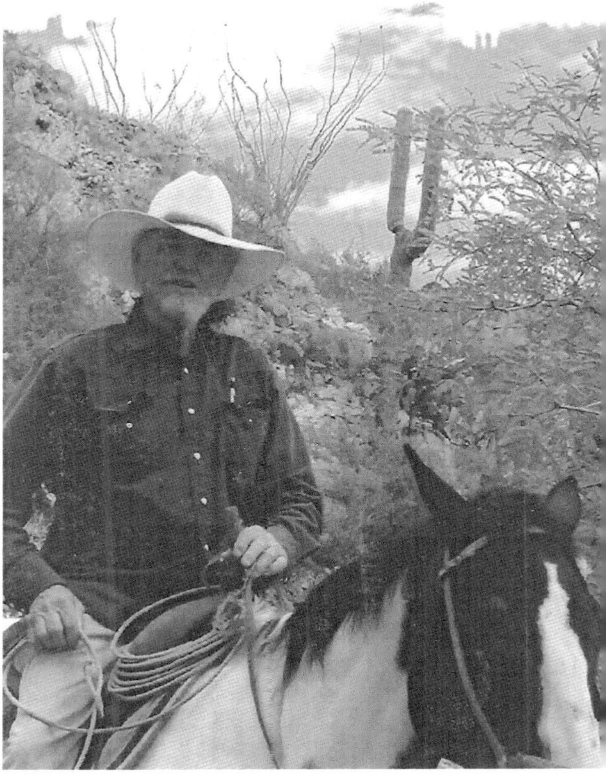

The Perennial Cowboy

Joe Goff may be in his 80s, but age doesn't stop him from working his ranches. From sunup to sundown, Goff is on the range taking care of his cattle and his land. Goff lives in the ranch house he helped his father build. His ranches bound the Santa Catalina Mountains on three sides and are worked by him and his children. (Courtesy Joe Goff and Dawn Doubek.)

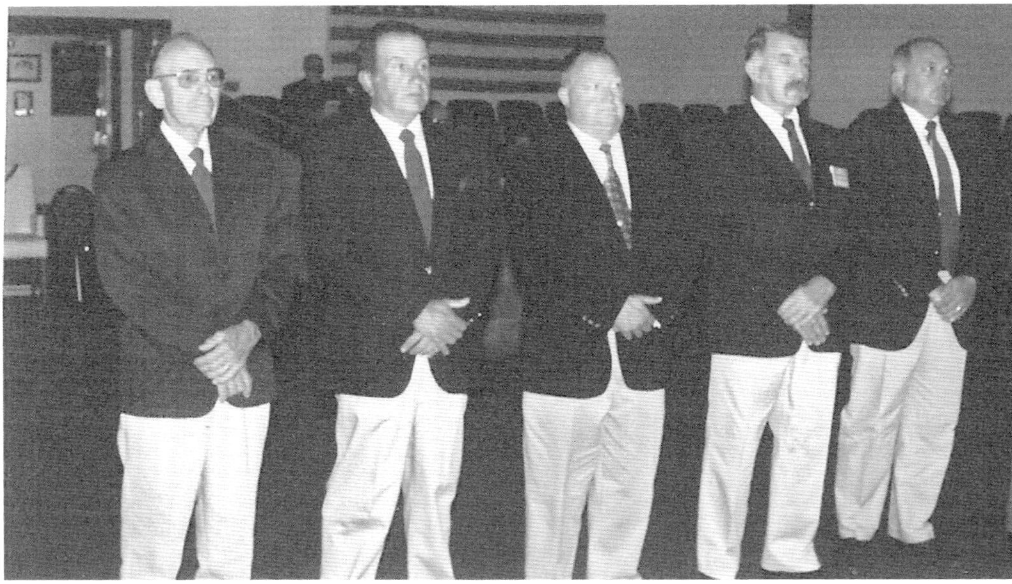

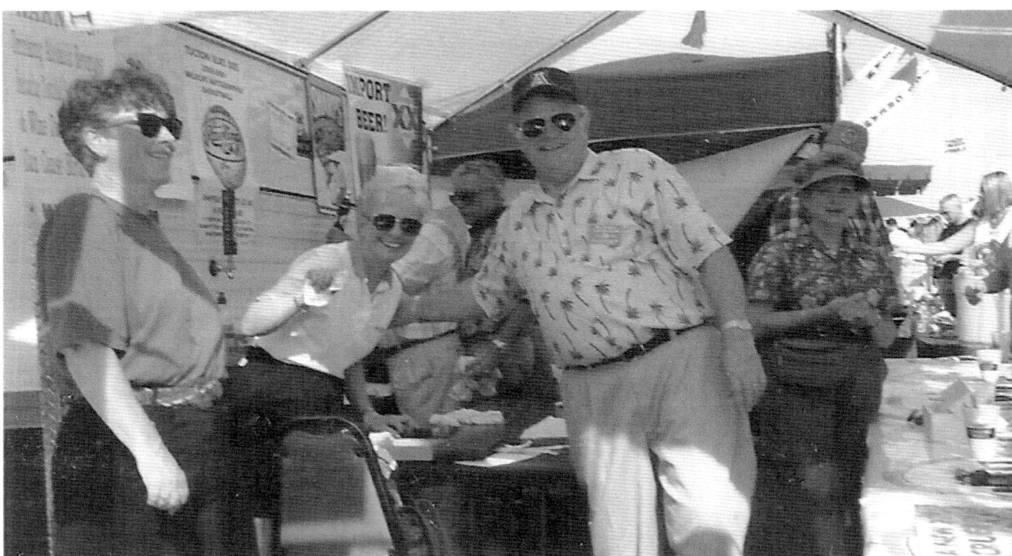

All for Charity

In October 2000, Richard Varian (top, left of line) and William Anderson (bottom) were two of the founding members of the Elks Lodge in Catalina. Varian had a degree in physics and a long career in the aerospace industry. He started the lodge's Clothe-A-Child Program and was responsible, along with his wife as co-chair, for managing a scholarship program that donated thousands of dollars to students in the Tucson area. After his retirement from a successful career at Johnson and Johnson, William Anderson turned his gregarious personality toward establishing an Elks Club in Catalina. He was the driving force behind the lodge's many fundraising events. Anderson was the official greeter and on the House Committee. Both men had served in the military. Varian was a Navy radar technician, and Anderson served in the Air Force. (Courtesy Catalina Elks Lodge #2815.)

With Honor and Courage

Lt. Col. Leo Thorsness received the Medal of Honor for his actions in Vietnam. His citation reads "for conspicuous gallantry and intrepidity in action at the risk of his life above and beyond the call of duty. As pilot of an F-105 aircraft Lieutenant Colonel (Leo) Thorsness and his wingman attacked and silenced a missile site, and then destroyed a second missile site. In the attack on the second missile site, Lt. Colonel Thorsness' wingman was shot down by intensive antiaircraft fire, and the 2 crewmembers abandoned their aircraft. Lieutenant Colonel Thorsness circled the parachutes to keep the crewmembers in sight and relay their position. During this maneuver, a MIG-17 was sighted in the area. Lieutenant Colonel Thorsness immediately initiated an attack and destroyed the MIG. Because his aircraft was low on fuel, he was forced to depart the area in search of a fuel tanker. Upon being advised that 2 helicopters were orbiting over the downed crew's position and that there were hostile MIGs in the area posing a serious threat to the helicopters, Lieutenant Colonel Thorsness, despite his low fuel condition, decided to return alone through a hostile environment of surface-to-air missile and antiaircraft defenses to the downed crew's position. He spotted 4 MIG-17 aircraft in the air and immediately initiated an attack damaging 1 and driving the others away. When it became apparent that an aircraft in the area was critically low on fuel and the crew would have to abandon the aircraft unless they could reach a tanker, Lieutenant Colonel Thorsness, although critically short on fuel himself, helped to avert further possible loss of life of a friendly aircraft by recovering to a forward operating base, thus allowing the aircraft in emergency fuel condition to refuel safely. Lieutenant Colonel Thorsness' extraordinary heroism, self-sacrifice, and personal bravery involving conspicuous risk of life were in the highest traditions of the military service and have reflected great credit upon himself and the U.S. Air Force for which he received the Nation's highest award, The Congressional Medal of Honor." (Courtesy the Congressional Medal of Honor Society.)

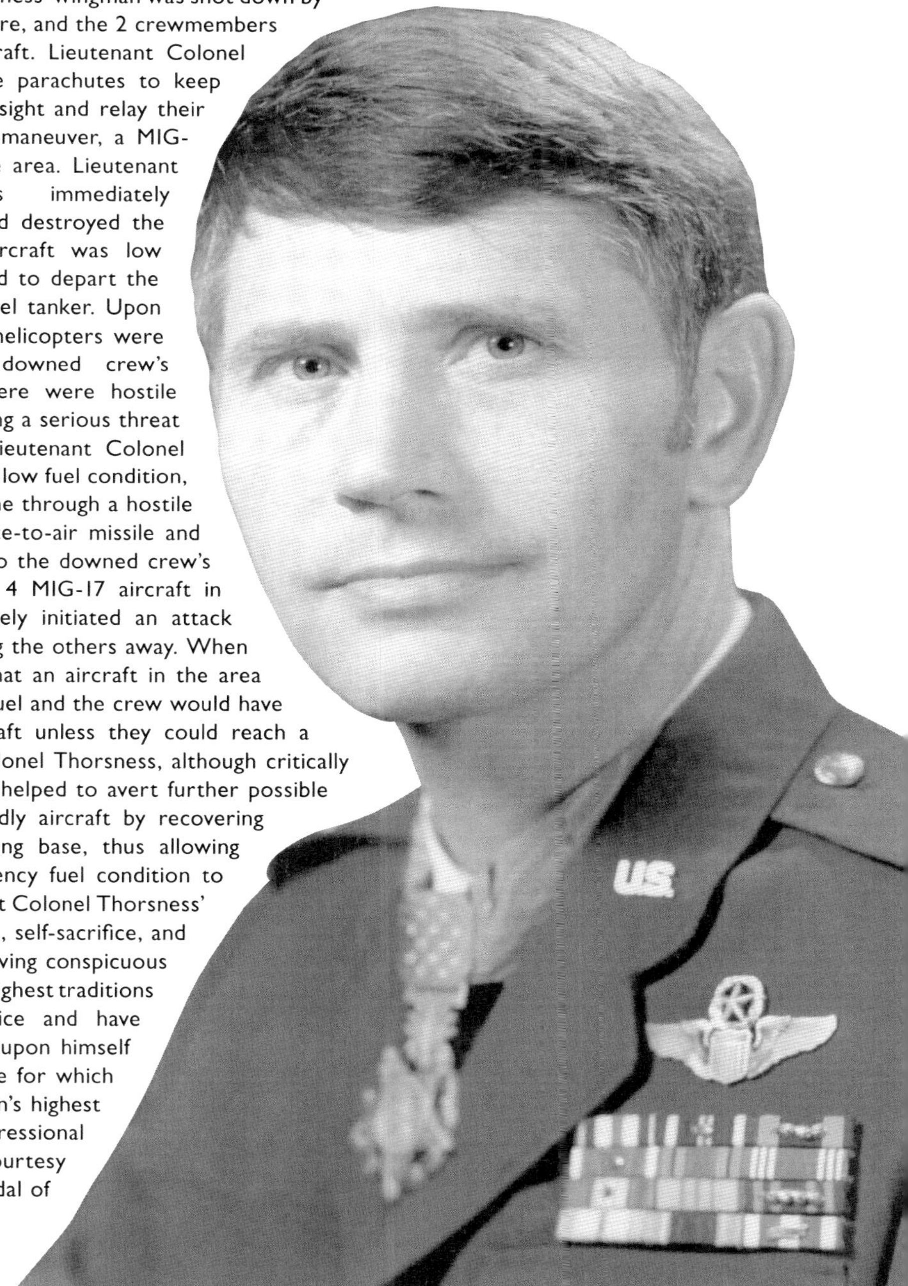

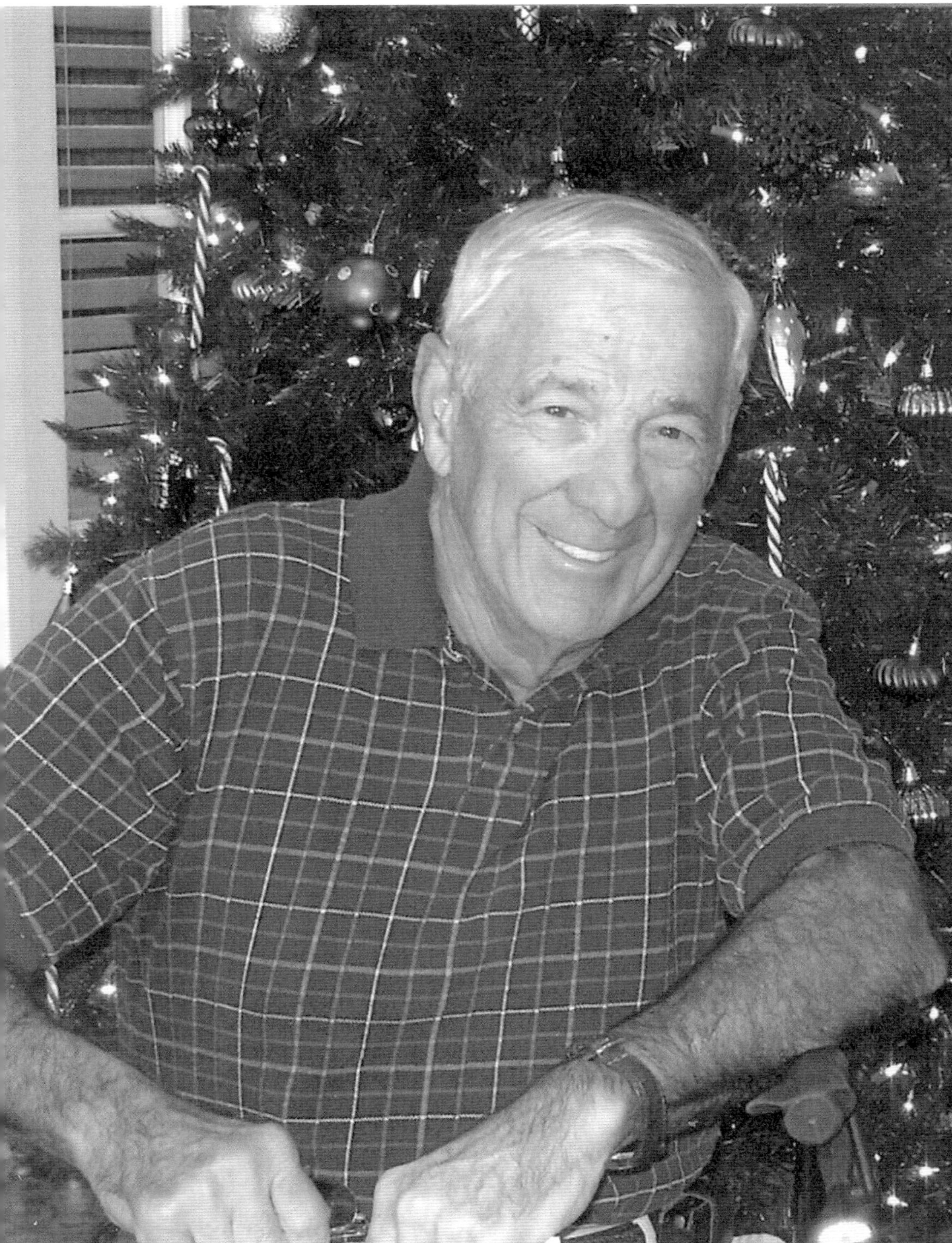

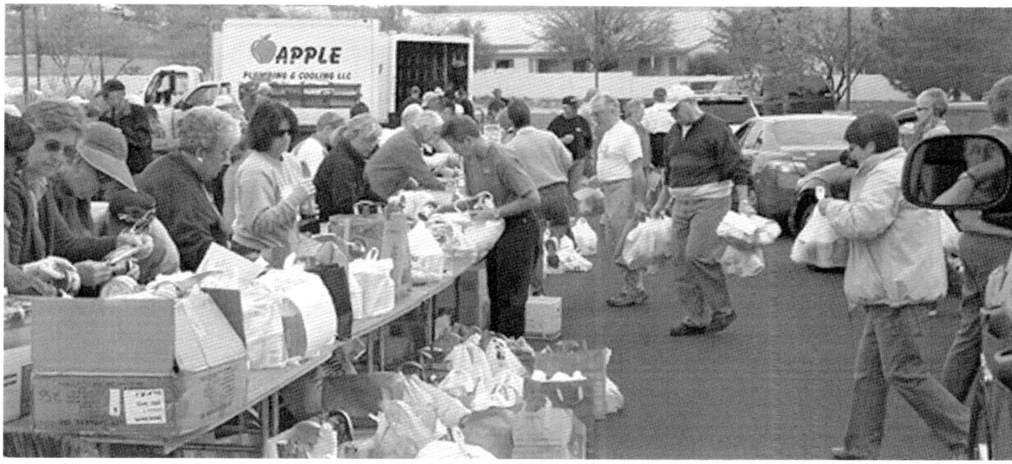

Caring for a Community

When Al Trice moved to Catalina in 1995, he saw a stressed community. He went to work implementing solutions. He helped found Catalina Community Services (CCS), a nonprofit organization that services the community's needs. CCS collects food and maintains a year-round food bank for residents in need. It also has a clothing shop where villagers can find items for all members of their family. All this comes from donations. Trice served on the Village Council, organized and served as director of the local Junior Achievement program, and served as president of the SaddleBrooke Home Owner's Alliance, Number One. He is the chair of the Oro Valley Hospital Board of Trustees, and chair of the advisory board of the Rancho Vistoso Urgent Care Center. (Courtesy Al Trice, CCS pictures Mike Marriott.)

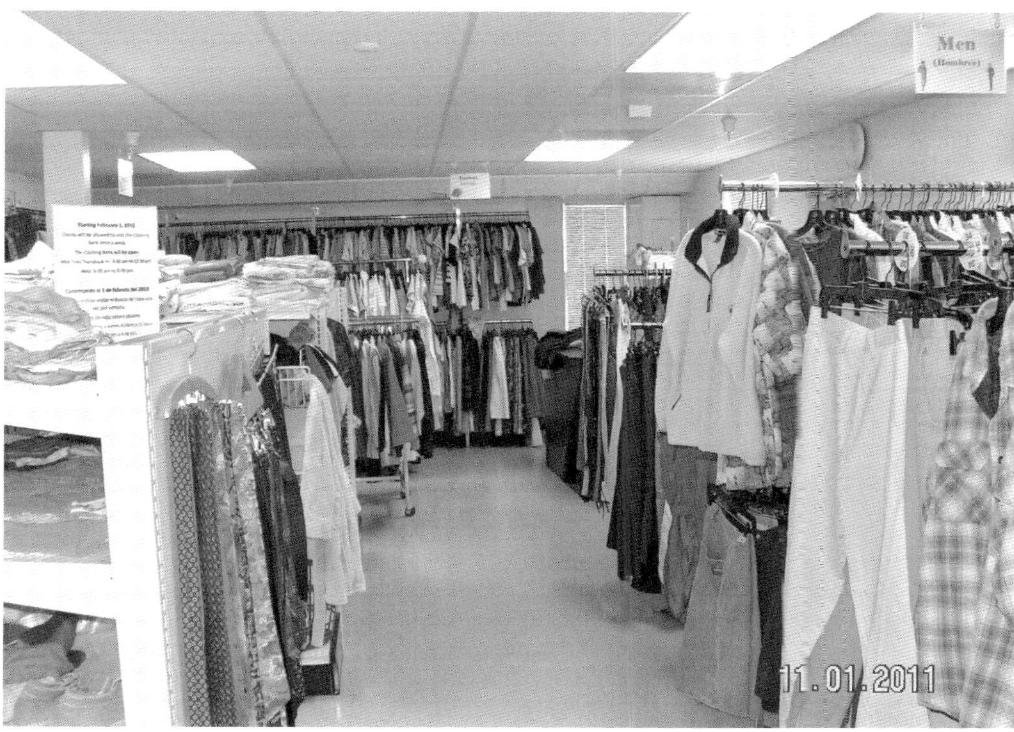

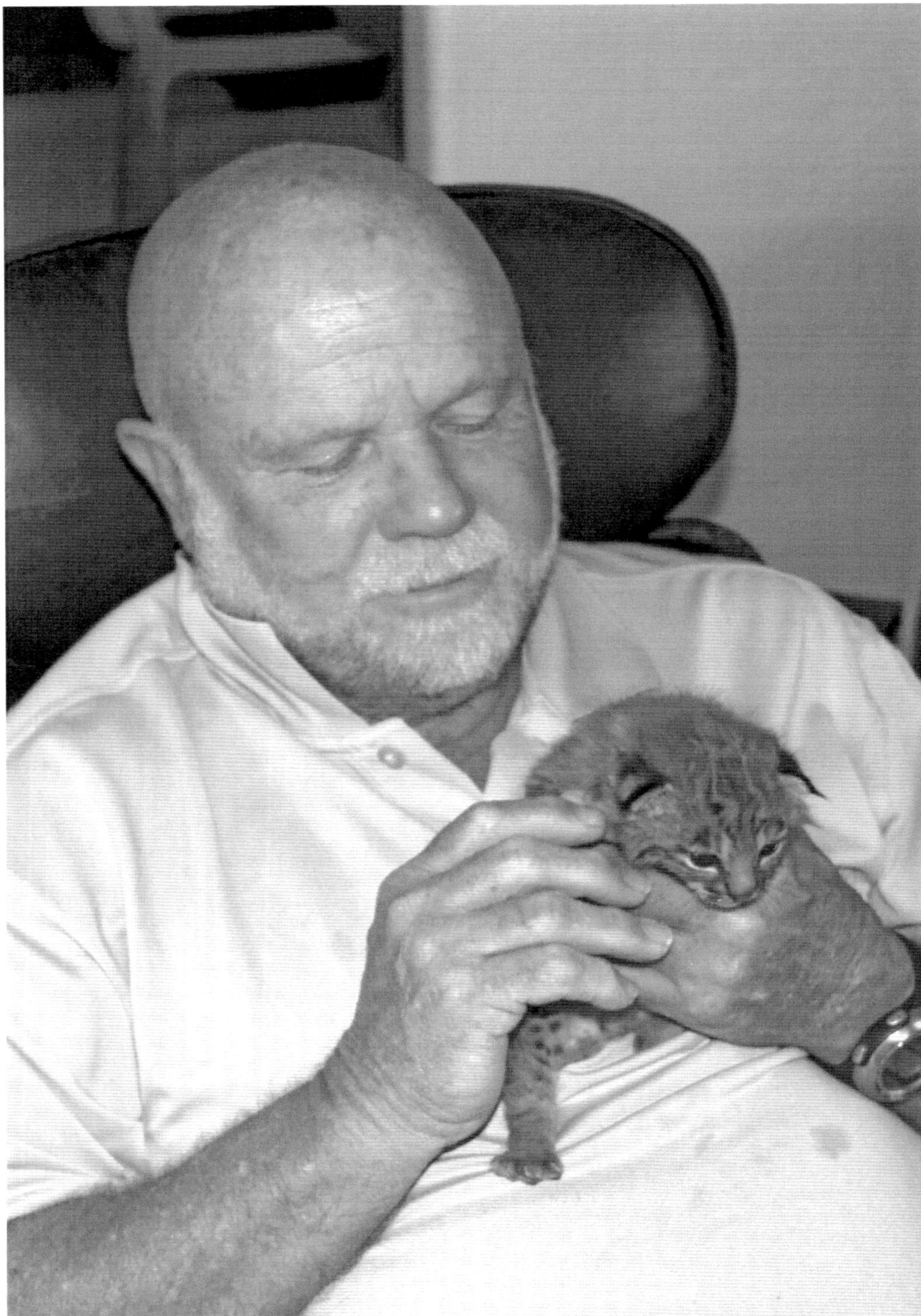

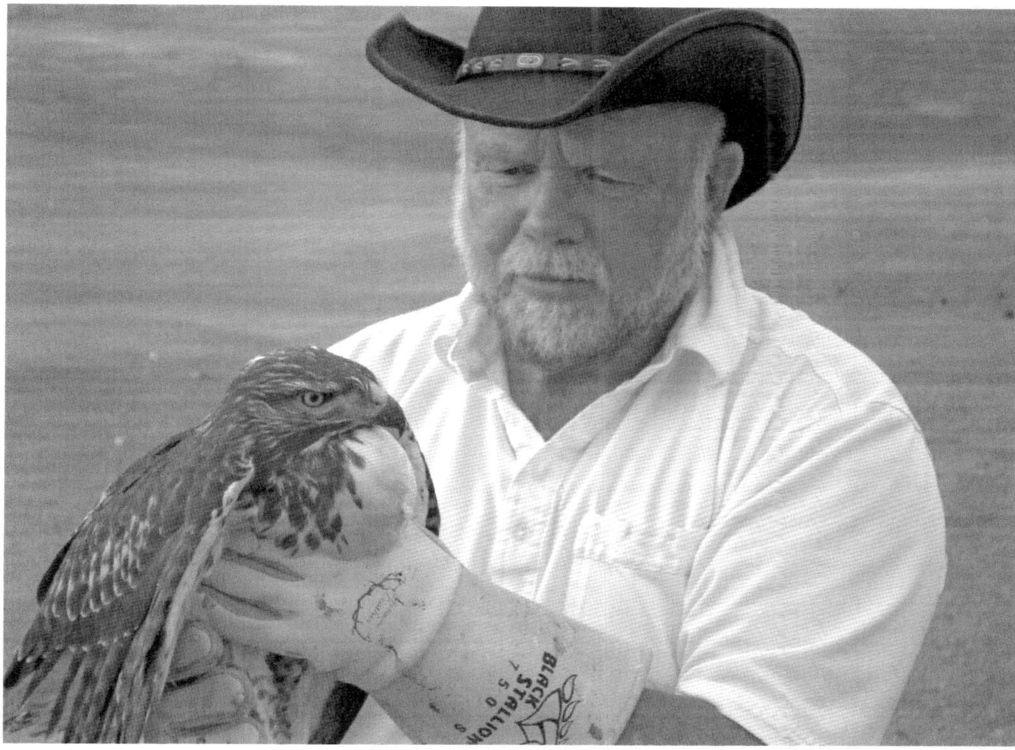

The Wild Man

When Jim Cloer was a boy, he collected wild animals. Some of his collections were ill received, such as the box of snakes he brought home. During his college years, he shared his house at different times with many animals, including a porcupine and an ocelot. The ocelot liked to take night dips in the neighbor's pool, which caused the town to pass an ordinance against keeping exotic animals as pets. After a stint in the Marine Corps, he attended college, then went on to teach a variety of unrelated subjects including computer programming, woodworking, math, and science. He holds a master's degree in arts and natural sciences. Although he says he is retired, he volunteers his time giving science programs in local schools and at Catalina State Park. (Courtesy Jim Cloer.)

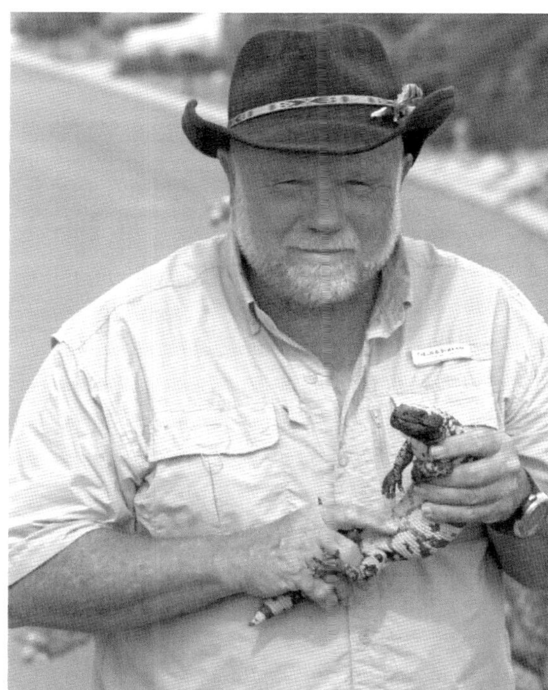

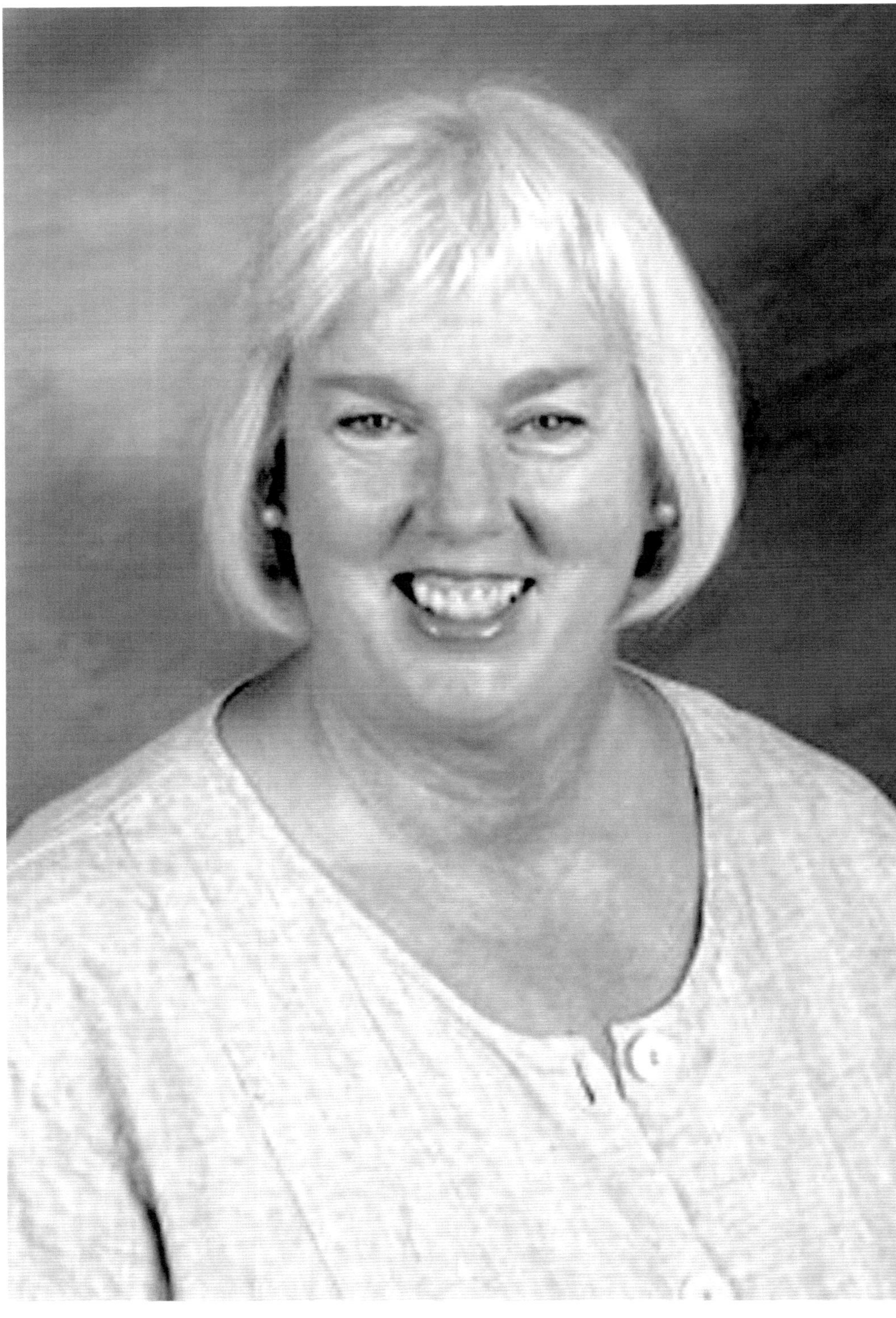

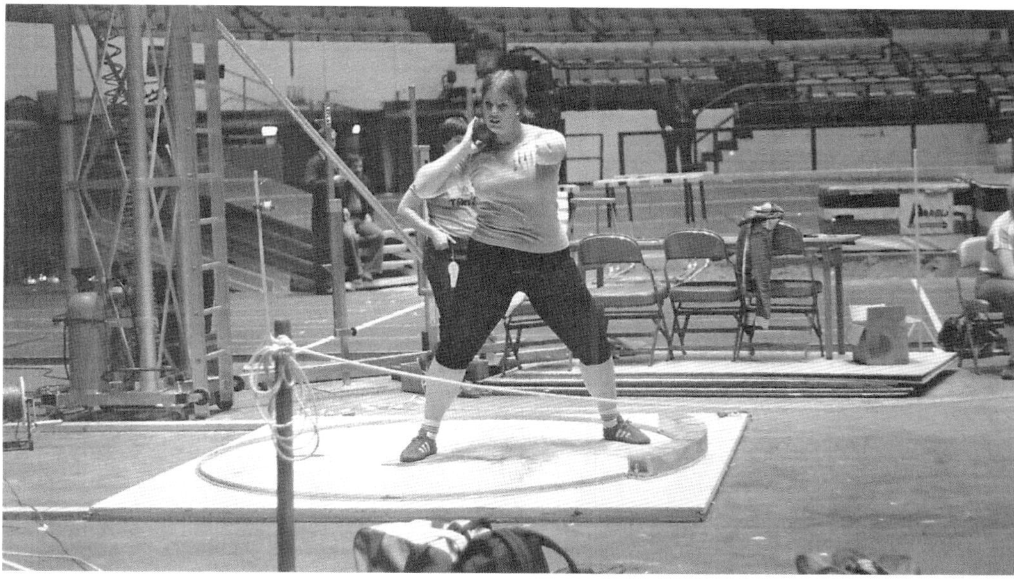

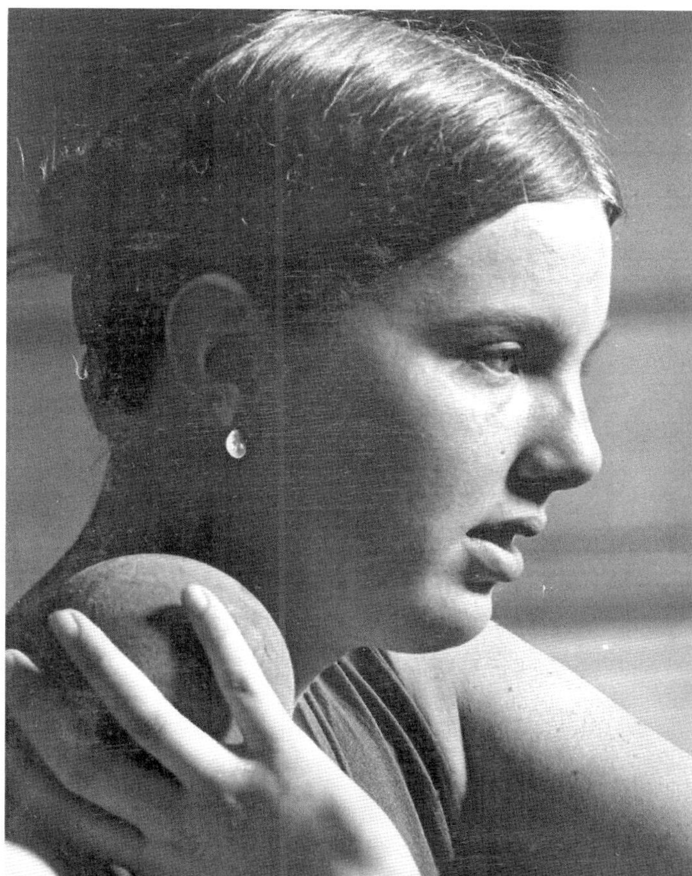

The Olympian Athlete
Maren Seidler received an official weight women's discus on her sixth birthday. Although that was not to be the event she broke records in, the discus did get her interested in track and field. At 11, she put a shot 35 feet. She was the first American woman to throw beyond 60 feet. Seidler earned 11 first-place rankings in the United States, and broke the American women's shotput record 11 times. Her late husband, a writer for the *San Jose Mercury*, was constantly amazed at what she could do. She was at the 1972 Olympics in Munich when Palestinian gunmen executed 11 Israeli athletes. The bond between Olympic athletes is strong. "They murdered people in my family," said Seidler. She was inducted into the US Track and Field Hall of Fame in 2000. (Courtesy Maren Seidler.)

The Cycle Master

The Tucson biking lanes are filled with cyclists from the SaddleBrooke Cyclemasters, which Jim Sanderfer founded in 1992. The club began with half a dozen riders and has grown to over 200 members, making it the second largest cycling club in Arizona. An eclectic, seasoned rider, Sanderfer holds the El Tour de Tucson (111 miles) record for the fastest time on a push scooter. He is a platinum level El Tour de Tucson rider, holds two *Guinness Book of World Records* marks in perimeter cycling, and is ranked 34th worldwide for total perimeter mileage. Sanderfer now rides casually and focuses his talents on writing. He authored two books, and is a syndicated columnist and professional resume writer. A retired Army officer, Sanderfer has a PhD in human resources and psychology. (The El Tour de Tucson Team, Sanderfer, Bud Chase, Dick Dall, Nancy Donehower, Roy Donehower, Courtesy SaddleBrooke CycleMasters, other photos courtesy Jim Sanderfer.)

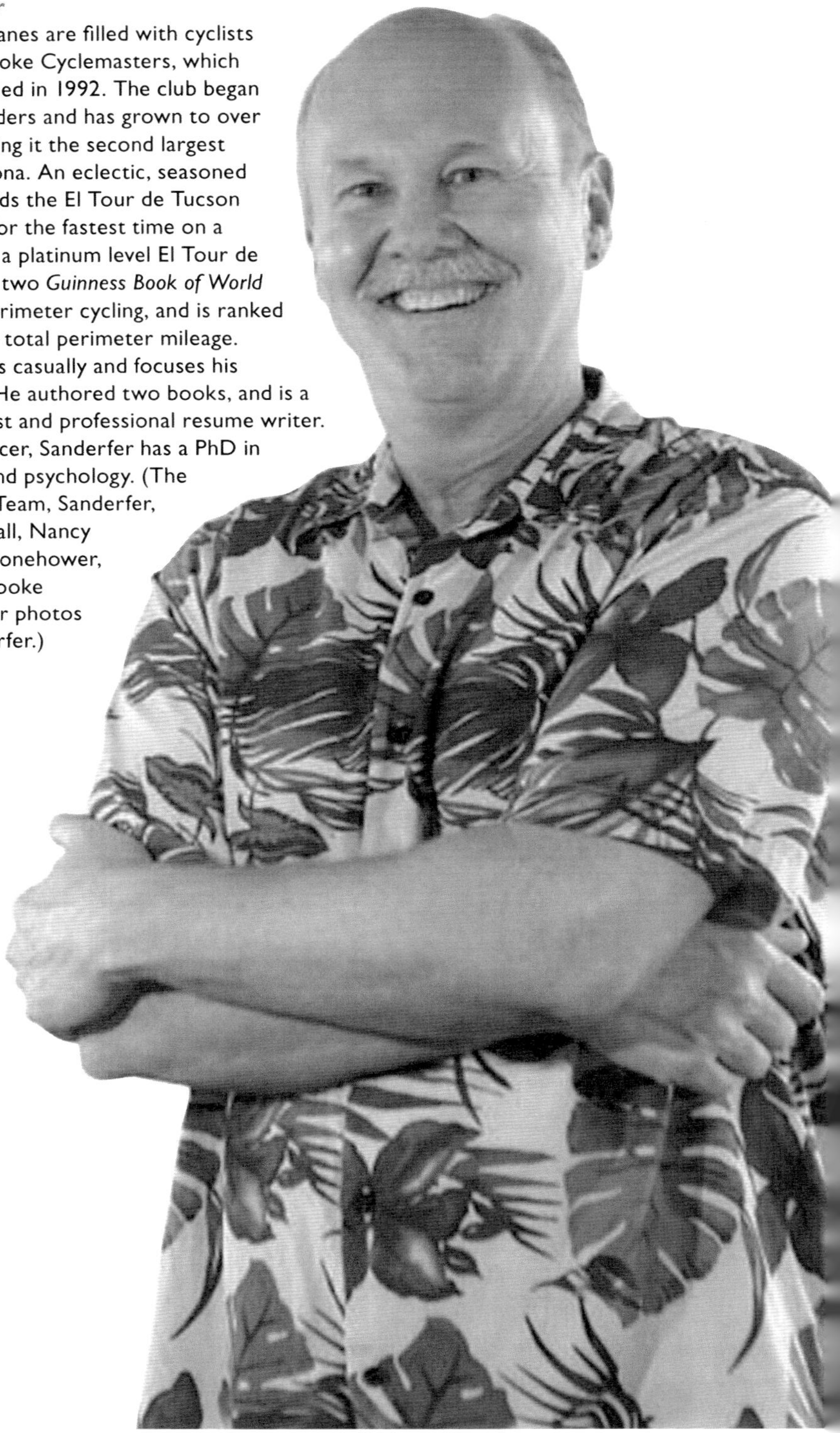

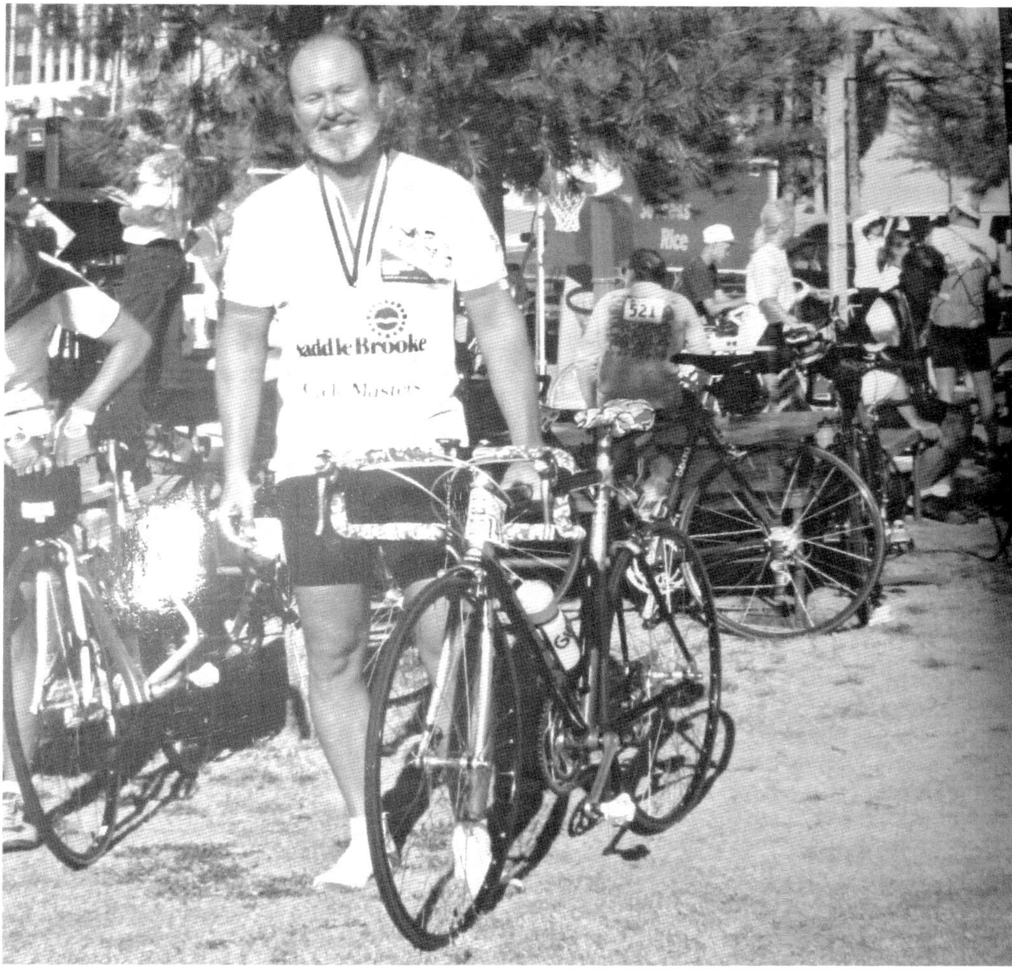
521
Rice
SaddleBrooke
Cycle Masters

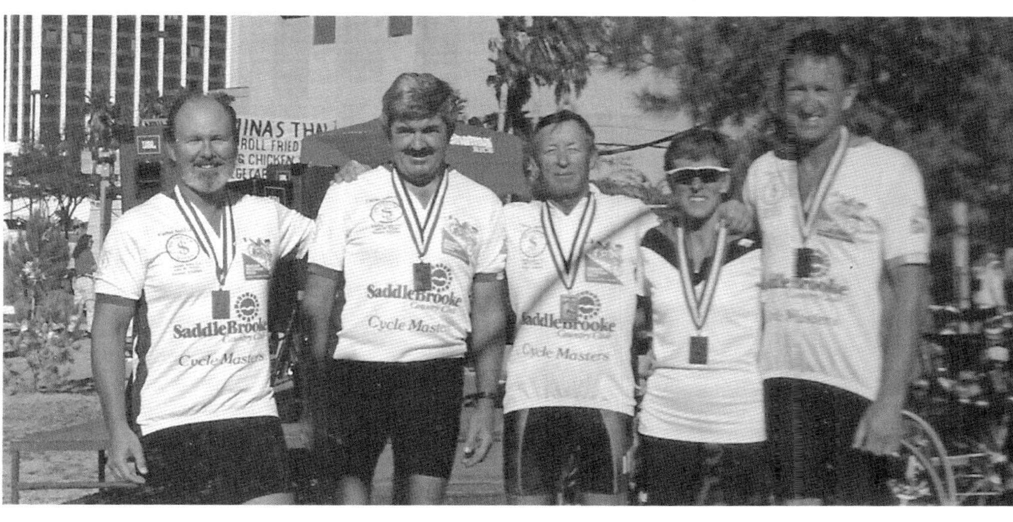
SaddleBrooke
Country Club
Cycle Masters
CHICKEN

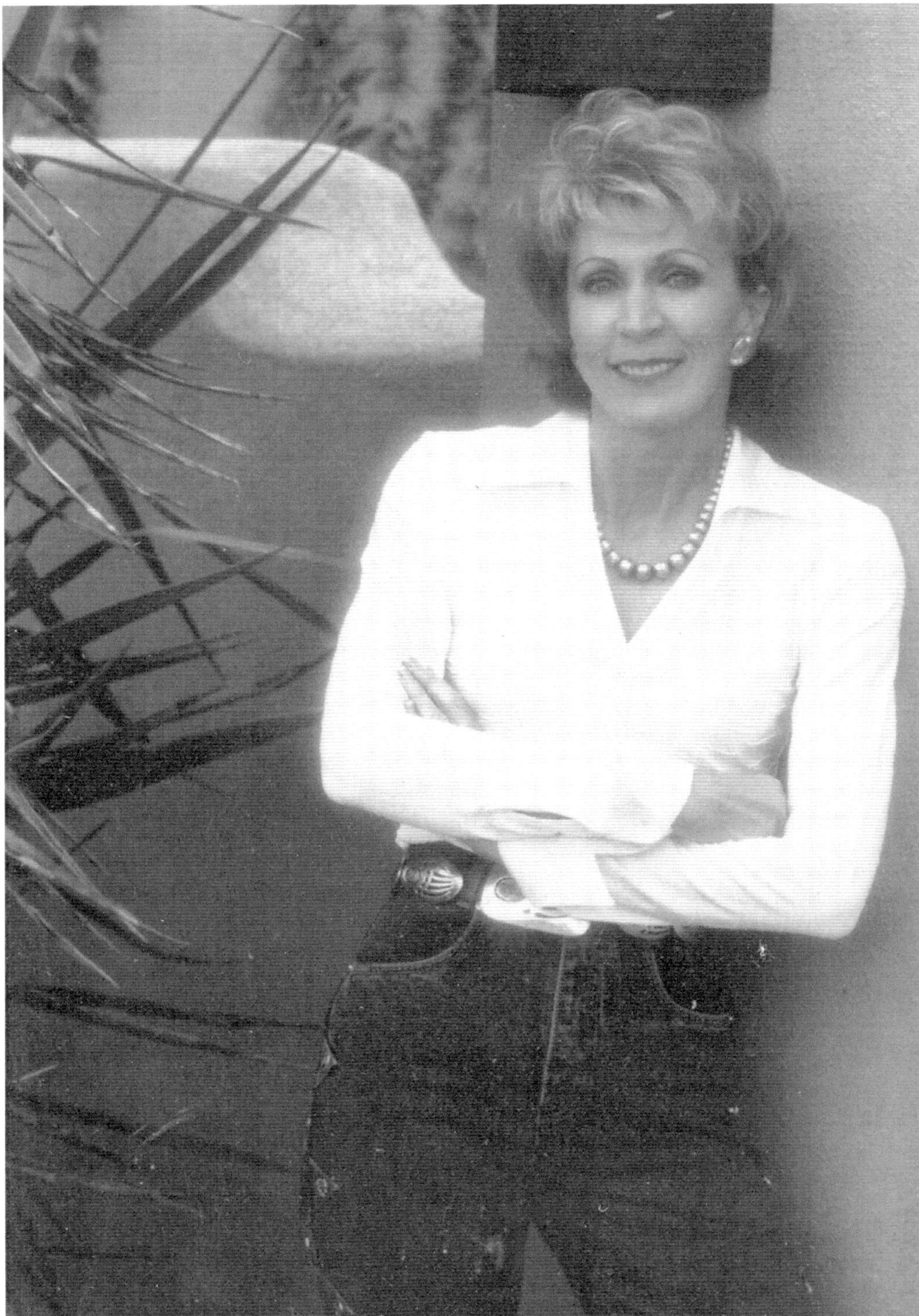

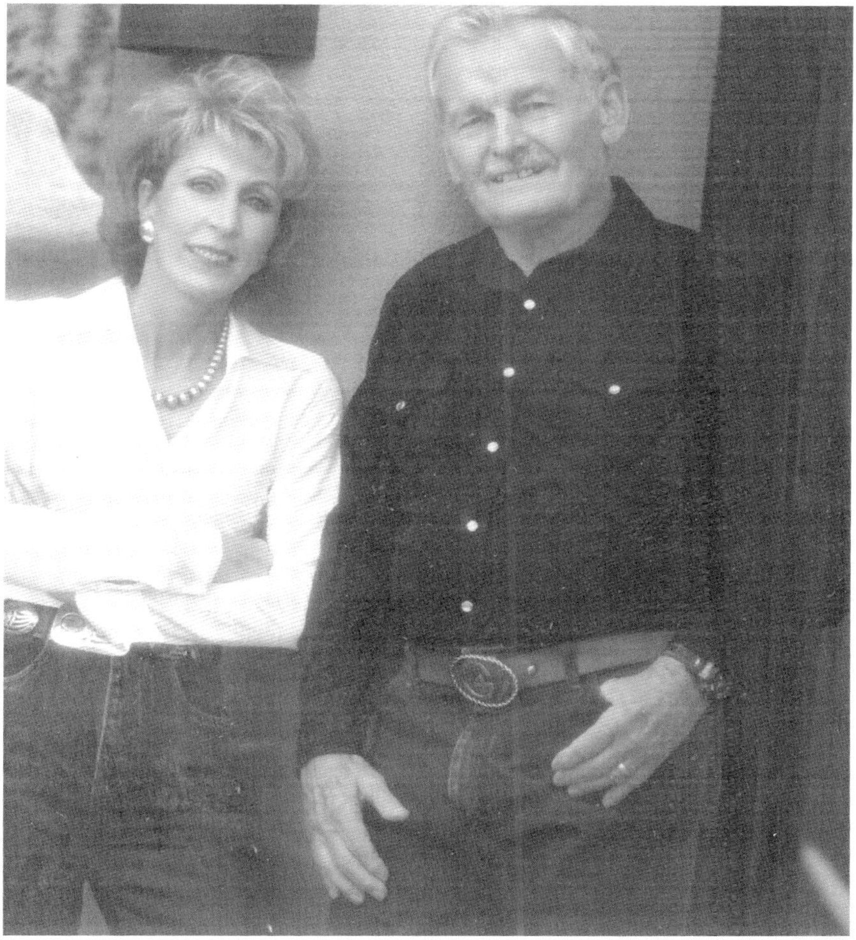

The Voice for Real Estate

Vicki Cox Golder was set to enter the University of Arizona on a full scholarship to study pharmacy when she learned her mother had died in a car accident. Her father had died 18 months earlier. Now her three younger siblings were orphans. Her goal now was not college, but keeping the family together. Although only 19, married, and with a son, she obtained legal custody of her sisters: Mary, 15; Dawn, 13; and Denise, 11. Her best option for earning a living was real estate. She started out in the field in 1973. By the time she was 25, she had her broker's license and her own office. In 1994, Golder served as president of the Arizona Association of Realtors, and took a central role in rebuilding the government affairs program, making it one of the top five organizations in the state for political access. She was elected president of the National Association of Realtors, taking office in 2009. With her election she became "The Voice of Real Estate" on national legislative and regulatory priorities. Although her business responsibilities are enormous, she has not neglected her small community, or her home state. She founded the Catalina Village Council, and the Helping Hands Program. Golder is a member of the Pima County Planning Commission, headed up the unsuccessful incorporation movement, and is on the district Ampi School Board. She is shown with her husband and on the evening of her inauguration as president of the National Association of Realtors, her son Lloyd introduced her, and her sister Dawn was there to give her support. Even today she still focuses on family, finding time for her husband, two sons, and three grandchildren. (Courtesy Vicki Cox Golder.)

The Pearl Harbor Sailor (RIGHT)
He was only a young kid at the time, scared out of his mind, and all he knew how to do was follow orders. So with enemy planes divebombing around him, naval vessels on fire and sinking, Joe Owens drove his boat through dangerous waters delivering supplies to the ships that remained in the port of Pearl Harbor. He was only 100 yards away from the USS *Arizona* when she was hit. The supplies turned out to be ammunition. It was December 7, 1941. Owens served 30 years in the US Navy, retiring as a commander. During his Navy career, he served on destroyers, destroyer tenders, and aircraft carriers as the weapons officer. He saw action in the Pacific during the Second World War, including at Midway and Guadalcanal. When he retired, he went to work for the Northrop Corporation in their drone program. Owens was a member of Rotary for 47 years and held many positions within that organization including president. (Courtesy Mrs. Joe Owens.)

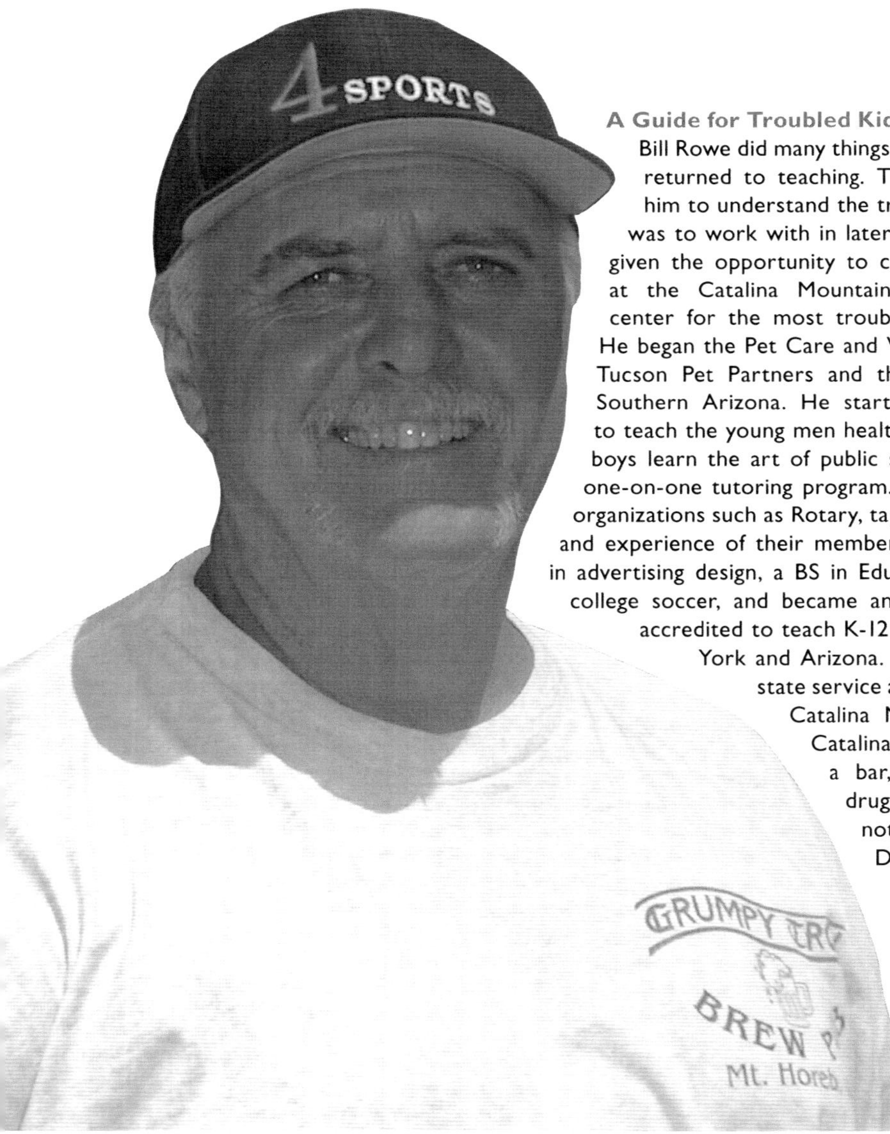

A Guide for Troubled Kids
Bill Rowe did many things in his life, but he always returned to teaching. That profession enabled him to understand the troubled young adults he was to work with in later years. In 1996, he was given the opportunity to create his own position at the Catalina Mountain School, a detention center for the most troubled youths in Arizona. He began the Pet Care and Visitation Program with Tucson Pet Partners and the Humane Society of Southern Arizona. He started a speakers' bureau to teach the young men healthy life skills, helped the boys learn the art of public speaking, and offered a one-on-one tutoring program. He worked with local organizations such as Rotary, tapping into the expertise and experience of their members. He earned an AAD in advertising design, a BS in Education, two letters for college soccer, and became an Eagle Scout. Rowe is accredited to teach K-12 in both his native New York and Arizona. He began his career in state service as an art therapist at the Catalina Mountain School when Catalina had a two-lane road, a bar, two cafes, boatyard, drugstore/post office, and not much else. (Courtesy Dawn Doubek.)

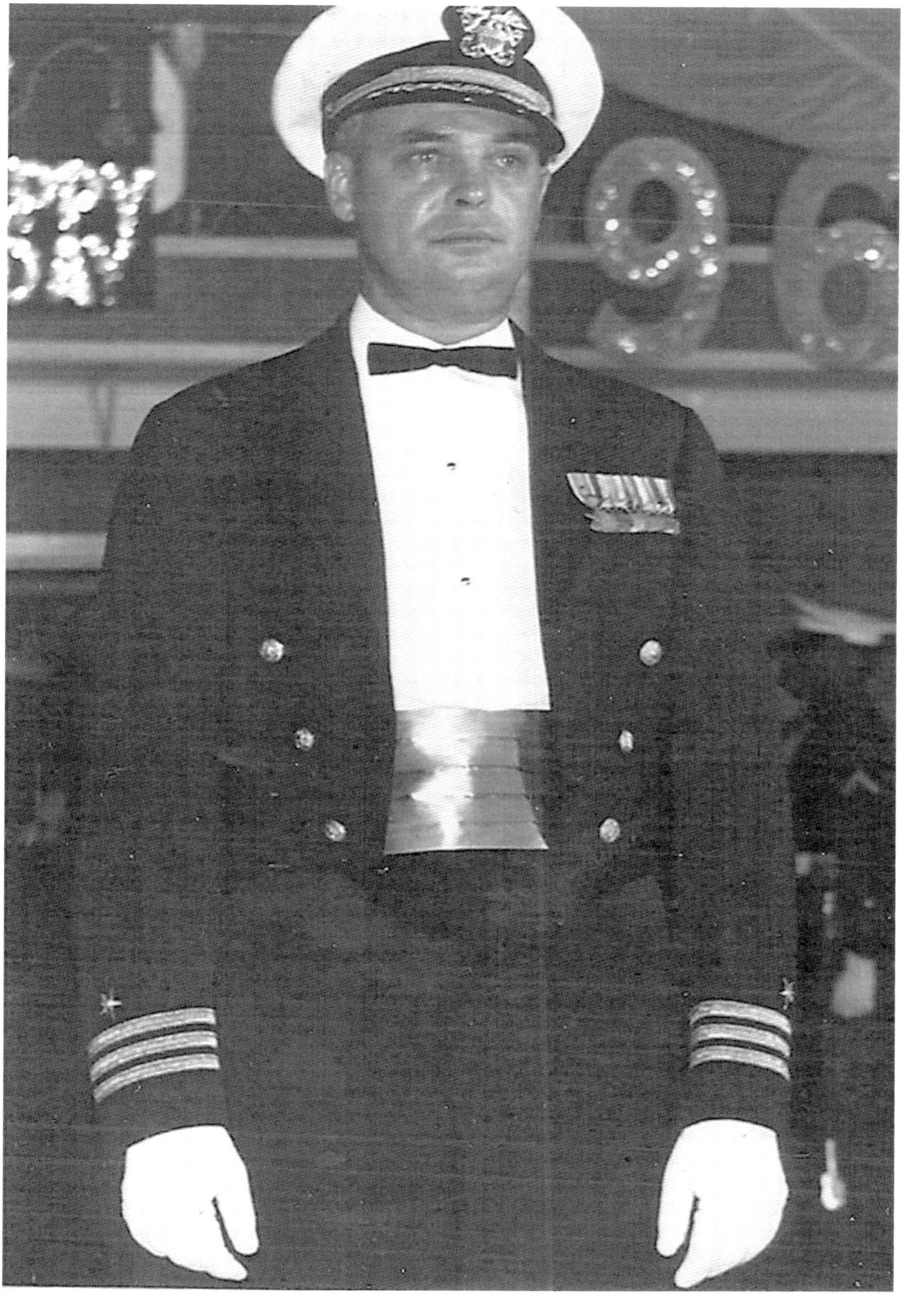

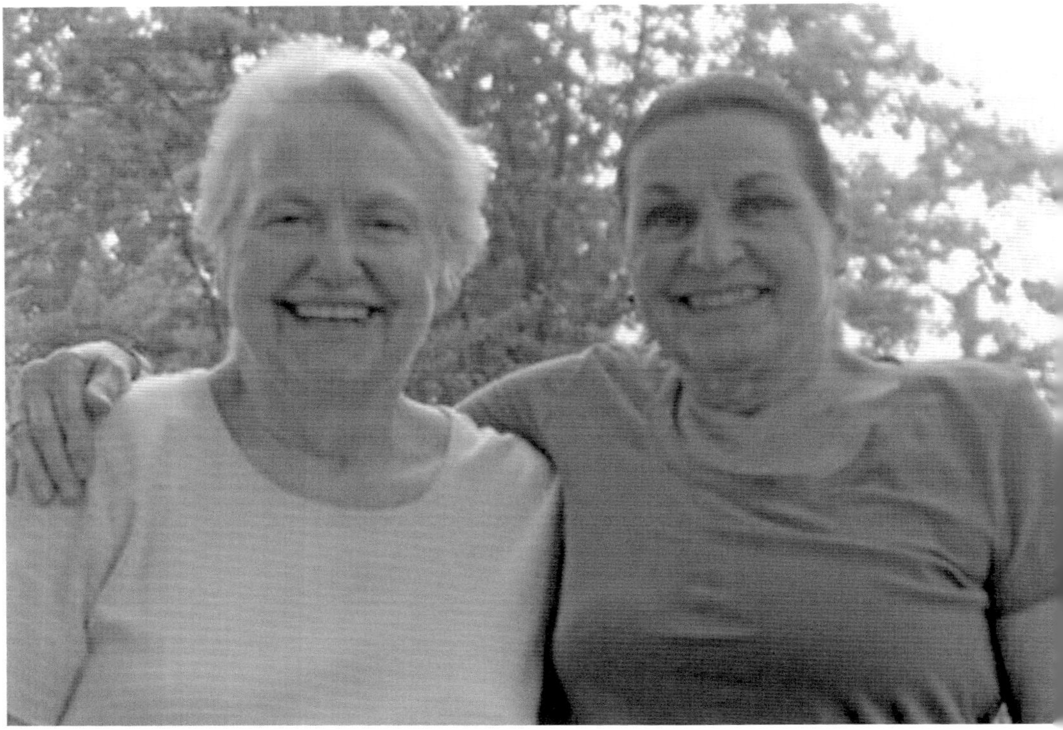

A Community Outreach

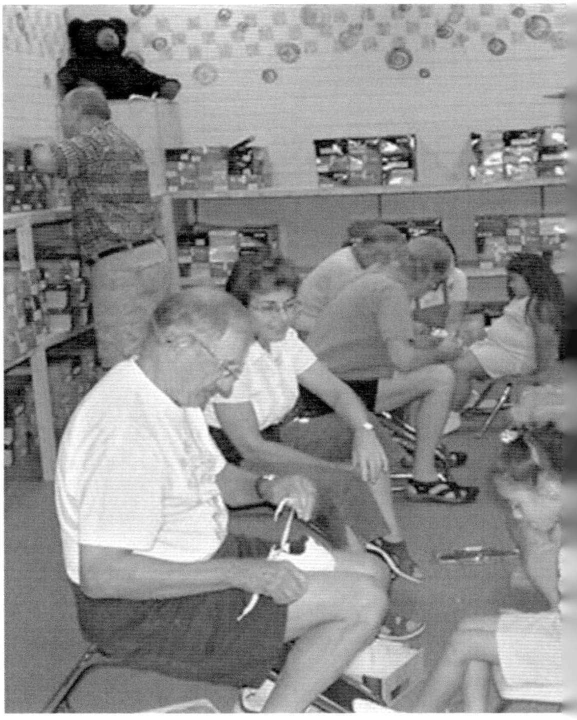

In 1996, when Dorothy Steffano (left in photo above) heard the children of the neighboring copper mining towns of Oracle, San Manuel, and Mammoth had no clothes for school, she and her friends Anita Eagle and Cyrene Shockett formed the SaddleBrooke Women's Outreach program. Dorothy Steffano was the first president and The Kids' Closet venture was chaired by Harriet Schultz (right in photo above) and Elaine Stamm. The first year Community Outreach provided 358 children with school clothing. In the 2010–2011 school year, Community Outreach clothed 36,000 schoolchildren. It also has a tutoring program and awards scholarships to needy and deserving students. It is a national award-winning organization with over 200 volunteers. Money is raised through the Clothe-A-Child Program, donations, and annual events such as their golf tournament, a walkathon, a home and garden tour, and other special programs. (Founders courtesy Dorothy Steffano, Kids' Closet courtesy Community Outreach.)

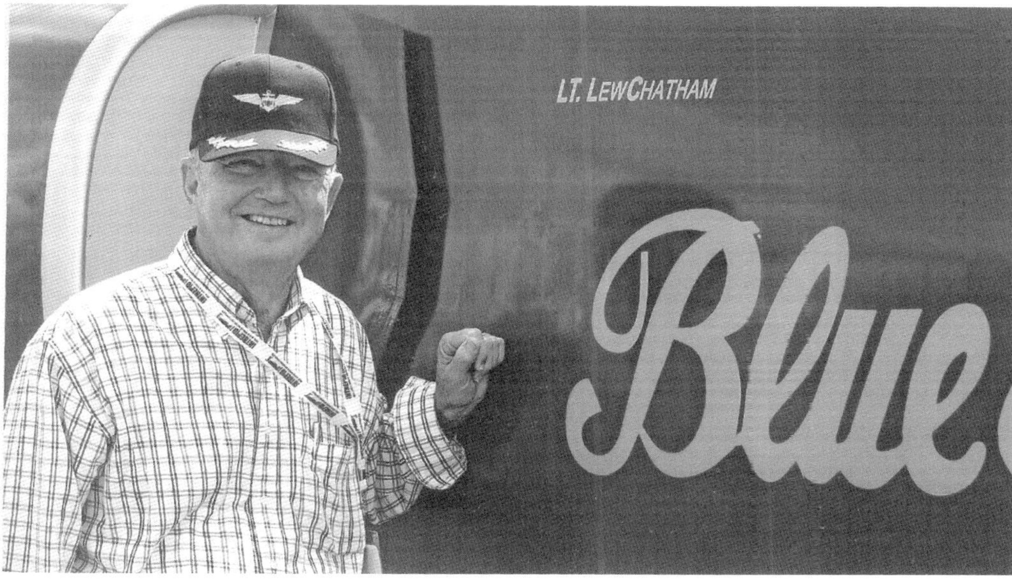

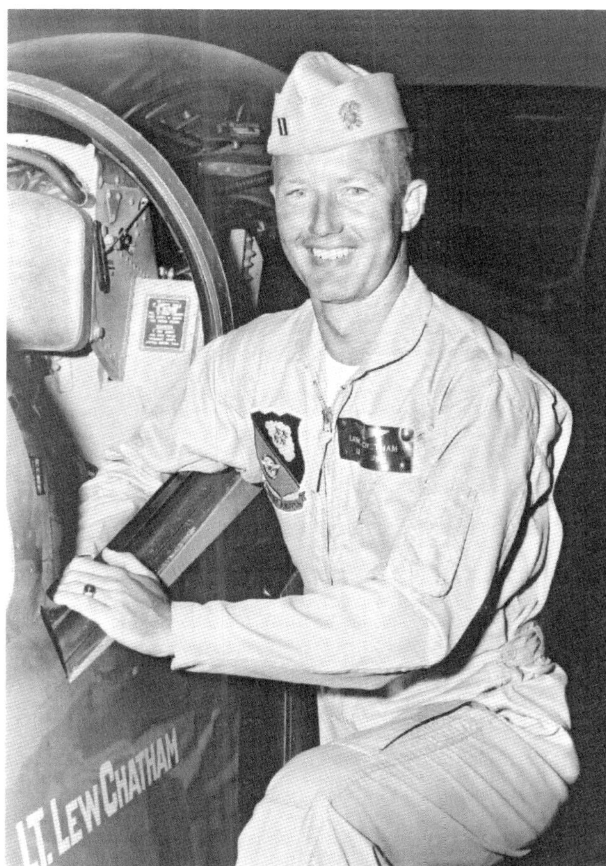

The Blue Angel
From 1961 to 1963, Rear Admiral (Retired) Lew Chatham flew Lead Solo with the Blue Angels, the US Navy's Flight Demonstration Squadron. In his career, he logged approximately 5,000 flying hours in over 30 different aircraft, and 1,100 carrier landings. Three hundred of his carrier landings were at night. Chatham flew 336 combat missions in Vietnam. His many commands include the oiler the USS *Hassayampa*, the carrier the USS *Kitty Hawk*, and two carrier battle groups. He was awarded the Legion of Merit six times, the Distinguished Flying Cross four times, and earned the Strike/Flight Air Medal 35 times. His Blue Angel aircraft is on display on the deck of the USS *Intrepid*, now a museum permanently docked in New York Harbor. (Courtesy Lew Chatham.)

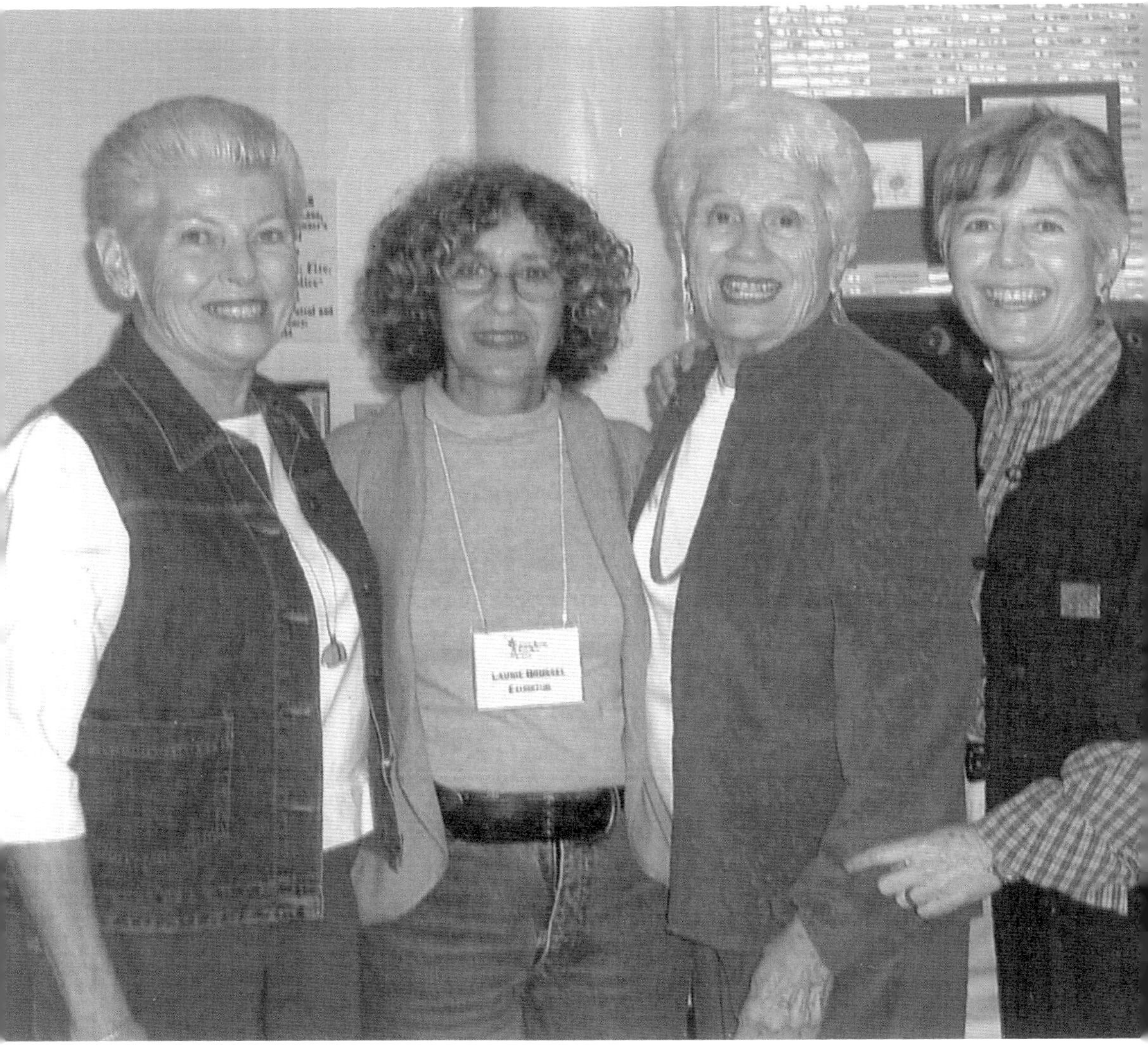

Teaching the Power of Art

In 2006, five members of the SaddleBrooke Fine Art Guild took their talents, and their compassion, out into the surrounding community and started teaching art to the elderly. They designed classes to teach various styles and donated the materials needed to complete each project. Their two-hour classes average 10 students each, and they teach twice a month at different senior facilities in the area. The art lessons stimulate the students, giving them newfound confidence, a new focus, and a chance to socialize. The artists are (left to right) Judy Weiner, Laurie Brussel, Dorothy Bachman (Resident Artist), Harriet Hason, and Robbie Summers. The teachers mount an art show once or twice a year to show off the work of their students. All of the instructors enjoy teaching these special students and look forward to these classes. The artists feel they have been rewarded by the people they have met and the opportunity to add something special to the life of their senior students. The students, in return, have taught them lessons in life and experience. (Courtesy Harriet Hason.)

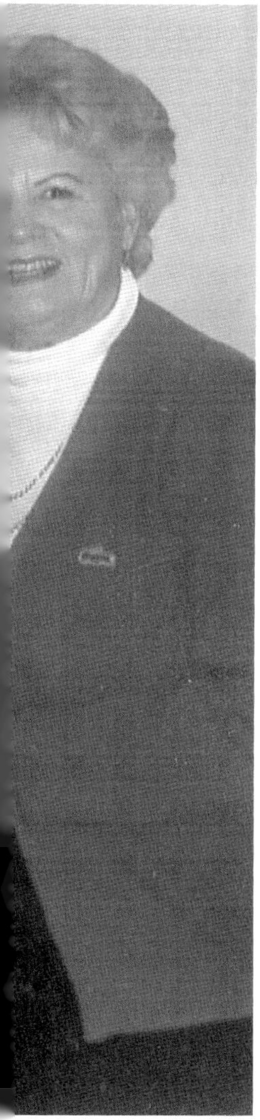

A Scouting Way of Life

Dick Marion served 38 years as a scout executive for the Boy Scouts of America. Under his leadership as district scout executive, in Pennsylvania enrollment swelled from 26,000 scouts to 82,000. As CEO he led a staff of 60 employees and over 10,000 volunteers. He has received the Patrick Henry Award for Patriotic Achievement, the Distinguished Eagle Scout Award, the St. George Award, the Mary H. Hart Award, and the James E. West Fellow award. He was one of the founding members of the SaddleBrooke Rotary Club Foundation, which every year funds charitable needy projects and goods for people of all ages, but mostly for young men and women. He volunteered his time as teacher, tutor, and counselor at the Catalina Mountain School, a state facility for boys in trouble. In Catalina, he was active in his church Sunday school, where his special joy was working with the three- and four-year-old children. (Courtesy Richard Marion.)

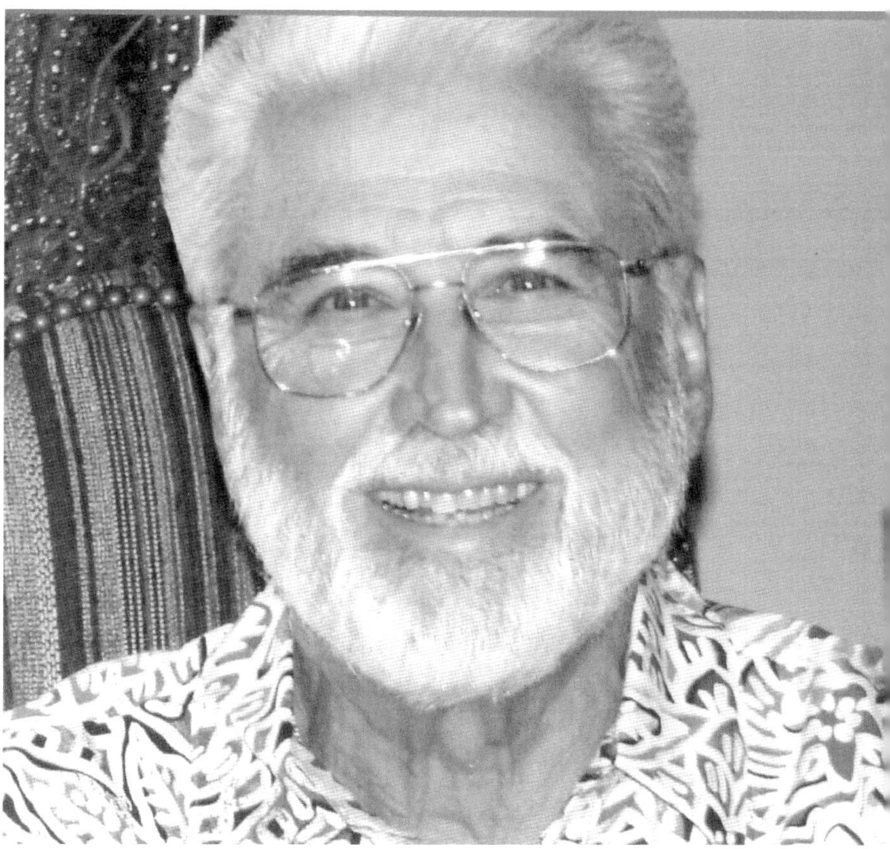

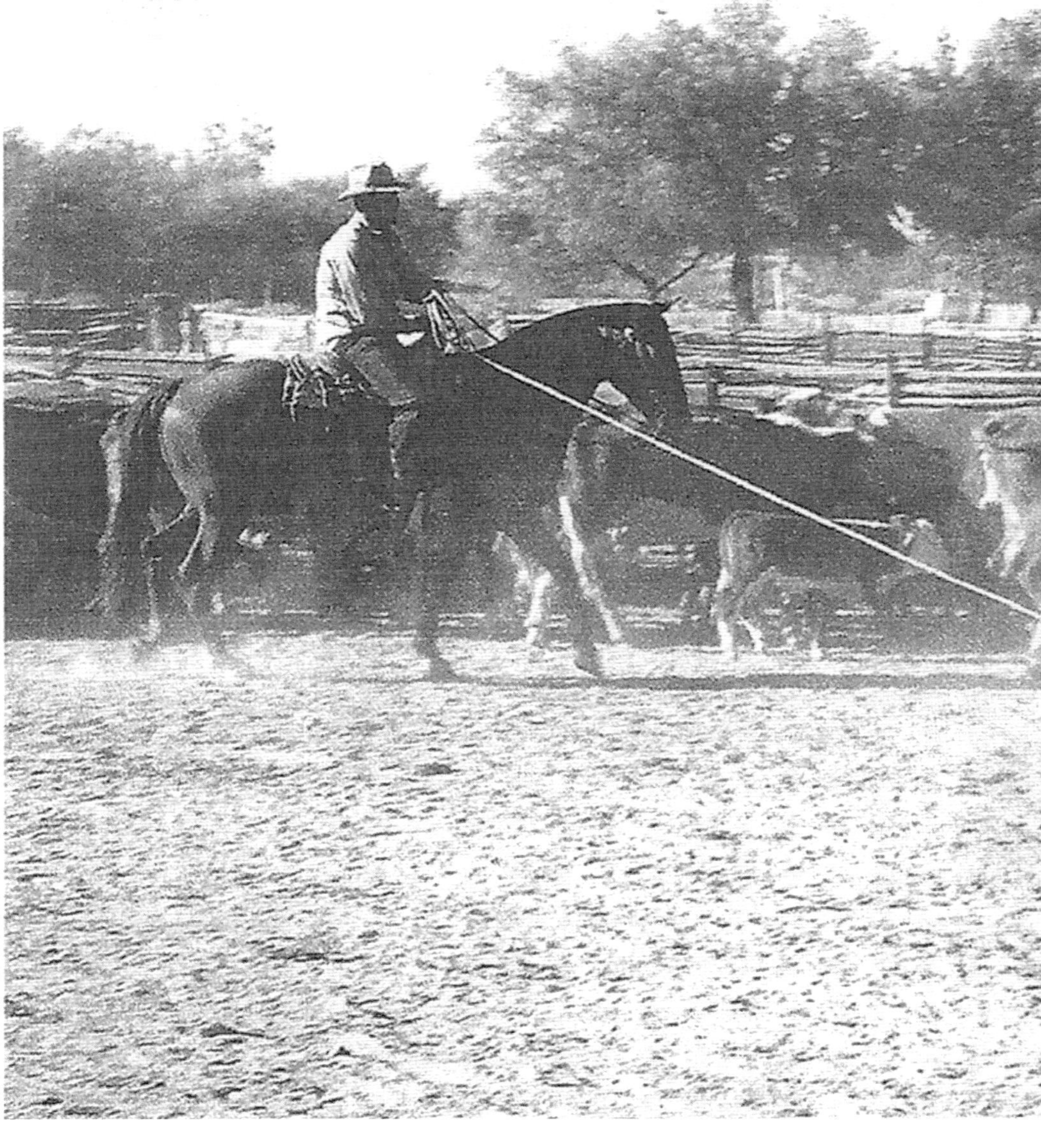

The Cowboys' Cowboy

In his day, there wasn't a wrangler, cowboy, or rancher that didn't know Joseph Thomas Fanning. He worked on just about all the ranches in the Santa Catalina area, including the Steam Pump Ranch, the Golder Ranch, the Rooney Ranch, the Romero Ranch, and the Rail N. He was born in Tucson on May 4, 1934, and died there on June 19, 2004. He was the kind of cowboy character movies were made about. Every cowboy on the big screen and little screen had a bit of Joe Fanning in him. He knew and performed every job on the ranch, not only the working and caring of the cattle, but the maintenance of the ranches and lands he worked. The Rivera family was just one that learned their skills from Fanning. He lived hard and worked hard and to this day remains a legend in the area. (Courtesy Fanning family.)

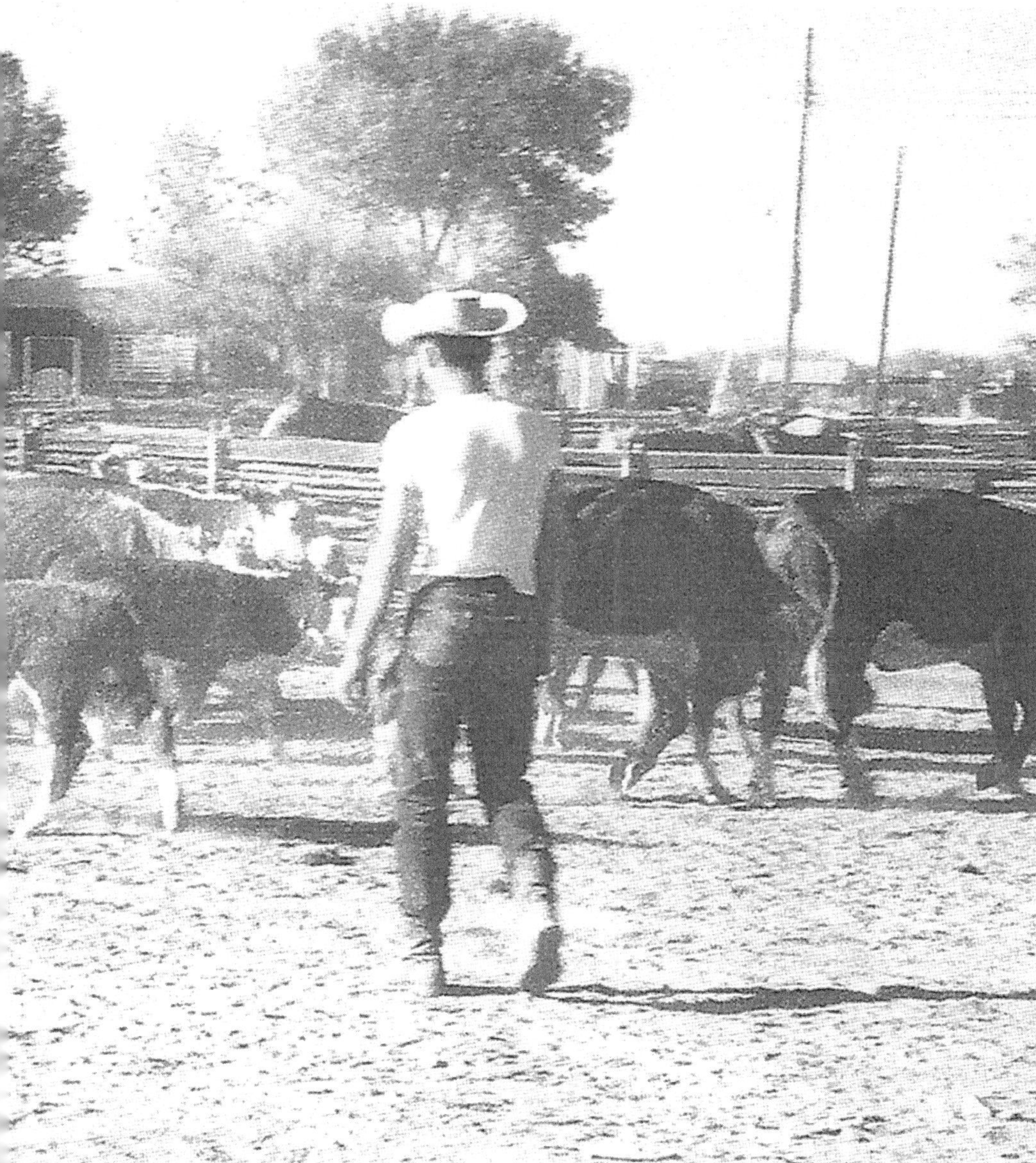

BIBLIOGRAPHY

"Citizens of the Decade," *Explorer*, May 7, 2003

Lawson, Jan. *Marana History*. Marana Chamber of Commerce Publication, 2005, pp. 2–3.

Marriott, Barbara. *Annie's Guests: Tales from a Frontier Hotel*. Tucson, Catymatt Productions, 2002.

Marriott, Barbara. *Canyon of Gold: Tales of Santa Catalina Pioneers*. Tucson, Catymatt Productions, 2005.

Marriott, Barbara. *Images of America: Oro Valley*. Charleston, Arcadia Publishing, 2008.

Martin, Douglas. *An Arizona Chronology: The Territorial Years 1846–1912*. Tucson, University of Arizona Press, 1963.

INDEX